City Builders And Vandals
In Our Age

by Caleb Maupin

REVOLUTIONAIR
ideas that change lives

Published by REVOLUTIONAIR, Denver, Colorado

City Builders And Vandals In Our Age

Author: Caleb Maupin
Publisher: Eve Chen
Copyright © 2019 Caleb Maupin
All rights reserved
Printed in the United States of America

For additional copies, contact your favorite bookstore or email info@calebmaupin.com. Quantity discounts are available.

ISBN-13: 978-1-64606-123-5
First edition: First Printing, July 2019

CONTENTS

iv

Part Two – Capitalism in Crisis

Part Three – The Middle Eastern Theater

ACKNOWLEDGEMENTS

I want to thank all the people who made this book possible.
I extend my appreciation to Katy Seward for her proof-
reading, and to Eve Chen, Andy Hart and the Birdie Media
Team for their assistance in the publication process.

I also want to give special appreciation to George Ehrhart,
Paul Shepard, Michael Ladson, Brent Lengel, Ramiro Funez,
Donald Courter, Mnar Muhawesh, Steve Gong, Jessica
Coco, Dakotah Lily, Gavin Lockhard, Nick Maniace, Alex
Kalmikov, Lloyd Clark, Kiki Dewar, Felicity, Dr. Wilmer
Leon, Daniel Burke, Rachel Brown, John Stachelski, Joe
Gail, Sander Hicks, Bill Dores, Frances Dostal, Allison F.,
Manuel O., Dari D., Timothy Connelly, Meches Rosales-
Maupin, and everyone else who in one way or another helped
the contents of this book to come into being.

"The same dream came to me, sometimes in one form and sometimes in another, but always saying the same or nearly the same words: Cultivate and make music."

- Socrates on his deathbed, recounted in Plato's *Phaedo*.

CITY BUILDERS AND VANDALS IN OUR AGE

AN INTRODUCTORY ESSAY

Throughout human history two distinct trends have most certainly been present among us.

There have always been city-builders; innovators, scientists, philosophers, unifiers, heroes, poets, painters, architects, preachers, prophets, dreamers, visionaries, egalitarians, solidarity builders, rationalists, optimistic non-conformists, bright-eyed rebels, advocates for the downtrodden, inspirers, motivators, in essence, those individuals who push civilization toward a higher state of being, driven by an inner flame of creativity and boldness.

And these city-builders have always stood in opposition to the efforts of the vandals; raiders; machine breakers, hate mongers, ignorance celebrators, jealousy peddlers, demagogues, cultists, hedonists, self-destructive stoics, wreckers, persecutors, lynch mob leaders, dope pushers,

2

snake oil salesmen, sadists, crucifiers; vulgar emotionalists, crass pornographers, bullies, bombers, and worshippers of darkness and primitivism.

The designations of left and right in politics are rather new relative to the history of human civilization.

On May 5th, 1789, the people of France formed a national assembly. This was the body that would lay the basis for the revolution and the toppling of the feudal monarchy. Barron de Guaville described the scene saying: "We began to recognize each other: those who were loyal to religion and the king took up positions to the right of the chair so as to avoid the shouts, oaths, and indecencies that enjoyed free rein in the opposing camp." In 1791, those who sat on the left side of the French national assembly, the opposing camp to those defending the old regime, began referring to themselves as the *Innovators*. Soon, society at large began referring to them as the *left*.

The concept of left and right in politics did not spread beyond France for at least half a century after that. The idea of Socialism is even newer, emerging as a vaguely defined concept in the early 1800s in France, and not first used in the English language until 1822. Marxism did not originate as a movement until 1848. These concepts, *left, right, socialism, Marxism* are anything but eternal and in their short life they have already encompassed a wide variety of diverse ideals and figures.

However, these two distinct trends, city-builders and vandals, have existed since the dawn of human history and class society. From the very moment we began domesticating and animals and growing crops, there were those who wanted to perfect our ability to do so and drive us toward a more advanced way of being. And from the moment of civilization's birth there have been those who wanted us to regress back toward hunter-gatherer civilization and reduce ourselves to a lifestyle closer to that of lower primates.

The essence of the ongoing battle that has raged between civilizations and cultures, within civilizations and cultures, and even within individuals themselves has boiled down to this question: *Will human beings utilize their gift of rationalism and creativity to progress toward greater achievements and a better world? Or will they reject the distinct essence of human-ness and descend toward the conditions of less intelligent species?*

City Builders & Vandals In Our Age

I

The Legacy of Gilgamesh, Confucius and Socrates

In describing the uniqueness of the human species, Frederick Engels, Marx's close collaborator, observed: "the animal merely uses its environment, and brings about changes in it simply by its presence; man by his changes makes it serve his ends, masters it. This is the final, essential distinction between man and other animals." Engels' observation was correct, and it has been mastering the environment and creating better conditions for human beings, so that we might live longer and in better comfort that has been the task of the city builders in every age.

As civilization dawned, the city building tendency manifested itself on every continent and among every people. No region or society had a monopoly on innovation. In the Americas, the Incas and Mayas built pyramids and beautiful metropolises. In Africa, we saw the rise of city states like Timbuktu and Carthage, and eventually the wonders of Egypt. Confucius, and his brilliance, lives on to this day in the unfolding victories of Chinese civilization after 5,000 years.

In what is now Iraq, we saw the birth of a civilization called Mesopotamia. The central myth of this society was told in the *Epic of Gilgamesh*. The legend told of the protagonist, Gilgamesh battling the Bull of Heaven, a mighty and powerful creature. Gilgamesh was able to defeat this massive animal by employing his intelligence. The narrative explains that despite being smaller and weaker, human beings are indeed superior to even the largest and most powerful beasts. The spark of creativity and the ability of rational thinking and collective effort makes us superior to all other species, no matter how large and powerful. The modern-day tradition of bull fighting can be traced back to Mesopotamia where the legend of Gilgamesh was acted out in a ritual to demonstrate the distinction between humans and animals.

The great thinkers of Athens articulated notions of democracy and wrangled with the nature of truth and reality. Socrates, the founder of western philosophy, was put to death because his ideas were too threatening to the status quo. Socrates was accused of corrupting the minds of the youth and creating sympathy for Sparta, the rival city state.

The words of Socrates on his deathbed, as recounted in Plato's *Phaedo*, point toward the common mindset of city builders in every age. Socrates told his followers when he knew his execution was imminent: "The same dream came to me, sometimes in one form and sometimes in another, but always saying the same or nearly the same words: Cultivate and make music."

The dying teacher urged his students to give up their attachment to the bodily sensations of pain and pleasure: "The lovers of knowledge are conscious that their souls, when philosophy receives them, are simply fastened and glued to their bodies: the soul is only able to view existence through the bars of a prison, and not in her own nature; she is wallowing in the mire of all ignorance; and philosophy, seeing the terrible nature of her confinement, and that the captive through desire is led to conspire in her own captivity."

Socrates believed that human beings were not simply animals avoiding pain and seeking pleasure, but that they had a higher intellectual ability, a soul capable of reasoning and construction. Socrates' bravery in becoming a martyr for the cause of civilization set a bold example for heroes of the future. Socrates became more powerful after death than he was in life. His ideas were preserved by those he taught and were utilized in training great minds for thousands of years; illustrating a kind of immortality for progressive thinkers.

Reactionary thought and vandal mindsets certainly manifested themselves, as humanity marched onward in spite of them. The Roman Empire was a great manifestation of barbarism and savagery. Rome was a military society founded on holding back history, and plundering other peoples, living off tribute and slaves, extracted at the point of a spear. The founding myth of Rome presents a message that seems to be completely opposed to the founding myth of Mesopotamia, and illustrates the difference between the two civilizations.

The legend of Rome's founding told of two twin brothers abandoned by their father and left to die by the river as infants. Romulus and Remus, according to the legend, were never loved and cared for by humans, but rather were nursed and raised by a "she-wolf." The Romans believed that the strength which enabled the two co-founders to establish the mighty empire, flowed from their lack of humanity. The lack

8

of human affection and the exposure to the wild predator mentality was believed to have enabled Romulus and Remus to grow into effective conquerors who could establish a slave society. In the Roman Empire, cruelty, sadism, and indifference toward the suffering of others were a celebrated traits, actively cultivated by the rulers.

As Rome's agricultural and industrial output gradually decreased, with a highly inefficient slave system of production in its plantations and mines, Rome continued to make up the difference by conquering other peoples. The German scholar Karl Kautsky reflected on Rome's reactionary nature, writing: "The slave economy... did not denote a technical advance, but a step backward. Not only did it make the masters impotent and incapable of working, and increase the number of unproductive workers in society, but it also cut down the productivity of the productive workers and checked the progress of technology, with the possible exception of some luxury trades....Like every mode of production that is founded on contradictions, the ancient slave economy dug its own grave. In the form it finally took in the Roman world empire, it was based on war. It was only continual victorious wars, continual subjugation of new nations, continual extension of the territory of the Empire that could supply the masses of cheap slave material it required."

The Roman Republic had a hereditary senate, elected representatives and elements of democracy for the simple reason that this was a better way of motivating its citizenry to plunder. A population that feels somehow involved in the business of governing, and the distribution of loot, is far more motivated to join wars of conquest than those who simply exist as subjects of an autocrat. However, the limited democratic procedures within the city state empire proved to be too dangerous to the small elite of families who held the actual power.

The Death of Julius Caesar

The typical Roman was a hedonist who bet money on coliseum fights and chariot races, while seeking pleasure from orgies, drunkenness and over-eating often to the point of induced vomit. The archetype of a shallow, pleasure-hungry sadist was actively cultivated by the Empire with gladiatorial shows, infanticide, and other barbaric practices designed to stimulate the primitive side of the human mind.

For the minority of Romans, whose intellect would not allow them to be satisfied by hedonism, the stoic cults emerged to satisfy their need to find deeper meaning in life. For the stoics, the sadism of Roman life was replaced by a glorified masochism, dressed up in spiritual and philosophical pretensions. Romans who wanted more meaning in their lives than physical pleasure and cruelty would induce states of supposed mysticism with ritualized self-mutilation, flagellation, or even starvation. The stoics would drug themselves in order to have hallucinations, believing this to be a way of connecting to divinity. The stoic Romans would worship some new god imported from part of the Empire, forming little cults in the hopes of finding truths concealed by the official imperial gods.

The stoic Romans, who longed for something more out of life would often be preyed on by philosophical conmen like Seneca. These charlatans preached on the supposed ethical merits of poverty while demanding huge sums in tribute from their flock. The apparent hypocrisy of various stoic gurus and preachers became the subject of many Roman comedies.

While the Romans who rejected the hedonism and cruelty of the Empire were more intelligent and had potential to create real change, their ability to break with societal norms was simply channeled into another avenue of self-destruction.

Yet, even within this nightmare of historical reaction called the Roman Empire, the city-building tendency within humanity asserted itself. Gaius Julius Caesar, a military man born among the aristocracy, emerged in the late Roman Republic to present a progressive vision. Michael Parenti's award winning work of political science and historiography *The Assassination of Julius Caesar: A People's History of Ancient Rome* tells of a maligned populist and reformer, who championed every day Romans against the wealthy landowners. Parenti writes: "He used state power to effect some limited benefits to small farmers, debtors, and the urban proletariat, at the expense of the wealthy few. No matter how limited these reforms proved to be, the oligarchs never forgave him. And so Caesar met the same fate as other Roman reformers before him."

Parenti's book recounting the life and death of Julius Caesar was the 2004 Online Review of Books Non-fiction Book of the Year. The same year that Parenti published his widely praised text, the Caucus for New Political Science gave him the Career Achievement Award. Parenti's scholarship was groundbreaking because it showed Julius Caesar in a completely different light, challenging the narrative put forward by William Shakespeare and the Roman historians who favored the perspective of the wealthy elite.

Parenti draws from the words of those who demonized Caesar to show that their contempt was rooted in their own class interests. Parenti quotes sources such as the Greek biographer and essayist Plutarch who accused Caesar of "stirring up and attaching himself to numerous diseased and corrupted elements in polity." Parenti also quotes Appian, another Roman historian, who described Caesar as having introduced "laws to better the conditions of the poor".

The specifics of Caesar's reforms show him as a thoroughly progressive-minded leader. Caesar sent the unemployed proletarians of Rome to rebuild city states throughout the empire in the hopes of making them thriving centers of trade. Caesar constructed public libraries, giving the citizenry access to written records and information. Caesar cracked down on money lenders, lifted the restrictions and penalties on debtors, and imposed luxury taxes on the decadent rich. Caesar granted Roman citizenship to all doctors and teachers, hoping to reward and cultivate the kind of people who could make Rome a center of science, civilization, and culture.

Caesar was appointed by the Senate for a 10-year term as the Imperator, or Roman head of state. On three occasions, Caesar was offered a crown, but each time he declined to become a monarch. Despite being a strongman Caesar remained an advocate of democracy and he was loved by the people. His power came from the thousands of Roman proletarians, free citizens with no property, who saw him as their champion against the wealthy landowners and senators. This mobilization of the people, as a *populari* or a populist made Caesar far more powerful than any king or emperor could be.

Caesar's vision for reconstructing Roman society involved mobilizing millions of people, not as plundering raiders extracting tribute, but as city builders continuing the great project of *making music* for which Socrates had been executed by a similarly cruel, short-sighted elite. Parenti explains: "The Senate aristocrats killed Caesar because they perceived him to be a popular leader who threatened their privileged interests".

The greatest sin of Julius Caesar in the eyes of the Roman elite was his talk of land redistribution, ensuring that a tiny oligarchy would not maintain a monopoly over the main sources of wealth for Roman society, the mines and plantations. Parenti quotes Plutarch in describing how Caesar's land reform law "provided that almost the whole of Campania be divided among the poor and needy."

Caesar also talked of granting citizenship to people throughout the rest of the Empire. Parenti quotes Roman historian Cicero who bemoaned that Caesar planned to confer "citizenship not merely on individuals but on entire nations and provinces". If people in Central Europe, Persia, North Africa, and other conquered lands could join with the Roman people in setting the policies and enjoying the fruits of the Empire, the civilization might be more sustainable.

Having championed the common people, Julius Caesar was stabbed to death in the hall of the Roman Senate. Parenti explains the assassination: "Caesar was branded a traitor to his class by members of that class. He committed the unforgivable sin of trying to redistribute, albeit in modest portions, some of the wealth that the very rich tirelessly siphon from state coffers and from the labor of the many. It was unforgivable that he should tamper with the system of upward expropriation that they embraced as their birthright. Caesar seems not to have comprehended that in the conflict between the haves and the have-nots, the haves are really have-it-alls. The Roman aristocrats lambasted the palest reforms as the worst kind of thievery, the beginning of a calamitous revolutionary leveling, necessitating extreme counter measures. And they presented their violent retaliation not as an ugly class expediency but as an honorable act on behalf of republican liberty."

The assassination of Julius Caesar, though it was met with riots and rebellions among the people, ultimately doomed Roman civilization. Some of the very Senators who had stabbed Caesar wept by his funeral pyre because they realized that their empire needed a progressive thinker, a strong leader, an advocate of kindness, compassion, and solidarity to lead it toward something better. But yet, in love with their own profits, the greedy and rich had stabbed to death the very person who could save their empire from its own self-destructive, vandal tendencies.

Vandals Bring On the Dark Ages

The demise of the Roman Republic, marked by the stabbing of its greatest advocate and creation, was a historical turning point that paved the way for the Empire's eventual decline and fall. With any notion of democracy being too dangerous to the rich and powerful, Rome descended into a naked autocracy, with a string of emperors who claimed to be gods, leading it further and further down the road to decay. After the eventual fall of Rome came the dark ages and huge setbacks for civilization in Europe.

As Rome declined, the weary and demoralized public began to give stoics the upper hand. In its final years Romans began trading in Bacchus, the God of pleasure and orgies, for a sanitized and redacted image of Jesus Christ, first worshipped secretly among the Jewish craftsman.

The Roman Emperor Constantine is said to have seen a cross in the sky and heard the words *In hoc signo vinces* (under this sign, you shall conquer), inspiring his conversion to Christianity. However, history showed the opposite of what was supposedly promised by the divine voice. As Rome adopted a symbol representing a humble carpenter who preached a gospel of loving one's enemy, the savage empire crumbled.

The fact that the Roman Empire fell almost simultaneously with its official embrace of Christianity has long been met with defensiveness by Christian scholars and historians. St. Augustine's book *The City of God,* considered to be one the most vital theological works in the history of Christianity, was intended to address this point. However, no defensiveness is really necessary. The teachings of Jesus Christ were obviously not intended for the purpose of building a society based on plunder, and the fact that they would play a role in the demise rather than strengthening of such an empire should not be surprising.

In the twilight years, the once powerful militarist city state could not even raise its own armies. The Germanic tribes, the Vandals, the Austro-Goths, the Vista Goths, who played a pivotal role in Rome's ultimate demise did not even battle Roman centurions. The decaying empire was so weak that it fought the Germanic tribes, not with its own soldiers but by hiring other Germanic tribes to fight on its behalf. As it reached its end, an empire founded on military plunder was so weak that it could not raise its own army to defend itself.

Despite the reactionary nature of the Roman world order, the fall of Rome made conditions far worse. It took 1100 years before Europe's population returned to what it had been at the height of the Roman Empire. The average height of people dramatically decreased due to a decline in nourishment and caloric intake. In their orgy of destruction, the Barbarian tribes made a point of burning books and records, and attempted to erase scientific progress.

The Barbarians of central Europe had essentially beaten the Romans at their own game. The dying Empire was brought down by pagan tribes who worshipped Odin, a god of valor and grit who seemed to embody the animalistic tendencies of Romulus and Remus. Unlike the Romans, the Goths and Vandals did not even construct cities, but lived in the woods as nomadic raiders, plundering what prior civilizations had built, and ushering in an era of huge setbacks and very little human progress.

A New Order Forged By Revolutionaries

After centuries of feudalism and serfdom, it was a change in political theory, sparked by changes in the economy, that paved the way for something better. The Renaissance was not a random occurrence. In Italy, Britain, Bavaria, and other parts of Europe, the dawn of the Silk Road from Asia and travelers observations of other civilizations in the Middle East, China, and elsewhere, inspired a strand of progressive thinking.

The achievements of the Islamic Enlightenment, an age of reform in the Arab world, as well as China's great advances gradually trickled into the western world, despite brutal institutions that sought to repress them. Much like Socrates had experienced, often those who promoted science and questioned the backward nature of things were met with repression. Often those accused of alchemy or heresy were tortured, imprisoned, or burned at the stake. Yet, despite so many setbacks, the flame of human progress was not extinguished. New ideas were smuggled in and secret societies of educated people began to form, in order to share the forbidden knowledge. One after another, forward-thinking monarchs who aligned themselves with the new layer of travelers and thinkers, began to encourage scientific research as well as ground-breaking artistic endeavors.

The music of Bach, the paintings of Michelangelo, and the empowerment of figures like Leonardo Da Vinci and Thomas Moore, all flowed from a new mindset regarding the nature of government. In the dark ages the feeling was that human beings were obliged to serve their natural superiors. However, the paradigm shift that defined the Renaissance of the 14th to 17th centuries was the notion of statecraft, the feeling that those who govern have an obligation to improve the conditions of the citizenry, to serve the people. With a few forward thinking monarchs allowing new thoughts to bloom, the inner light of humanity began to glow once again in Europe.

When Copernicus composed his earth-shaking text *On The Revolution of Heavenly Spheres* in 1543, the text was simply a presentation of what he had discovered with mathematical calculations and his primitive telescope. The text had no mention of politics in it, but the political implications were explosive.

Copernicus had argued that the scientific method was a superior mechanism for finding truth, and that what the Catholic Church claimed about the earth being the center of the universe was false. Those who accepted the scientific method and belief in rational thinking began to refer to themselves as *revolutionaries*. The *revolutionaries* believed that the earth revolved around the sun, and more importantly, they believed in science and human reason. Across Europe, the revolutionaries conspired, sometimes openly and sometimes in secret, to challenge the feudal order and replace it with something that would no longer restrain human progress.

The Korean invention of the printing press, utilized for the first time in Europe by Johaness Gutenberg, opened the door to the protestant reformation. By the late 1700s revolutionaries were on the upswing, speaking of a new order protecting *natural rights* or the *rights of man*. Talk of *Life, Liberty and Property and Liberty, Egalite, Fraternity* swept the world, and feudalism fell amid a wave of optimism. Jefferson's *Declaration of Independence*, marking the first step toward the creation of the modern United States, is awash with the slogans and sentiments of the era. It speaks of human-beings as being "endowed by their creator with certain inalienable rights." It speaks of the moral imperative to revolt against unjust social conditions. As the 19th Century dawned, red banners and declarations of liberty were on display across the western world. Kings and nobles were beheaded. Millions of peasants marched into battle in order to topple old principalities and to forge modern nation states with their muskets and bayonets.

The old order, of course, scoffed with contempt at those who brought about its demise. Robert Thomas Malthus coined the term *overpopulation* proclaiming that the unrest was all due to the birth rate expanding faster than the food supply. The Spanish Inquisition, anti-semitic pogroms, and various episodes of genocide and repression marked the vengeful scorn of a dying order.

As capitalism dawned, the feudal lords were replaced by factory owners, and the power of kings was usurped by bankers. Peasants were driven from their lands and pushed to urban areas where they became wage workers. A new social order emerged from the ashes of the old.

The dawn of the new social system, hailed as "glorious," was wrought with horrors and inhumanity. A genocide cleared the Scottish highlands. Millions of Irish people were starved in a man-made famine. Colonialism in Africa and the Americas, the slaughter of native people, and the transnational slave trade laid the foundations of what would eventually become the global market.

The Emergence of Scientific Socialism

Political and economic theorist Henri de Saint-Simon looked on to the new French society created in a massive revolution and saw millions who were left hungry and destitute. He invoked Christianity and moralism and built cooperatives while providing charity to the poor. Saint-Simon began to speak of *socialisme* as an alternative to selfishness and individualism of the new society, where profits ruled and self-interest seemed far less restrained than ever before. The Welsh industrialist and social reformer Robert Owen followed after Saint-Simon, becoming the first to speak of *socialism* in the English language, and constructing egalitarian model cities in New Lanark and New Harmony.

The Utopians followed a long tradition of seeking to construct an ideal world, but the first time science was applied to this project came amid the 1848 German Revolution.

As a young man, the socialist revolutionary Karl Marx was a participant in a massive revolt that sought to create a German nation state. The uprising was part of the Spring of Nations, a series of rebellions that swept Europe demanding the creation of democratic republics, social equality and better conditions for the people. Like most of the 1848 uprisings, the German revolution failed.

Marx's faction in the 1848 revolution, the Communist League, and presented a documented called *The Communist Manifesto* to express its beliefs. The text presented arguments for a new social order beyond capitalism. However, unlike like Saint-Simon and Owen, Marx's arguments were not rooted in moral criticism and religious sentiments, but rather rooted in an analysis of the history of human society and how it develops.

Marx began his famous document with the words: "The history of hitherto existing society has been the history of class struggle…" He explained the constant drive of human beings toward a higher mode of production, fueled by the conflict between different social classes. Prior to this opening statement, Marx's preamble declares "A spectre is haunting Europe — the spectre of communism!" arguing that the ideas he presented were well alive all across Europe, and the 1848 Manifesto was simply the first place to give a concise, popular voice to them.

Marx spoke of the working class, the proletariat, "a class of laborers, who live only so long as they find work, and who find work only so long as their labor increases capital. These laborers, who must sell themselves piecemeal, are a commodity, like every other article of commerce, and are consequently exposed to all the vicissitudes of competition, to all the fluctuations of the market."

He called for the working class to rise up and take control of society, rescuing it from the irrational greed of factory owners, "The proletariat will use its political supremacy to wrest, by degree, all capital from the bourgeoisie, to centralize all instruments of production in the hands of the State, i.e., of the proletariat organized as the ruling class; and to increase the total productive forces as rapidly as possible."

The Marxists argued that factory owners lived by extracting surplus value from those they hired, and operated only according to what was profitable. As a result the new society unfolding across Europe was plagued by economic crises, war, hunger, and poverty amidst plenty. While the bourgeoisie had done great things by breaking apart feudalism, Marx argued, its new society presented fresh contradictions that could only be resolved by the working class rising up. Marxism argued that with the workers controlling the means of production, the economy could be rationally planned and human progress would no longer be restrained by the *anarchy of production*.

As Marx's close collaborator Frederick Engels later explained, the purpose of the communist revolution was to establish a society where growth and human progress were unlimited. According to Marx's theory, with a state-run economy, humanity could be unleashed to gradually deconstruct all forms of social hierarchy and oppression: "In a higher phase of communist society, after the enslaving subordination of the individual to the division of labor, and therewith also the antithesis between mental and physical labor, has vanished; after labor has become not only a means of life but life's prime want; after the productive forces

21

have also increased with the all-around development of the individual, and all the springs of co-operative wealth flow more abundantly—only then can the narrow horizon of bourgeois right be crossed in its entirety and society inscribe on its banners: From each according to his ability, to each according to his needs!"

The ultimate vision was for human productivity and creativity, after perhaps thousands of years, to establish so much material abundance that the need for any form of coercion or authority would fade away: "In proportion as anarchy in social production vanishes, the political authority of the State dies out. Man, at last the master of his own form of social organization, becomes at the same time the lord over Nature, his own master — free."

According to Marx, the workers revolution would lead to a centrally-planned economy, and this would be the first step toward an ideal world in which people could simply take what they wanted and do what they felt like doing *("From each according to his ability, to each according to his needs").*

Marx's economic work explained the natural instability of profit-centered economies, describing workers' competition with machines, the falling rate of profit, and the drive toward cyclical market crises due to advances in technology. Marx stated that the more effectively a capitalist can carry out production, the fewer people he hires. In capitalism, human beings ability to survive and prosper is tied to their inherent profitability to those who own the centers of economic power. Therefore, he argued that capitalism leads to a situation where abundance and efficiency creates unemployment, and poverty persists amid plenty.

Marx's political writings analyzed the 1851 *coup d'etat* in France in which Louis Bonaparte marched into power with his "party of order" seeking to restore order and liquidate a nation-wide episode of unrest and instability. Marx described how in a time of crisis, factions among the ruling class begin to violently suppress each other, in the hopes of taking dramatic economic actions and stabilizing a naturally unstable system.

Marx helped form the International Workingmen's Association (IWA), commonly called the *First International*, in the hopes of spreading communist ideas across the world and uniting revolutionaries of different countries. Within the First International, Marx frequently polemicized with anarchists like Mikhail Bakunin and Ferdinand LaSalle who advocated left-adventurist violence and did not see revolution in a scientific way.

Marx analyzed the Paris Commune of 1871, where French workers, who saw the capitalist government surrender to the invading Prussian armies, established a short-lived, working class regime to defend their city. Marx had originally opposed the communards' uprising, but after it was underway, praised it as an example of workers "storming heaven" and taking great risks to advance history and defend their communities. Marx said that the Paris Commune of 1871 was the first *Dictatorship of the Proletariat* and that similar uprisings would soon sweep the world.

Eventually, the First International broke apart due to factional disagreements between Marx's allies and anarchists. However, Marx observed the formation of the German Social Democratic Party (SPD) in 1875, and composed a pamphlet called *The Critique of the Gotha Program* pointing out nonscientific aspects of its founding document. Eventually the German SDP adopted Marx's ideas as its official ideology.

Though Marx never visited the United States, he was employed by the *New York Tribune*, an American newspaper owned by abolitionist Horace Greely. From London, Marx composed columns praising Lincoln and called the US Civil War the *Second American Revolution*. Describing why working class people across the ocean felt enthusiastic about supporting the anti-slavery war, Marx wrote: "The workingmen of Europe feel sure that, as the American War of Independence initiated a new era of ascendancy for the middle class, so the American Antislavery War will do for the working classes. They consider it an earnest of the epoch to come that it fell to the lot of Abraham Lincoln, the single-minded son of the working class, to lead his country through the matchless struggle for the rescue of an enchained race and the reconstruction of a social world."

Marx's followers played a key role in this war, with German communists who fled to the United States forming the Ohio Ninth Infantry Regiment and fighting against slavery on the battlefield. Textile workers in Britain, organized into Marx's IWA, refused to work with cotton picked by slaves and held demonstrations supporting Lincoln and his *Second American Revolution*. While the British textile factory owners saw the US South as a cheap source of cotton, and London and Wall Street insurance cartels saw slave exports as an opportunity to make profits, Marx argued that the interest of the working class people were on the other side. Marx wrote: "Labor in white skin cannot emancipate itself where the black skin is branded."

Imperialism & The Crisis of Marxism

The Marxist movement proliferated across Europe, most especially after the death of its founding 'prophet' in 1883. The Socialist International (Second International) emerged as a continent-wide mass movement, with the German SPD as its flagship organization. Millions of working class people joined Marxist, labor, and social-democratic parties. Unions fought for the rights of factory workers. Universal male suffrage, restriction on the length of the workday, and union representation on the job was established in many parts of Europe. Socialist deputies were elected to many parliaments. Marx's writings were broadly distributed, and institutes of Marxist studies were established.

The United States was not left out of the rise in socialist consciousness. Activist Edward Bellamy's science fiction novel *Looking Backward* was published in 1888. The text told of a beautiful, futuristic USA in which the rule of profits had been eliminated, and human beings lived in comfort and cooperation. The book created a sensation across the USA as a bestseller. People inspired by the novel formed *Nationalist Clubs* to promote the vision Bellamy's narrative presented. Among those who promoted his socialist vision was Edward Bellamy's cousin, Francis Bellamy. Francis Bellamy was a Baptist minister who later composed the US Pledge of Allegiance.

The Daniel DeLeon's Socialist Labor Party of America and eventually the much larger Socialist Party of America, led by Eugene Debs, began to spread the Marxist gospel of social revolution and rational economics across the American heartland. Debs traveled in a red train car from city to city, calling for the working class to take its place as the master of

US society. Upton Sinclair, Ida Tarbell, John Reed, Lincoln Steffens, and other socialist journalists exposed the crimes of the rich and powerful. The Industrial Workers of the World organized the desperately low income and immigrant trade and industrial workers who were rejected by American Federation of Labor for being "unskilled."

In the first decades of the 20th century, Marxism was everywhere in the western world, and the working class was more organized than ever before. Yet, socialist revolutions did not occur. Scholars began to write about "the crisis of Marxism" because it seemed that while Marx's ideas had widely proliferated, they did not manifest themselves in the predicted proletarian revolution they were intended to create.

The crisis of Marxism and the lack of revolutions and uprisings, occurred because the global economy was changing. Factory owners were being usurped by bankers. As international corporations based in western capitals spread themselves across the world, the living standards for some strata in the homelands were rising.

Writing from Russia, Lenin described this new global order as "Imperialism: The highest stage of capitalism."

Lenin wrote:

"Imperialism is a specific historical stage of capitalism. Its specific character is threefold: imperialism is monopoly capitalism; parasitic, or decaying capitalism; moribund capitalism. The supplanting of free competition by monopoly is the fundamental economic feature, the quintessence of imperialism.

Monopoly manifests itself in five principal forms:

(1) cartels, syndicates and trusts—the concentration of production has reached a degree which gives rise to these monopolistic associations of capitalists;

(2) the monopolistic position of the big banks—three, four or five giant banks manipulate the whole economic life of America, France, Germany;

(3) seizure of the sources of raw material by the trusts and the financial oligarchy (finance capital is monopoly industrial capital merged with bank capital);

(4) the (economic) partition of the world by the international cartels has begun. There are already over one hundred such international cartels, which command the entire world market and divide it "amicably" among themselves—until war re-divides it. The export of capital, as distinct from the export of commodities under non-monopoly capitalism, is a highly characteristic phenomenon and is closely linked with the economic and territorial-political partition of the world;

(5) the territorial partition of the world (colonies) is completed."

The rise of the international market led to bankers supplanting factory owners with industry depending on credit and lending in order to function. Unlike industrialists, bankers have a fundamentally anti-progressive historical position in relationship to the world. For example, figures like Henry Morgan, Andrew Carnegie and Henry Ford ultimately sought to see living standards in the United States

27

increase. They viewed their own profits as rising alongside advances in technology and scientific progress. The various captains of industry could be ruthless in breaking strikes and crushing those who challenged their power and profits, but they still built libraries, financed public works, and on some level believed that their own advancement, accompanied the advancement of the country and human civilization.

The financial elite of creditors that usurped the factory owners and came to rule the world in the "monopolistic associations" which Lenin described, had a completely different relationship with the world and with human history itself. This current represents nothing more than a financial middle man, accumulating its position and making profits through the lending of money, not production.

The imperialists maintained their *super profits* by *super exploiting* countries across the developing world. In order for Wall Street and London to maintain their position as monopolist rulers of the global market, it was necessary to tear down any level of development that was taking place across the developing world. Great nations had to be reduced to the level of captive client states. The world had to be made poor and kept poor, so that Wall Street and London could be made rich.

The financialization of capital led to a new level of stability, and also resulted in stratifying the working class of western countries. As skilled workers and craftsmen saw their wages increase, they became far less interested in solidarity with industrial workers deemed to be "unskilled." English-speaking, US-born, and white workers in the United States banned foreign-born, non-English speaking, and non-white workers from their labor unions. Most of the labor unions in the American Federation of Labor were openly racist, allowing only whites to join.

Lenin labeled this layer that emerged among the working class as the *Aristocracy of Labor*. It was made up of workers with higher pay, who sympathized with the western capitalists against lower paid workers and people in the colonized world. As the labor federations and Marxist parties became dominated by the labor aristocrats, they became far less interested in revolution. They also became far more sympathetic to militarism, and hostile to foreign nations. Essentially, a section of the working class was being unconsciously bought off, and becoming loyal to the bankers and their governments.

The Atlanticist Pathology: A Mindset 'From Hell'

The dawn of imperialism, a new stage of the capitalist economy greatly changed social relations. It resulted in a state of mind unfolding in the western world that can accurately be described as the Atlanticist Pathology.

The ruling class of Britain, led by its royal family, boasts about being descended from the Normans, a Germanic tribe of vandals and Odinists, who seized England at the famous Battle of Hasting in the year 1066. The Viking raiders of the sea and vandal tribes of the forests did not build cities, they raided them. They stole from those who had constructed. They went to what had already been created and looted it, and, in some cases, destroyed it.

As the British industrialists subordinated themselves to entities like the East India Company and the various finance houses of the London Stock Exchange, this same predatory and destructive means of existence came to dominate the international markets. Various geopolitical analysts have referred to "Atlanticism" as a trend among western nations throughout history who have prioritized control of the trade routes and maritime dominance over economic development on the mainland.

The Queen's Empire infamously burned down the various looms of India and Bangladesh, and as the colonizer, forced a civilization that had been weaving for thousands of years to import its cloth from Britain. China faced two *Opium Wars* in response to the Emperors efforts to raise living standards and stop the inflow of destruction and plunder. British bankers established the Hong Kong Shanghai Banking Corporation, HSBC Bank, for the purpose of controlling China's economy and keeping a great civilization poor. Heroin and opium became a central aspect of British imperialism. With the force of the British military, various parts of the world were seized, economically looted and reduced to mere captive markets for British products.

Britain was simply the first in line when it came to imperialism. Germany, France, Belgium and eventually the United States soon moved in to the globalist model of international capitalism. The western powers began seizing parts of the developing world and, with economies centralized around banking institutions and monopolies protected by the state, extracted immense profits by crippling the developing world.

From 1885 to 1908, Belgium oversaw a genocide of roughly 15 million people in the Congo Free State, an African colony under personal direction of the King. Most of those who perished were worked to death in the process of extracting natural rubber.

The United States seized the Philippines during the Spanish-American War, and then from 1899 to 1913, fought against Filipino resistance. Between 250,000 and a million Filipino civilians were killed over the course of the fighting.

As Britain rose to be the top superpower of capitalism in its imperialist, monopoly stage, the writings of Adam Smith came to be the celebrated view on economics. *Free trade* and *free competition* in one big, global market was to tear down international borders and allow the "superior" ones to rise to the top. Language lifted from Charles Darwin's biological texts was used to justify the horrendous atrocities carried out to secure London's position as imperialist top dog. The notion of "survival of the fittest" was nothing new among thieves and criminals, but Darwin's work allowed the British to proclaim their destruction and impoverishment of people across the world as simply the natural order of things.

The British settlers gunned down entire African villages with primitive machine guns, justifying their crimes with social-Darwinist rhetoric about *inferior races*. Rhodesia emerged as an apartheid plantation state named after the great imperialist Cecil Rhodes in the territory that is now Zimbabwe. Rhodes described the colonization of the world and the enlistment of British workers to be settlers and overseers across the planet as a matter of ensuring social peace and preventing class struggle and revolution. In 1895, Rhodes wrote: "I was in the East End of London (a working-class quarter) yesterday and attended a meeting of the unemployed. I listened to the wild speeches, which were just a cry for 'bread! bread!' and on my way home I pondered over the scene and I became more than ever convinced of the importance of imperialism.... My cherished idea is a solution for the social problem, i.e., in order to save the 40,000,000 inhabitants of the United Kingdom from a bloody civil war, we colonial statesmen must acquire new lands to settle the surplus population, to provide new markets for the goods produced in the factories and mines. The Empire, as I have always said, is a bread and butter question. If you want to avoid civil war, you must become imperialists."

The rise of the *Atlanticist Pathology* involved promoting a generalized vandal mindset among the population. The British homeland, much like the Rome, developed a domestic culture designed to breed sadistic raiders and vandals. In Victorian Britain, parents were taught never to hug their children, and to greatly restrict their affection. Sadistic corporal punishment became standard for school children, with rattan canes imported from Asia as treasured implements for inflicting pain. A puritanical and shame-based attitude toward matters of sexuality became widespread. War was glorified in every aspect of life.

As British imperialism rode high across the planet, plundering and destroying what is now labeled the 'global south,' at home, Britain was cultivating a culture of insanity. It was the British empire that introduced humanity to what is now described as the 'serial killer,' a pattern of criminal behavior in which a man murders women in a sexualized manner.

London's infamous 'Jack the Ripper' grabbed headlines in 1888 with his killing and mutilation of prostitutes in London's Whitechapel, the very "working-class quarter" where Cecil Rhodes had his revelation about the importance of imperialism less than a decade later.

As the gruesome details of the murders were reported in the press, the *London Times* received thousands of letters from individuals hoping to take credit for the unsolved crimes. Most of the letters were anonymous, but they revealed that beneath the surface, many British people, raised in an atmosphere glorifying war, plunder, and punishment amid sexual repression, secretly cherished fantasies about engaging in similar behavior.

With so many imposters stealing his spotlight, the actual Whitechapel murderer sent a body part from a victim in a package to prove that he was the real 'Jack The Ripper.' The letter containing half of a human kidney was signed 'From Hell.'

Soon, this pattern of serial killers who sexualized their murders became a widespread phenomenon across the western world, declining only in the past few decades. An article from *The Guardian* newspaper, published in 2018 quotes criminologists noticing this pattern of homocidal behavior has seen "a clear downward trend from the 1989 peak."

Whatever progressivism had been at the foundations of the revolutions to topple feudalism seemed to be pushed into the background with the rise of imperialism, capitalism in its monopoly stage. The new global economic order became an expression of the *Atlanticist Pathology*. The vandals had seized control of the high seas, and as pirates they proceeded to raid and plunder the entire world. The city builders were in retreat.

The Party of New Type

The ultimate conclusion of the Crisis of Marxism was millions of workers being sent to their deaths in the First World War. As the western imperialists battled each other for control of the world, with the British and Americans blocking the rise of their rivals in Germany and Austria, the result was mass killing as had never been seen before.

Blame for this horrendous catastrophe of destruction and death could not simply be placed on capitalism, but on the bankruptcy of the massive socialist movement that could have stopped the war. The various parties of the Second International had spoken of class solidarity, but when the *Guns of August* roared in 1914, they abandoned their internationalist principles and sent their rank and file off to die.

Lenin was a Russian revolutionary who lived in exile, and from Britain he observed that the stratification of the working class in western countries was shifting the revolutionary energy to the countries of the east. Like a voice crying out in the wilderness, he had warned Marxists around the world about the decline of social democracy. Lenin explained how capitalism was now in its monopoly stage of imperialism. While Marxists had opposed all nationalism, Lenin argued that it was national liberation, and the struggle of countries across the world to break free from the imperialist financial order, that would give birth to socialism.

While Marx's manifesto had ended with a reference to Germany, and most Marxists believed that the Communist-revolution would break out in the western developed countries, Lenin said the opposite. Lenin said that the revolutionary upsurge in the 20th century would take place in the east and in the colonized world. As western capitalism kept countries in chronic poverty as captive markets and spheres of influence, they would be forced to adopt socialism in order to break free. The Marxists of the third world would sit at the center of united fronts against imperialism, as whole nations fought to be free.

From exile, Lenin pitched his vision of a new revolutionary organization to seize control of Russia. He called it a *Party of New Type* and what eventually became of it was known to the world as *Bolshevism*.

The Bolshevik movement, despite espousing a strictly materialist and Marxist perspective, carried with it many features from Russia's cultural and spiritual past. With his groundbreaking work *What is to be done?* Vladimir Lenin rejected the liberal democratic model for political parties. The *vanguard* organization Lenin created was a kind of secret society made up of those who gave *the whole of their lives* to be the *tribune of the people*. Instead of putting forward a Marxist program, the party engaged in *agitation*, stirring up the masses to greater confrontation, while reserving ideology (*propaganda*) for the advanced and recruitable.

The Bolshevik movement was founded in exile by Russian intellectuals and middle class radicals who sought to mobilize the industrial working class to topple the Czarist autocracy and replace it with a socialist-oriented state. Like Rosa Luxemburg, Eugene Debs, and others, the Bolsheviks opposed the First World War, and denounced the various "socialist" parties that supported the imperialist bloodbath. Lenin described the Second International and its member parties as a 'stinking corpse.'

The name "Bolshevik" literally means "Majority Group." The name was selected after the majority of those who met with Lenin in 1903 agreed to form his *"Party of New Type"* while the minority of those in the room ("Mensheviks") rejected the plan. However, most of the people who eventually fought in the streets to bring the Bolsheviks to power were probably not aware of this meeting and the origins of the name. To the average Russian worker, "Bolshevism" essentially came across as "Majoritarianism." The Russian Social Democratic Labor Party (Bolshevik) in their call for a *revolutionary dictatorship of the workers and peasants* fought for the majority of Russia's people against the minority of wealthy factory owners, landlords, and the Czarist autocracy.

After the Czar stepped down following Russia's February Revolution in 1917, Lenin returned from exile to seize the moment. It is widely understood that in order to return to the country, Lenin received some level of support from German intelligence agencies who wanted to see Russia withdraw from the war. Lenin travelled to Russia on a sealed train so his arrival would not be anticipated.

When Lenin arrived, he presented his famous April Theses, reorienting the Bolsheviks to be dedicated to ending the war and defending the "Soviets" or councils the people had formed during the uprising. Lenin instructed his political organization to change their name. Instead of calling themselves *social democrats* the Bolshevik organization adopted the label of *communists* in order to distinguish themselves from the failed Marxist movement in Europe.

The platform of the Bolshevik Party included many planks such as the nationalization of banks, the separation of church and state, and granting women the right to vote. However, the slogan for which the Bolsheviks were known was "Peace, Land, and Bread."

The Bolsheviks entered an alliance with the Russian capitalists who were tied in with German capital. The Bolsheviks continued to lead strikes demanding an end to the war. The Bolsevhiks defended the continued existence of the Soviets, which evolved into a kind of dual government structure in Russia's urban centers. In September of 1917, the Bolsheviks repelled the Kornilov Reaction, and prevented a military regime from taking power in Saint Petersburg which would have aggressively continued the war.

In October of 1917, Lenin's *Party of New Type* seized power on a platform of *All Power To the Soviets* and created a new government. Soviet Russia eventually became the Soviet Union, granting autonomy to various nationalities that had been part of the Russian Empire.

Following the Russian revolution, various uprisings took place across Europe. As the First World War ended, German soldiers rose up against the Kaiser. Hungarian workers took up arms and seized government buildings. This explosion of revolutionary anger, as a horrific war was ending, shook the world, but only in Russia were the revolutionaries able to keep power.

The Bolsheviks withstood invasion by 15 different countries, and fought a lengthy civil war to maintain their Soviet government. The Russian people starved and suffered amid an economic blockade, and massive internal turmoil. Originally the Soviet government had maintained three major political parties, the Bolsheviks, the Left Mensheviks, and the

Left Socialist Revolutionaries, all of which recognized the Soviet Constitution and held seats in the government.

However, as the blockade and internal turmoil escalated, both the Left Mensheviks and the Left Socialist Revolutionaries launched armed revolts against the Bolsheviks. A member of the Left Socialist Revolutionary Party even shot Lenin, severely wounding him. As a result of these conditions, the Soviet government was forced to become more authoritarian, and all other parties were outlawed. Openness and civil freedoms are based on a level of stability and development, but a society under siege is forced to become rigid and militarized. Soon, even factions within the Bolshevik Party were no longer permitted. Ironclad discipline was needed in order to hold the country together in the face of relentless efforts to crush socialism.

After Lenin's death in 1924, Leon Trotsky and his followers among the Bolsheviks held on to the illusion that Europe's factory workers would soon rise up. Describing his theory of Permanent Revolution, Trotsky wrote: "The completion of the socialist revolution within national limits is unthinkable. One of the basic reasons for the crisis in bourgeois society is the fact that the productive forces created by it can no longer be reconciled with the framework of the national state... The socialist revolution begins on the national arena, it unfolds on the international arena, and is completed on the world arena. Thus, the socialist revolution becomes a permanent revolution in a newer and broader sense of the word; it attains completion, only in the final victory of the new society on our entire planet."

However, among a population that was weary of war and chaos, this call for marching into Europe in a crusade, to

behead every last king and capitalist, fell on deaf ears. Josef
Stalin, a Georgian Bolshevik organizer who had grown
up in poverty, took the helm of the Soviet government on
a platform of building *socialism in one country* rejecting
Trotsky's bloodthirsty fantasy of *permanent revolution.* Under
Stalin's leadership the Soviet government signed treaties with
the western countries and focused on raising living standards.

Socialist Construction & The Rise of Eurasia

Prior to his death, Lenin explained the goals of the
Soviet government this way: "There can be no question
of rehabilitating the national economy or of communism
unless Russia is put on a different and a higher technical
basis than that which has existed up to now. Communism is
Soviet power plus the electrification of the whole country,
since industry cannot be developed without electrification.
This is a long-term task which will take at least ten years to
accomplish, provided a great number of technical experts are
drawn into the work."

The vision was put into practice in 1928 after the defeat of
the Trotskyite and Bukharinite opposition, and the triumph
of Stalin's vision of Socialism in one country. Stalin's five
year economic plans completely transformed the Soviet
Union into an economic superpower. By 1936, the USSR
was the world's top steel manufacturer, and had constructed
the world's largest hydro-electrical power plant. The Soviet
Union had brought running water and electricity to every
household and wiped out illiteracy among the population.
New universities had been constructed across the country,
and modern apartment buildings had replaced rural villages
with huts.
Interviewed for a 1998 PBS documentary called *Red Flag,*

part of the *People's Century* documentary series, Tatiana Federova, an elderly female construction worker described her memories of the Five Year Plans: "We wanted to do something with our own hands, to glorify our country -- not just with words but with deeds. And we did it. We built the metro, we built Magnetogorsk, we built the railway. We did it all with such comradeship, enthusiasm and happiness. And if today I could live again, despite all the big difficulties, I would have done the same things again...Stalin set a task: build this or build that and, thanks to the fact that people trusted him and this enthusiasm of young people, it was possible. Remember, people were illiterate, lived in virtual darkness, wore birch bark shoes. Even now I think it's like something out of a fairy tale. It was one of the most difficult times to build this country. To build these great construction sites would only be possible through unity, the unity of the people and the love of the people to their idol."

The secret behind this massive success in economic construction was socialist-central planning. The Soviet state had the ability to do what the chaos of the market cannot do, unleashing growth. The Soviet Union had eliminated the anarchy of production, the chaos of the market, and thus enabled a backward, under-developed society to rise to the level of a global superpower. The Stalin era was marked by mobilizations of the population to achieve collective goals toward the overall rebirth of the country.

Maurice Dobb, an economics lecturer at the University of Cambridge, summarizes with actual numbers the economic progress that was made by socialist planning in the USSR between 1928 and 1938 in his text *Soviet Economics Development Since 1917*. In this single decade, the Soviet Union multiplied its rate of electrification tenfold. During this period coal production increased by three and a half times, and 20 new tramway systems were built, along with 80 new bus systems. The number of hospital beds in rural areas doubled. By 1938, the Soviet Union had a larger tractor production apparatus than any other country in the world, and also led the world in locomotive production. American Radio personality Frazier Hunt, writing for *The New York American* in 1931, emphasized how dramatic the Soviet Union's explosion of economic growth really was. He said "Japan, westernizing and industrializing itself 50 years ago, was doing child's play compared to what the Soviet Union is doing today…Already, almost overnight, the USSR has become an industrial country."

One of the great achievements of the Soviet Union's rapid industrialization was the creation of the Dnieper Dam located in Ukraine. When this hydro-electrical facility was completed in 1932, it was the largest such facility in the entire world at the time. The Soviet government hired technicians from General Electric, the American corporation, to oversee the project and then mobilized thousands of people to build this massive power plant that brought electricity to the Soviet countryside. In 1941, as Nazi invaders poured into Ukraine, the local residents dynamited the dam so the Nazis could not seize it and use it for their war efforts. The Dnieper Dam was then reconstructed after the war.

It must be noted that the economic renaissance created by socialism in Russia and the surrounding republics that made up the Soviet Union, took place while the western world was experiencing the Great Depression. Writing for *The Nation* in November of 1931, Louis Fischer observed: "The Soviet frontier is like a charmed circle which the world economic crisis cannot cross. While banks crash, while production falls and trade languishes abroad, the Soviet Union continues in an orgy of construction and national development. The scale and speed of its progress are unprecedented."

The Soviet Union was a center of scientific and technological innovation. Soviet scientists invented space travel and LED lights. The Soviet Union created the AK-47 rifle, the most efficient weapon ever invented. The first mobile phone ever created was patented in 1957, by Soviet engineer Leonid Ivanovich Kupriyanovich.

While western countries freely adopted Soviet technology, the *Coordinating Committee for Multilateral Export Controls* functioned as an agreement between 16 NATO Countries banning the sale of high technology to the USSR. The *New York Times* described the treaty as "organized to ensure that strategic technology, such as computers, machine tools and microelectronics items that could be used for weapons and other military applications, did not fall into the hands of the Soviet Union." Though the USSR was prevented from collaborating with western computer companies, and had nowhere near the level of resources to invest in such endeavors, the Soviet Union actually went as far as manufacturing its own home computer system in 1985, the Elektronika BK-0010.

In the contemporary United States, statements to the effect of the "Soviet Union completely failed" or "socialism has never worked anywhere" are quite common. These statements simply spit in the face of well-documented evidence and do not acknowledge the economic miracles that took place during the golden years of the Soviet Union. From 1917 to 1960, the life expectancy of the Soviet people nearly doubled. Medical care was made widely available in even the most remote parts of the country. The overall living conditions for the population within the Soviet Union improved tremendously due to socialist central planning. Despite the shortcomings of Soviet society in terms of human rights and consumer goods, no society had ever raised its technological level and living conditions so rapidly.

As the Soviet Union was rapidly industrializing, the world's press marveled at what it had accomplished. Among the voices praising the Soviet Union were Albert Einstein, H.G. Wells, the young Nelson Mandella, and British intellectuals Sidney and Beatrice Webb. In his autobiography, published in 1969, the well-loved African-American scholar W.E.B. Dubois wrote: "What I saw in the Soviet Union was more than a triumph in physics; it was the growth of a nation's soul, the confidence of great people in its plan and future... We have begun to recognize the Soviet Socialist Republic as giving its peoples the best education of any in the world, excelling in science and organizing industry at the highest levels."

After repudiating the Trotskyite opposition, the Soviet Union very much became a society marching in line with the legacy of city builders throughout human history. When the 1956 edition of the *Encyclopedia Britannica* was published, the entry for Josef Stalin acknowledged the vast improvements of living conditions proclaiming: "He had found Russia working with wooden plows and left it equipt with atomic piles."

Victories for All Humanity

The advances that the Soviet Union brought to humanity were not merely technological. The socialist state founded

by the Bolsheviks spawned the music Shastokovich,
great advances in modern ballet, as well as the cinematic
breakthroughs of Sergei Eisenstein, the father of montage.
The New York Times glowed with admiration for the Soviet
Union's cultural achievements in 1931, writing: "There
seems to be no parallel in history to the drive for learning
in all branches of knowledge, from reading and writing to
the abstruse sciences, now in progress in the Soviet Union...
Before the revolution only about 7,000,000 children attended
school; now there are 23,000,000. The whole school system
is growing by leaps and bounds; the teaching is according to
the most scientific methods, it is carried on in 70 languages,
there being over 100 peoples going to make up the Soviet
Union. A system of compulsory schooling has been adopted
and everywhere applied...There is a whole deluge of books
pouring from the printing presses, the Soviet Union being
already the world leader as a publisher of books—not to
speak of their superior quality. The theatre, the swiftly-
growing radio and motion pictures, are also tremendous
educational instruments."

The Soviet Union inserted a very big shift into global
consciousness with its condemnation of racial prejudice and
discrimination. The Soviet Union, from its inception, rejected
the idea that one race is superior to another, something that
was widely accepted in most of the world at that time. W.E.B.
Dubois wrote about how the lack of racial prejudice in the
USSR was something he, as a Black man from the United
States, was deeply impressed with: "The Soviet Union seems
to be the only European country where people are not more or
less taught to look down on some class, group or race. I know
countries where race and color prejudice show only slight
manifestations, but no white country where race and color
prejudice seem so absolutely absent."

Internationally, the Soviet Union championed the rights of various marginalized people, most notably African Americans in the United States. The USSR presented William L. Patterson's text *We Charge Genocide* to the United Nations, exposing the horrors of Jim Crow segregation. It was only in the context of the Cold War, and constant ridicule in the Soviet press, along with communist-led protests for civil rights at home, that the leaders of the United States moved to adjust issues of racial injustice. Soviet influence pushed the United Nations to begin making statements condemning any form of racial or ethnic supremacy. It is primarily due to the Soviet Union's gigantic efforts on the international arena, that in our contemporary world, opposition to racism has become so widespread.

The Soviet Union's project of creating a socialist society spread to China when Mao Zedong and the Communist Party took power in 1949. Fidel Castro's revolution in Cuba, Kim Il Sung's revolution on the Korean Peninsula, all resulted in huge advances in living standards. No matter how flawed the socialist societies of the 20th century were, they each abolished illiteracy, created universal housing, and implemented a new level of industrialization. While the *Atlanticist Pathology* and the economic global order of imperialism would have kept these countries as agrarian, underdeveloped, captive markets, it was socialist planned economies that brought electricity, running water, and industrialization to so much of the planet.

Socialist improvement of basic living conditions for people across the planet included major infrastructure projects. For example, in 1960 the Soviet Union and the Arab Socialist Egyptian leader Gamal Abdul Nasser together launched the construction of the Aswan Dam, the largest hydroelectric facility in the Middle East. When the dam was completed in 1967, the facility brought power to almost every village in Egypt, most of which had never had electricity. The Aswan Dam increased the amount of irrigated land in Egypt by a third, and enabled Egypt to produce more of its own food than ever before. Not only did the dam greatly increase agricultural output, but it also shielded Egypt's farms from many of the frequent droughts that plague the region.

In the context of the Cold War, the western world was forced to relent and tolerate some level of development among its allies. Bonapartist regimes in South Korea, Iran, Chile, Argentina, and elsewhere oversaw some basic economic development, hoping to stop the spread of Communist revolution during the 1950s and 1960s. The words of US President John F. Kennedy, "Those who make peaceful revolution impossible make violent revolution inevitable" were the sentiments of the time. Intending to stop the spread of the Marxism-Leninism, the western bankers loosened their grip, and allowed some countries within their own sphere to break the chains of poverty.

In 1963, the Kennedy administration worked with the Shah of Iran to implement his *White Revolution*, redistributing land and building railways. As historian Ervand Abrahmanian explained "The White Revolution had been designed to preempt a Red Revolution."

In 1968, the United States facilitated Japan lending millions of dollars to South Korea, so that the dictator Park Chung Hee could oversee the creation of the POSCO steel corporation. With huge amounts of government oversight and state control, the bonapartist Park regime in South Korea brought in lots of foreign investment. The hope of western leaders was that South Korea would be prevented from joining China and its northern countryfolk in socialist revolution, if a prosperous middle class could be established.

The period of 1951 to 1973, labelled as the *Post World War Two Economic Expansion* by economists, is the longest and largest period of economic growth in all of world history. Never before has humanity experienced so much construction and progress taking place. This period of uninterpreted growth across the planet involved construction and central planning in the Soviet Union and other socialist countries, bonapartist state-sponsored development in Asia, and many developing capitalist countries, along with the height of the Keynesian welfare states and social democracy in Europe.

The notions that "socialism does not work" or "socialism makes people poor," commonly stated in US media and discourse, are simply laughable when observing the actual economic data. Socialism's triumph in the USSR, and expansion into China and Eastern Europe, ultimately resulted in the greatest overall episode of human progress and advancement ever achieved. It should be noted that the global, post-war boom ended with the collapse of the Bretton-Woods Financial System in 1971, and the subsequent oil crisis of 1973. These setbacks, that halted a massive wave of growth, came from the capitalist world, not some inherent flaw in socialism.

The results of Lenin's conspiracy in exile, to seize control of his homeland with a *party of new type* were massive. Many great strides forward for humanity were taken as a result of socialism being put into practice, regardless of the widely-heralded short comings and setbacks.

47

II

History does not march in a straight line. Zigzags and regressions often follow great advances. The progress of humanity can often be observed in patterns such as *one step forward, two steps back.*

Between the moment when socialism as the 20th century incarnation of the city-building tendency was in ascendency, and the situation facing the planet today, is a period marked by many disasters and regressions. These setbacks have allowed the *Atlanticist Pathology* to rebound and to mask itself in many new disguises.

The result has been a high level of political confusion. The political compass that defined the Cold-War era is now broken. *Left* and *Right* are harder to define than ever. A clear-headed analysis is needed in order to assess where we stand today in terms of the global economy and geopolitics. The clash between city builders and vandals persists, though the ideological division between the two camps is not as clear.

Revolutionary Intelligentsia & The Broad Masses

Among those in the world who call themselves leftists, socialists communists or Marxists two distinct psychologies exist.

No matter where you go in the world, you can always find a revolutionary intelligentsia. These are younger people of middle-class origin who become attracted to revolutionary ideas out of a desire to tear down the unjust world around them. The revolutionary intelligentsia is always a small minority within society. They are known for their boldness, courage, and their outrage at inequality. They strive to create chaos and disorder. In their youthful passion, they seek to dethrone oppressors and correct injustice with explosive displays of heroism.

The Marxist movement certainly originated among such a revolutionary intelligentsia in Europe, but such sentiments long predate it. Before Karl Marx was even born, William Blake, the English poet famously wrote: "I shall not cease from mental strife, nor shall my sword sleep in my hand, until we have built Jerusalem in England's green and pleasant land". Such feelings of passion and rebellion among a privileged intellectual strata were key in toppling feudalism, not just in Blake's England, but all across Europe.

Like Trotsky, who sought for the Soviet Union to be only a temporary military holdout in his fantasy of global permanent revolution, the revolutionary intelligentsia is wedded to a spiritual conception of a relentless struggle to create Utopia, despite all costs. Some of the most admired figures in world history, such as Joan of Ark and Che Guevara seemed to give voice to this mindset by choosing lives of struggle.

However, for those who approach the question of historical progress scientifically, not merely romantically, a certain truth must be acknowledged. Though the revolutionary intelligentsia may be brave, forward thinking, creative, and intelligent, it is not capable of giving birth to a socialist society. Socialist revolutions have always been made by the broad masses of people, who turn to revolutionary and anti-capitalist ideas, motivated by very different desires.

While the revolutionary intelligentsia has always existed, no matter what the state of affairs in society, the broad masses of people generally avoid revolutionary and anti-capitalist politics. Only when economic hardship and war make their lives increasingly less stable, when society can no longer function in the old way, do the broad masses of people take up history's challenge. In such times they are forced by material conditions to examine the nature of the crisis and seek a way out. In times of great crisis, the millions who normally avoid politics and ideology, will turn to socialists and revolutionaries for a solution.

The broad masses approach socialism with completely opposite desires from the revolutionary intelligentsia. The broad masses of people do not desire chaos. They turn to socialism because they see it as bringing order and stability. Socialism is appealing because it will ensure that they are no longer desperate, hungry, or living in great uncertainty. Socialism offers the hope, not for vengeance or some kind of cathartic uprising to correct injustice, but rather, for reducing their pain and creating a more stable and safe world.

The Bolsheviks won the support of the Russian people by offering *Peace, Land and Bread*, not by promising *Permanent Revolution*. Immediately following the revolution, Lenin insisted that a treaty withdrawing from the war be signed in order to keep the trust of the masses, who had supported the Bolsheviks due to their anti-war platform. The Bolsheviks had risen to power promising to end Russia's involvement in the First World War, redistribute land, and raise the living standards, and they kept this promise.

In China, Mao Zedong won the peasants and the broad masses of Chinese people over, not with promises of *storming heaven* but with talk of *land to the tiller*, *New Democracy*, and defeating the Japanese invaders.

At the height of its strength during the 1930s depression, the Communist Party USA (CPUSA) thoroughly understood this. As Americans were unemployed and hungry, William Z. Foster proposed *A Revolutionary Way Out of the Crisis* as the slogan for his 1932 presidential election. In the 1940 election, the CPUSA ran Earl Browder for President, with an even more explicit articulation of these sentiments in his slogan *The Way Out*. Both of these electoral campaigns received the votes of tens of thousands of people, despite being driven from the ballot in various states.

The strength of the CPUSA during the height of its power in the 1930s was its unemployment councils and labor unions that provided relief for the desperately poor while advocating on their behalf in local community struggles. A 1936 article that was wildly hostile to the CPUSA published in *Fortune* magazine admits the source of the party's increasingly popularity at the time: "Not long ago a government official toured the country, penniless and clothed in tatters, to see for himself how unemployment relief was being handled. He learned a great deal. 'Even the communists taught me something,' he told reporters. 'I learned that the power the communists have is gained principally because they will listen to people who are down and out and will work for them and fight for them."

The Black Panther Party of the 1960s and 1970s also drew its strength from providing services to those in need. After expelling Eldridge Cleaver's faction that advocated ultra-leftist adventurism and violence, the organization shifted toward community service. The Black Panthers, following the examples of successful revolutionary organizations around the world, launched a free breakfast program, healthcare clinics, and other programs described as *survival pending revolution.*

The typewritten statement launching the *Free Breakfast for Children Program* in 1969 and appealing for financial support, issued from the national office of the Black Panther Party explained its purpose: "One of the greatest forms of oppression is hunger. Children must be fed and the Free Breakfast for School Children is another key to liberation by halting the staunch form of oppression - HUNGER. One who looks into the face of a hungry child knows that his need is immediate. One can delay an asking face with a cold heart. A child does not understand hunger surveys made by the government, but he can relate to a full stomach every morning."

While these words may sound mild, the US federal government realized how potentially revolutionary this program was. In May of 1969, shortly after the program was launched, FBI director J. Edgar Hoover issued a special memo pointing out how effective the program was in winning mass support for the Black Nationalism and Communism among African-Americans. Hoover wrote:

"The BCP (Breakfast for Children Program) promotes at least tacit support for the Black Panther Party among naive individuals and, what is more distressing, it provides the BPP with a ready audience composed of highly impressionable youths. Consequently, the BCP represents the best and most influential activity going for the BPP and, as such, is potentially the greatest threat to efforts by authorities to neutralize the BPP and destroy what it stands for".

It is abundantly clear, to those who seriously study the history of revolutionary politics, that what attracts the broad masses of people to socialist ideas in times of crisis, and what captures the imagination of the revolutionary intelligentsia, are distinctly different. Around the world, effective revolutionary organizations that ultimately succeed in taking power, win support from those who are suffering and want a new order that will protect them from capitalism's irrationality.

This reality of two different motivations behind revolutionary anti-capitalism has become apparent to the western intelligence agencies in their efforts to beat back socialism and secure Wall Street's domination of the planet. Open and direct efforts to manipulate the revolutionary intelligentsia and separate it from the socialist countries of the world and the masses of the American people have completely redefined politics in our contemporary world.

The Synthetic Left

The CIA's program known as the Congress for Cultural Freedom (CCF) was created explicitly for the purpose of manipulating left-wing artists and intellectuals in order to weaken the influence of the Soviet Union. CIA's website boasts that this program was one of its most successful operations.

The CIA's article summarizing its CCF program goes into great detail about how the operation was conducted. To lead the program, Sidney Hook, a New York City Trotskyite Professor was selected. The program involved covertly funding and circulating a publication called *Partisan Review*, which highlighted intellectuals like Susan Sontag, Irving Howe, Isaac Duetscher, Noam Chomsky, George Orwell, and others. The idea was to cultivate intellectuals and leftists who were critical of western capitalism, but who strongly opposed anything that would challenge it on the global stage. The website boasts that the CCF program was carried out by: "a cadre of energetic and well-connected staffers willing to experiment with unorthodox ideas and controversial individuals if that was what it took to challenge the communists at their own game."

Through the CCF program, the CIA covertly funded the work of Jackson Pollack, a painter who refused to depict people, scenery, or even clear shapes, but simply splattered paint onto his canvas. His *abstract* and *modern* art was viewed as a celebration of western freedom, contrasted with the *propaganda* art of the Soviet Union in which the artist sought to espouse a political message. Among academia, the Frankfurt School and the "Neo-Marxism" were pushed forward with the covert help of US intelligence agencies. Herbert Marcuse, who had been employed by the US State Department and US intelligence agencies, became the selected academic spokesperson for the *New Left*.

Efforts were made to portray "Stalinism" and the pro-Soviet communist parties as authoritarian and out of touch. Sidney

Hook is quoted as saying "Give me a hundred million dollars and a thousand dedicated people, and I will guarantee to generate such a wave of democratic unrest among the masses--yes, even among the soldiers--of Stalin's own empire, that all his problems for a long period of time to come will be internal. I can find the people."

The efforts to control the revolutionary intelligentsia and separate it from the revolutionary movements across the planet, went beyond academia and leftism. Much like the Roman Emperors, in order to control their population imported cults and exotic gods from across the empire, the US intelligence agencies began importing primitive sects from Asia.

CIA director John Foster Dulles wrote: "The religions of the East are deeply rooted and have many precious values. Their spiritual beliefs cannot be reconciled with Communist atheism and materialism. That creates a common bond between us, and our task is to find it and develop it". The CIA followed Dulles' instructions, and some of the most primitive eastern cults were not only supported in Asia, as they worked against the Chinese Communist Party, but brought to the USA to flourish among intellectuals who might have otherwise become Marxists.

The Dalai Lama's regime in Tibet was particularly repressive with serfdom, executions, torture, and mutilations. During the 1950s, hundreds of thousands of people died as the United States airdropped Buddhist monks with stockpiles of weapons into the mountains of Tibet to foment civil war against the Peoples Republic of China. The Dalai Lama's oldest brother, Gyalo Thondup, was among those who killed communist literacy volunteers and burned healthcare clinics in the hopes of reestablishing the feudal kingdom. The efforts of the CIA to popularize the Dalai Lama and his Tibet separatist movement are documented in the book *The CIA's Secret War in Tibet* published by the Heritage Foundation.

Yet, to American audiences, the Dalai Lama is presented as a *man of peace* and it is leftists and liberals who are among his adoring flock. This is particularly ironic when it is recognized that prior to the Cold War, the Tibetan kingdom was a fetish of right-wing extremists. The book *Seven Years in Tibet*, considered a sacred text among western advocates of Tibet separatism, was written by Heinrich Harrer, a card carrying member of Hitler's SS. Rightist intellectual Julius Evola, and the Nazi regime itself, praised Tibetan society under the Dalai Lama's rule for how authoritarian and traditional it was. Under the iron grip of the Dalai Lama, who functioned as any ancient god-king, no strikes or protests seemed to exist. Tibet's admirers in the 1930s saw the ancient kingdom that opposed science and maintained serfdom as the fascist ideal of a *natural order.*

Abhaya Caranāravinda Bhaktivedānta Svāmi was the first of many Indian *gurus* to be brought to the United States. In 1966, he established the *International Society for Krishna Consciousness*, commonly known as the Hare Krishna Movement. The organization actively recruited young peace activists, students, teenage runaways, and other demographics that commonly make up the revolutionary intelligentsia to a far-right wing brand of Hinduism. Many other *mystics* and gurus, who are considered to be far-right extremists and fanatical anti-communists in India, trickled into the United States.

In India, these religious teachings were associated with

massacres of Muslims, assassinations of trade unionists, child marriage, and the caste system. These sects generally oppose any effort to correct social injustices, arguing simply that the poor should live a humble life in the hopes of being reincarnated into a better position.

Those who align themselves with these most right-wing and authoritarian elements in India were carefully selected to become favored teachers among peace activists and left wingers in the United States. The Hare Krishna movement became a staple of anti-war rallies in the United States.

In addition to anti-communist politics and eastern cults, the use of narcotics has also become an aspect of left-wing activity in western countries. The revolutionary movements around the world had always fought to liberate working people from the horror of addiction. Wiping out the scourge of heroin and opium is one of the Chinese Communist Party's greatest achievements. The CPUSA forbid its members from using drugs, and many socialist organizations in US history have even discouraged the drinking of alcohol. Marxists have generally seen drug addiction as a horrific scourge of capitalism, in which people turn to substances in order to numb their pain. Marx famously compared organized religion to opium, saying it was the "heart of a heartless world, and the soul of soulless conditions."

However, covert efforts by the US government, aimed at cultivating a *synthetic left* and preventing the rise of any effective socialist movement, reversed this longstanding position among Marxists and socialists. During the early 1960s, the CIA launched a program called MK-ULTRA and began to conduct experiments and distribute hallucinogens to college students. In the places where young people were opposing the Vietnam War or marching for civil rights, LSD, marijuana, heroin, and cocaine always seemed to be present.

Dr. Timothy Leary, a fired Harvard Psychology professor, traveled across the United States urging young people who protested the Vietnam War or marched for civil rights to use narcotics. His slogan was "Tune in, Turn on, Drop out" and he became a national figure, speaking on many college campuses and appearing frequently on national TV.

On August 17th, 2010, the retired Fidel Castro devoted one of his columns in Cuba's daily newspaper *Granma,* to quoting the work of Lithuanian writer Daniel Estulin. Castro's column describes efforts to subvert leftism in the United States: "...Both in the United States and in Europe the big outdoor rock concerts were used to stop the increasing discontent among the population... According to recently released CIA documents (thanks to the Freedom of Information Act), Allen Dulles purchased over 100 million doses of LSD -- almost all of which flooded the streets of the United States during the late 1960s'...Thousands of graduate students served as guinea pigs. Soon they were synthesizing their own 'acid'...The overwhelming majority of anti-war protesters went into SDS (Students for a Democratic Society) on the basis of outrage at the developments in Vietnam. But once caught in the environment defined by the Tavistock Institute's psychological warfare experts... their sense of values and their creative potential went up in a cloud of hashish smoke".

The Malthusian concept of *overpopulation* and the belief the scientific progress is an affront to *mother nature* has also slipped into leftist discourse. While environmental problems and climate change are certainly a reality, the answer is obviously more scientific progress, not less. New, sustainable energy sources must be developed and utilized. The economy must be controlled in order for resources to be used in a logical way in line with long-term plans, not the short term interests of individual capitalists.

However, this is not the belief of most activists who call themselves environmentalists and ecologists. Rather than calling for a rational state-run economy, and scientific progress in order to overcome global warming, the dominant voices in the green movement tend to look backward.

Among *leftist* circles, one often now finds the belief that human beings are a cancerous tumor on the planet eating up precious resources. The Neo-Malthusian voices that speak in the name of *environmentalism* now call for drastically reducing living standards and the human population. Many great infrastructure projects in the developing world have been stopped in the name of ecology.

One of the central beliefs of many within the current that can accurately be described as the *synthetic left* is a rejection of historical progress. While the political designations of *left* and *right* can be traced back to the French Revolution, and the very concept of historical progress itself, so much has been distorted. This distortion is not accidental, but has been documented to be the result of intentional work by intelligence agencies.

Susan Sontag's Redefinition of Fascism

Through covert efforts, the revolutionary intelligentsia has not only been rendered harmless to the western system, but it has essentially been hijacked by it. Rather than acting as the champions of working class people against the rich and powerful, the *synthetic left* has largely become a battering ram serving neoliberalism and the efforts of the international financial oligarchy.

This is not only true within the United States, but also on the international arena. Today, US interventions are promoted with liberal-sounding language. Countries are invaded to *liberate the women*. Sanctions are imposed on countries out of supposed concern for the rights of the LGBTQ community. US media portrays the activists covertly funded to topple anti-imperialist governments as Guevara-esque *freedom fighters* while the independent and anti-imperialist governments are represented as cold, mechanical tanks, inhuman machines ruthlessly crushing individuals and their dreams of freedom.

This propaganda formula, where the western world is associated with freedom, consumerism and a lifting of restrictions, while anti-imperialist governments are equated with the fictional society in George Orwell's 1984 involved a careful restructuring of how progressive and socialist-oriented people view the world. A key part of this has been redefining the nature of fascism, and obscuring the fact that the USA and the Soviet Union were allies in the fight against Nazi Germany.

In 1935, Bulgarian Georgi Dmitrov, the Secretary of the Communist International defined fascism "as the open terrorist dictatorship of the most reactionary, most chauvinistic and most imperialist elements of finance capital." Fascism has always been understood by Marxists to be a form of right-wing terrorism and violence used to carry out mass repression in a time of political crisis. Fascism often represents the Marxist phenomenon of Bonapartism, where the capitalists suppress not only the workers and the oppressed, but also members of their own class in the hopes of restoring order amid ongoing turmoil.

As the revolutionary intelligentsia became coopted and prevented from being a force of opposition to western capitalism, a new definition of fascism emerged. Presently the political orientation has become so confused that often young leftists working to topple revolutionary and anti-imperialist governments on behalf of Wall Street and London will somehow believe they are engaging in "anti-fascist" heroism like the communists of the 1930s.

The pseudo-leftist intellectual Susan Sontag was the most explicit in redefining fascism to serve the global financial elite. Sontag, who was first published in the CIA-funded *Partisan Review* magazine, famously proclaimed in 1982: "Communism is fascism - successful fascism, if you will... communism is in itself a variant, the most successful variant of fascism." She made these statements at a rally in support of the Solidarity movement in Poland, in which Roman Catholic dock workers helped to topple the Marxist-Leninist government.

Though much of Sontag's work drew heavily from Karl Marx's teachings about capitalism, the origins of private property and the family, and his critiques of western society, she ultimately rejected all aspects of Marxism other than these. The only acceptable, non-fascist application of Marxism, according to Sontag, who is celebrated widely among post-modern leftists and liberals, is as a mechanism for deconstruction.

According to Sontag's analysis, presented in essays like her piece *Fascinating Fascism* published in 1975 in the New York Review of Books, fascism is essentially anything that seeks to construct, build, and unify. In her famous essay examining Nazi collaborator Leni Riefenstahl's photographic exhibit of African tribes, she defines the photographs as *fascist* for the following reasons: "…it is generally thought that national socialism stands only for brutishness and terror. But this is not true. National socialism - more broadly - fascism - also stands for an ideal or rather ideals that are persistent today under the other banners: ideal of life as art, the cult of beauty, the fetishism of courage, the dissolution of alienation in the ecstatic feelings of community… the family of man… Although the Nuba are black, not Aryan, Riefenstahl's portrait of them evokes some of the larger themes of Nazi ideology: the contact between the clean and the impure, the incorruptible and the defiled, the physical and the mental, the joyful and the critical".

According to Sontag, it doesn't matter if one explicitly preaches hate or authoritarianism, because any effort to build a stable, prosperous society is fascist. Sontag lists characteristics of Fascist Aesthetics as including: "extravagant effort, and the endurance of pain… the massing of groups of people; the turning of people into things; the multiplication and replication of things and grouping of people/things around an all-powerful hypnotic leader-figure or force. The fascist dramaturgy centers on the orgiastic transactions between mighty forces and their puppets, uniformly garbed and shown in swelling numbers. Its choreography alternates between ceaseless motions and a congealed, static, "virile" posing. Fascist art glorifies surrender, it exalts mindlessness, it glamorizes death".

She explains "mass athletic demonstration, a choreographed display of bodies are a valued activity in all totalitarian countries; and the art of the gymnast, so popular now in Eastern Europe, also evokes recurrent features of fascist aesthetics; the holding in or confining of force; military precision".

Explaining her belief that Communism is a variant of fascism she states: "In both fascist and communist politics, the will is staged publicly in the drama of the leader and chorus".

According to Sontag's analysis, which represents very clearly the feelings of the *synthetic, post-modern left*, any attempt to organize society and unleash collective human brilliance is *fascist* at its core. Sontag's logic follows that because of what the Soviet Union and China have achieved in terms raising living standards and transforming the lives of millions, it is the most successful, and therefore, the most dangerous form of fascism.

Marxism-Leninism is the equivalent of fascism because communists, like fascists, believe in right and wrong. Communists, like fascists, are motivated to support the cause of right in politics and encourage *extravagant effort* from their adherents, *fetishizing courage*. Communists, like fascists, form political parties and mass movements dedicated to their ideas. Communists, like fascists, seek to *create ecstatic feelings of community* and achieve *the dissolution of alienation*. Communists, like fascists, seek to create a *family of man* and breaking away from the central thesis of western liberalism, that individualism must prevail above all else.

To Sontag, the differences between fascists and communists do not seem to matter. The fact that fascists seek to restore order and preserve social hierarchies with mass violence and terror, while communists seek to control the means of production and use science to advance human progress is conveniently overlooked.

According to the *synthetic, post-modern left*, ideology itself is the problem. Concepts like right and wrong and morality must be abandoned. Everything should be considered a clash of different narratives, shades of gray.

All efforts toward social progress and collectivism must be rejected as *totalitarian* and all efforts to deconstruct or disrupt civilization must be celebrated as *liberation*. In essence, the *synthetic left* has purged Marxism and left-wing politics of the progressive, city-building tendency. Leftism, for the post-modernists, is purely a vehicle for deconstruction. It is in essence, vandalism, dressed in progressive clothing.

The Rise of the Color Revolutions

This reality, about the nature of the *synthetic left* became very apparent during the collapse of the Soviet Union and the fall of various socialist countries across the Eastern Bloc.

Zbiegnew Brzezinski's entire career involved fomenting discontent in socialist countries, and he learned how to manipulate the intelligentsia of frustrated intellectuals across the socialist world. Brzezinski combined his efforts with those of Hungarian billionaire George Soros. Soros funneled money to dissident groups, helping to create instability in the socialist countries.

The grievances which Brzezinski and Soros manipulated were very real. The socialist countries faced an economic blockade, preventing the inflow of consumer goods and western technology. In the face of constant military threats and covert efforts to overturn socialism, the Marxist-Leninist governments maintained a very authoritarian political system, not offering the freedom that many young people longed for. While the industrial workers of the socialist countries were largely content, it was the educated strata of the youth, often children of the privileged party bureaucrats, who felt stifled.

In each of the various countries that saw capitalism restored during the late 1980s and early 1990s, a group of confused young intellectuals played a central role. The young nonconformists among the intellectual strata of socialist countries were in awe of blue jeans, rock music, and western consumer goods. Most of these young dissidents did not believe they were marching to overthrow socialism, but rather marching simply for freedom. They believed that in following their revolution against the Marxist-Leninist government, they could keep guaranteed employment, healthcare, and housing, but simply add to it a higher level of civil liberties, artistic freedom, and an inflow of western consumer goods.

These illusions defined the Prague Spring of 1968 and were perpetuated up until the 1990s. The illusion was that *synthetic left* represented a more humane, less authoritarian form of socialism. In reality, it simply opened the door to free market plunder and the recolonization of eastern Europe by western capitalism.

The formula was replicated across the Communist Bloc. Young intellectuals mobilized to protest around vague demands for freedom. Sections of the police force and military would express sympathy with them. Western media would play up the idea that the tyrannical regime was on the verge of massacring the peaceful demonstrators, and amid the chaos and panic, a pro-US faction of the military would seize power. The new regime with the blessing of Washington would then proceed to dismantle the economic system, sell off state assets, and reduce the population to extreme poverty.

The vote to preserve the Soviet Union was overwhelming. The peoples of the smaller republics, which the US media often described as colonies that were longing for independence voted to preserve the USSR at even higher rates than the Russians did. The popular vote was ignored by the pro-western faction that seized power and the Soviet Union was dissolved.

In Russia, the first election following the fall of the Soviet Union resulted in mass victories for the Communist Party. Boris Yeltsin then used his emergency powers to dissolve the legislature. When the Communist deputies refused to leave their posts, Yeltsin sent the military to crush them. What followed was a bloody episode of street fighting in which 187 people were killed and 437 others were wounded.

This model of staging color revolutions to overthrow socialist and anti-imperialist governments continues up to this day.

The Arab Spring of 2011 was cheered on by social media and American TV networks in language that sounded almost Trotskyesque. Anne-Marie Slaughter, Samantha Power, and various figures within Hillary Clinton's State Department, spoke of a global strategy of toppling independent governments and socialist states as if it was a leftist political cause. The Silicon Valley elites and social-media monopolists joined the operation.

An essay by Anne-Marie Slaughter for *Foreign Affairs*, the publication of the Council on Foreign Relations proclaims: "The people must come first, when they do not, sooner or later they will overthrow their governments." Slaughter's text goes on talk about the evils of populism and why social media led revolutions and the responsibility to protect (R2P) clause in the UN charter, must be used to topple regimes that don't respect the free market, the *open international system* and freedom of information.

One is reminded of Trotsky's theory of an endless, borderless, permanent revolution except that Slaughter makes no pretense of being a socialist. It is a permanent revolution to preserve the rule of western monopolist bankers. It is the mindset of the revolutionary intelligentsia in service of the *Atlanticist Pathology*.

The claim that unregulated capitalism would bring prosperity was widely discredited in eastern Europe as the swift imposition of free markets resulted in a humanitarian crisis. In each nation, mass unemployment, mass starvation, and mass poverty accompanied western corporations looting of the country. Sex trafficking and heroin became a big part of the new order of capitalism in eastern Europe. The rate of suicide and drug-related deaths skyrocketed. In Russia, the rate of heroin addiction increased by roughly 900% in the decade following the fall of the Soviet Union.

Noami Klein's widely praised book *The Shock Doctrine* described the results of free-market policies in Russia: "more than 80 percent of Russian farms had gone bankrupt and roughly seventy thousand state factories had closed creating an epidemic of unemployment." She goes on to describe how 74 million Russians lived in poverty, and "25 percent of Russians – almost 37 million people – lived in poverty described as 'desperate'".

With its farms and factories closed down amid the dismantling of socialism, Russia became a "captive market" for the imperialists. It was forced to import its food from the United States, and steel and raw materials from western countries. Wealthy western capitalists saw control of the Russian market as a way to reap super profits. Among those who plundered Russia was Bill Browder of Hermitage Capital Management, now featured as an expert on Vladimir Putin on western television. He has also testified before the US congress.

Klien quoted Russian academic Vladimir Gusev who said: "The years of criminal capitalism have killed off 10 percent of our population". Indeed, the population of Russia decreased by 6.6 million between 1992 and 2006. US economist Andre Gunder Frank used the term economic genocide and was echoed Russian Vice President Alexander V. Rutskoi, who said children and the elderly had been the hardest hit.

Former US Senator Bill Bradley described what he observed in Russia when working with the Clinton administration in the 1990s: "30% unemployment, rampant inflation, pensions gone, savings gone, 30 or 40 years... it's all gone. No jobs. A few people doing very well, who bought all assets from the state, but the average person, no."

The rise of Russian President Vladimir Putin, now declared to be an enemy by the voices representing western capitalism, marked a turning point, as the Russian state apparatus stepped in to stop the chaos of the market. Putin's academic dissertation spoke of utilizing *national champions*, state-controlled mega corporations to reboot the economy. Putin gradually put his college thesis into practice. Gazprom and Rosneft were put at the center of an economy that was then reorganized around the state. Gradually moving back toward elements of central planning, the Putin government has raised living standards, restoring order from the disaster created by free markets under Yeltsin.

During the first eight years of Putin's presidency, poverty was reduced by 14% and wages doubled. Russia experienced industrial expansion of more than 70%. Between 2007 and 2014 Russia's Gross Domestic Product increased from $764 billion to $2096.8 billion.

Russia is no longer a captive market for the west. Russia's ability to grow its own food was almost wiped out during the 1990s, but in recent years the Putin government has constructed a modern, state-controlled agricultural system. Russia now exports more grain than any other country in the world, bringing in roughly $20 billion a year in revenue. Russia's agricultural exports jumped by 20% in 2018, and the state plans for the country to be an "agricultural superpower" by 2024, with a goal set for over $45 billion in revenue.

Looking over the results of Putin's economic policies Dr. Marshal Goldman of Harvard University wrote: "It is understandable why the Russian people regard Vladimir Putin as their savior." John Browne, the CEO of BP has praised Putin's policies saying "No country has come so far, in such a short space of time."

Putin is not a Marxist or a leftist and the Russian government does not espouse such politics. Putin's construction of a state-centered economy has been carried out in the name of Russian nationalism and the Orthodox Church, not social revolution and dialectical materialism. He doesn't offer permanent revolution but rather the hope that Russia can be allowed to experience economic growth and maintain its unique identity as a long-existing Eurasian civilization without western interference.

In the 21st century, the revolutionary intelligentsia's vague, psychological desire for chaos in order to achieve freedom no matter what the human cost has become a vehicle to tear down borders and spread capitalism across the planet. With slick romantic staging, the US State Department's efforts to topple populists and dictators who get in the way of Wall Street are presented almost like the contrived scenes from the Broadway Musical Les Miserables.

As a result of western capitalism hijacking revolutionary aesthetics, actual existing socialism has become more conservative in its messaging. Profits and instability are associated with western social liberalism, while governments presiding over state-run economies often align themselves with traditional values.

China's Great Adjustment

The organization founded by Mao Zedong and his comrades in the basement of a women's college dormitory in 1921, now has over 90 million members, and rules over the largest country on earth in terms of population. The Chinese Communist Party (CCP) has presided over one of the greatest economic miracles in history. While the Marxist governments

of the Soviet Union and eastern Europe crumbled in
the 1980s, the CCP was getting stronger. The Chinese
Communist Party is now arguably the most powerful political
organization in the world, with no other entity exercising as
much authority and operating in such a disciplined manner.

The Chinese Communist Party came to power in 1949 and
achieved solid economic achievements for the population
in its first years. With Soviet assistance, Mao Zedong
built the first steel mills in China, along with a network of
power plants, water treatment facilities and other critical
infrastructure.

While completing a stage of development which Mao
referred to as New Democracy the CCP mobilized the
population to wipe out opium addiction, prostitution, venereal
disease, and other social ills. Women were granted the right
to vote and the right to divorce, and allowed to become part
of the political process. Land was redistributed to peasants.
Eventually the peasants combined their independent tracts
of lands into communes and collective farms. University
education greatly expanded and illiteracy was wiped out. As
Deng Xiaoping explained: "In eight years, between 1949
and 1957, we had completed the socialist transformation of
agriculture, handicrafts and capitalist industry and commerce,
and thus entered the state of socialism."

However, the Soviet Union cut its ties with China's
leadership in 1961 withdrawing all of its economic assistance.
Only Albania fully sided with China against the Soviet
leaders. Blueprints were burned, buildings were left half
built, and the efforts to modernize the country slowed very
dramatically. In response to the Soviet Union's betrayal, the
Chinese Communist Party launched a campaign against

revisionism and rightism.

These efforts to be more revolutionary than the Soviet Union resulted in the rise of deeply problematic elements from within the Communist Party. The rhetoric of these figures paralleled the *synthetic left* in western countries. While their language seemed to be infused with communist ideology, they were largely unconcerned with raising living standards and fixated on punishing and purging people.

The peak of the ultra-leftist deviation within the Chinese Communist Party came in the final years of Mao Zedong's life with the rise of the Gang of Four. The urban youth were deported from the cities and sent to the countryside to engage in farm labor. The Gang of Four cultivated a culture of public humiliation and torture, along with continued disruptions of production and education. The rules were unwritten in an atmosphere of mob rule, where people were encouraged to shame and publicly torture their coworkers and neighbors for alleged anti-communist behaviors such as wearing make-up, listening to western music, owning anti-communist books, or not showing proper loyalty to Mao. Instead of trying to raise China's population from poverty, the Gang of Four focused on attempting to make a still deeply poor and under-developed country more egalitarian and pure in its application of revolutionary principles. The Gang of Four argued that economic development was not necessary to advance toward communism, saying that it was possible to "transition in poverty to a higher stage."

The pivot in China's political and economic model began in 1976, a few months prior to the death of Mao Zedong. It was the funeral of a prominent CCP leader named Zhou En-Lai that marked the turning point. Zhou En-Lai had been alongside Mao Zedong on the Long March, and helped lay the foundations of the People's Republic with him. Zhou was viewed as a moderate, who occasionally restrained the Gang of Four's extremism, and his funeral, became an outpouring of grief from educated young people who were deeply worried about the future of their country and felt stifled by the chaotic political atmosphere.

Chinese engineers, college professors, scientists, and innovators sobbed for Zhou En-Lai. The crowds at the funeral in Beijing broke into an explosion of anger and rioting that put the Communist Party on notice to a deep problem. Just like in Eastern Europe, the socialist system was stagnating. Creativity was being held back. The Soviet-style command economy desperately needed to be adjusted.

These riots, and Mao's death shortly afterward, paved the way for Deng Xiaoping to march into power in 1978. Deng ended the Cultural Revolution and launched his reform and opening up, heralded by the often quoted slogan "Poverty is not socialism, but to be rich is glorious."

In 1980, Deng Xiaoping explained a new strategy for building up Chinese socialism: "The fact that China is poor, has weak economic foundations and is backward in education, science and culture means that we have to go through a hard struggle... We want to make use of foreign funds and technology and to actively expand our foreign trade, but we must rely primarily on our own efforts. We are opposed to those absurd, reactionary concepts of "impoverished socialism", "transition in poverty to a higher stage", and "making revolution in poverty" touted by Lin Biao and the Gang of Four. But we are also opposed to the idea of turning China into a so-called welfare state right now because that's impossible. We can only improve our standard of living gradually, on the basis of expanded production. It is wrong to expand production without raising the people's standard of living; but it is likewise wrong — in fact impossible — to raise the people's standard of living without expanding production."

Deng gave particular attention to the strata of intellectuals who had been the basis of counter-revolutionary confusion in other socialist countries during this time: "Our teachers and scientists are faced with many difficulties in their living conditions, which urgently need to be overcome. Many intellectuals who are very capable earn well under 100 yuan a month. Given slightly better working and living conditions, they would be able to solve many more problems for the state and the people and create immense additional wealth. I could cite many other examples."

Instead of stifling intellectuals, the Chinese Communist Party found ways to utilize their skills in order to create economic growth. Model cities sprung up in places like Shenzen. Foreign investment poured into the country. As the living standards began to rise dramatically, it was clear that poverty socialism and the Cultural Revolution was dead, and *Socialism with Chinese Characteristics* was in bloom.

Many observers have argued that China "became capitalist" following Deng Xiaoping's 1978 reform and opening up. However, this is not the case. Engels described the nature of capitalism, writing "under capitalism, the means of production only function as *preliminary transformation into capital*." Mao Zedong, the founder of the Chinese Communist Party defined capitalism as a system of "profits in command." Capitalism is a system in which the major centers of economic power function in order to make profits for those who own them.

Socialism, on the other hand, is a system of rationally organized production. Frederick Engels explained the nature of socialism this way: "The proletariat seizes the public power, and by means of this transforms the socialized means of production, slipping from the hands of the bourgeoisie, into public property. By this act, the proletariat frees the means of production from the character of capital they have thus far borne, and gives their socialized character complete freedom to work itself out. Socialized production upon a predetermined plan becomes henceforth possible."

To be clear, socialism is not synonymous merely with state ownership. State ownership exists to some degree or other in every capitalist economy. In the Kingdom of Saudi Arabia, state ownership is very prevalent. However, the state-run oil company in Saudi Arabia simply generates revenue for the royal family. The Saudi government simply plays the role of facilitating oil production, carried out in order to make profits for the royal family.

In the aftermath of the Second World War, many major industries were nationalized in Britain, so they could be rebuilt with public funds. However, the state-owned postal service, railways, power plants and coal mines of post-war Britain existed simply to facilitate capitalist enterprises and their ability to make profits. The means of production still operated on the basis of preliminary transformation into capital, despite large scale state involvement.

The nature of socialism is defined by "socialized production upon a predetermined plan." Under socialism, rational planning allows production to take place according to the interests of society overall.

Deng Xiaoping was very clear that the socialist nature of China's economy would not change, despite the introduction of foreign investment and private enterprise. He explained: "At present some people, especially young people, are skeptical about the socialist system, alleging that socialism is not as good as capitalism. Such ideas must be firmly corrected. The socialist system is one thing, and the specific way of building socialism another. Counting from the October Revolution of 1917, the Soviet Union has been engaged in building socialism for 63 years, but it is still in no position to boast about how to do it. It is true that we don't have enough experience either, and perhaps it is only now that we have begun in earnest to search for a better road. Nevertheless, the superiority of the socialist system has already been proved, even though it still needs to be displayed in more, better and more convincing ways. In the future, we must — and certainly will — have abundant facts with which to demonstrate that the socialist system is superior to the capitalist system. This superiority should manifest itself in many ways, but first and foremost it must be revealed in the rate of economic growth and in economic efficiency. Otherwise, there will be no point in our trying to blow our own horn. And to achieve a high rate of growth and high efficiency, it is essential to carry out our political line consistently and unfalteringly."

Despite market reforms, the Chinese economy remains state-controlled. The party continues to lay out five-year economic plans. Major industries remain under public control. The government controls the banking sector and dictates the lending of money. Private companies receive instructions from the government and are not free to produce and operate simply according to the dictates of the market.

A great example of the non-capitalist nature of the Chinese economy is the results of the stock market crash on July 8th and 9th of 2015. During these events, the Chinese stock market dropped by roughly 30%. Over 1,400 companies filed for a trading halt.

The result of a similar drop on the New York Stock Exchange would be catastrophic. Food would stop being delivered. Society would come to a screeching halt. A 30% drop on the US stock market would most likely result in riots in the streets, as 55% of the US public is directly tied in to Wall Street.

Nothing even close to this happened in China. China's stock market is not the center of the economy. The bulk of China's economic activity is centered around the government and its apparatus of state owned banks and industries. The stock market functions simply as a kind of elite gambling casino for millionaires and billionaires and a mechanism for bringing in foreign capital. Less than 6% of the Chinese population is in any way tied to the stock market. The overwhelming majority of Chinese people and the Chinese economy is fully insulated from market turbulence.

In 2015, after the Shanghai stock market crashed on July 8th and 9th, the government swept in with "anti-selling measures" to prevent a panic on the market. The Communist Party announced that anyone caught short-selling would be arrested. All major shareholders were barred from selling stock for six months. The state-owned enterprises followed government direction, and were carefully managed in their activities.

As a result of the Communist Party stepping in and taking control, the Chinese stock market was speeding ahead, with numbers rising, just a week after a collapse that western media declared as the long-predicted "doomsday" of the Chinese economy.

Because the state has control, and the market exists simply to enhance the state's ability to expand the economy, the boom-bust cycle described by Marx in his analysis of capitalism is not a threat to China's growth. In China, profits are not in command, the Communist Party is. Explaining the nature of the Communist Party's achievements, Deng wrote: "China always used to be described as a heap of loose sand. But when our Party came to power and rallied the whole country around it, the disunity resulting from the partitioning of the country by various forces was brought to an end. So long as the Party exercises correct leadership, it can rally not only its whole membership but also the whole nation to accomplish any mighty undertaking".

The result of Deng Xiaoping's adjustment of the socialist system has been to raise 700 million people from poverty. It has also been the creation of state-controlled mega corporations like Huawei technologies, now the largest telecommunications manufacturer in the world. China also has the largest hydro-electrical power plant on earth, the Three Gorges Dam. The China Railways Corporation is now creating the fastest trains in the world, exporting and constructing high speed railway across the world.

In 2018, every day a new Chinese millionaire was created. China even has many billionaires, but the billionaires do not rule. Every inch of the country is controlled by the Chinese Communist Party, and even some of the richest people have received the death penalty if they stand in its way. Poverty alleviation, scientific breakthroughs, and technological achievements have defined China in recent decades.

Despite its dramatic economic successes, problems of corruption and violations of human rights continue to plague the country. The rise of Xi Jinping has marked a significant effort by the party to end bribery and enforce its regulations.

When visiting the United States in September of 2015, President Xi Jinping explained that his widely-maligned, anti-corruption crackdown was necessary for China's growth, and joked that it was nothing like the popular Netflix TV program *House of Cards*. Speaking to an audience in Seattle on September 22nd, he explained: "China will continuing fighting corruption. As I once said, one has to be very strong if he wants to strike the iron. The blacksmith referred to here is the Chinese Communist Party. The fundamental aim of the party is to serve the people's heart and soul. The party now has over 87 million members and unavoidably, it has problems of one kind or another. If we let these problems go unchecked we will risk losing the trust and support of the people. That is why we demand strict enforcement of party discipline as the top priority of governance. In our vigorous campaign against corruption, we have punished both tigers and flies — corrupt officials — irrespective of ranking, in response to our people's demand."

Xi has also worked to adjusts the Communist Party's relationship with religious groups. Under Xi Jinping's leadership the Communist Party has restored relations with the Vatican, and adjusted its policies in relation to Christians, Muslims, and Tibetan Buddhists.

In 2019, China successfully landed a spacecraft on the far side of the moon. The Chang-e 4 mission utilized some of the most advanced cameras and satellite technology to achieve its historic results. The motivations for China's mission to the moon were not purely academic or scientific. The moon is home to a large deposit of the rare element called Helium-3 which many believe could be utilized for fusion energy.

Alternative energy seems to be an obsession of the Communist Party. When China announced its new regulations regarding automotive vehicles in 2017, the *Wall Street Journal* described them with a tone of shock, reporting: "China has created the world's largest electric car market by sheer force of will."

With these swift regulations, the Chinese government declared that 10% of all cars manufactured in China and imported into China be fossil fuel free. China is now the leading creator and manufacturer of *New Energy Vehicles*. Sandra Retzer of the German Agency for International Cooperation was quoted as saying that when it comes to electric cars: "China is the only one in the race; it's all Chinese manufacturers."

China is rapidly expanding the extraction of the minerals necessary for electric car batteries with its international partners. China's state-run mining corporations are teaming up with local African enterprises to expand production.

The global oil-based apparatus of production is one the greatest threats to China, and also one of the largest barriers to human progress. The global oil market is dominated by Chevron, BP, Shell, and Exxon-Mobil, the four British and American super-major corporations that operate on the New

York and London stock exchanges. The big four super majors are closely tied in with big banks. Exxon-Mobil is the modern incarnation of John D. Rockefeller's Standard Oil and is closely tied to Chase Bank. British Petroleum (BP) is closely tied to HSBC, the British house of finance first established for the purpose of dominating the Chinese market (largely with opium imports). The autocratic Kingdoms of Saudi Arabia, Kuwait, and the United Arab Emirates have long functioned as vassals for the western oil bankers, as has the corrupt, US-backed government of oil-rich Nigeria.

Aside from a few OPEC outliers like Russia, Venezuela, and Iran, the western bankers of London and New York have cornered the international oil markets. Along with the French oil corporation Total, the big four US-British oil monopolies control roughly 88% of the global oil market. As long as crude oil remains the primary fuel driving the global means of production and transportation, Wall Street and London will rule the world.

As a country rising up from poverty and consuming more resources than ever before, China depends on a huge amount of oil imports in order to maintain its state-controlled manufacturing apparatus. While some oil comes to China via pipelines from Russia, the majority of China's oil imports come via oil tankers in the South China Sea. The supposed "escalation" in the South China Sea is simply a matter of China working to secure its oil imports, amid an increased US military presence. China is also in the process of creating an intercontinental canal in Nicaragua in the hopes of reducing the maritime dominance exercised by the USA via control of the Panama canal.

As long as China depends on oil, it remains vulnerable to

western penetration and threats. As a result of this unique position, China is necessarily and universally recognized as the primary promoter of alternative energy and renewable resources. In 2015, 24% of China's electricity was generated by wind power. China is also the world's largest manufacturer of solar panels.

China's most crucial foreign policy is its creation of the Asian Infrastructure Investment Bank, which carries out the projects of the Belt and Road Initiative. With Chinese assistance, countries across Africa, Central Asia, South America, and elsewhere have been able to build vital infrastructure like power plants, schools, railways, airports, water treatment facilities, and highways. This has resulted in a situation where the domestic economies of these long impoverished countries has been able to expand, with new trade access.

China's economic policies strongly differ from the neoliberalism of the IMF and the World Bank. While the Bretton Woods institutions push countries to strip down the government budget and reduce the role of the government, China is doing the opposite. China inflates the role of the state in developing countries, enabling them to more effectively stimulate domestic businesses. As developing countries become wealthier, China becomes wealthier at the same time. The model is referred to as "win-win cooperation." Prior to the rise of *Atlanticist Pathology* and imperialism, various industrial capitalist economists in the United States and Europe such as Alexander Hamilton, Henry Clay and Frederich List proposed similar models for global trade.

There should be no doubt that the Chinese Communist Party is guided in all things by Marxism-Leninism, Mao

Zedong Thought, Deng Xiaoping Theory, and Xi Jinping Thought, which has recently been added to the party's constituion. The October-December 2018 issue of the Communist Party's theoretical Journal *Quishi* made the following declaration: "The successful development of Chinese socialism in both theoretical and practical terms has put a spotlight on Marxism and socialism and inspired more of the world's people to believe in them. Going a step further, Chinese socialism now represents the mainstream of the world socialist movement, and has revived a sense of confidence within people around the world. It is becoming a standard bearer for the development of scientific socialism in the 21st century, and a pillar for a revitalization of world socialism".

The Nature of Socialism for the 21st Century

China sits at the center of a new block of anti-imperialist countries, which largely represent the contemporary incarnation of the city-building tendency. The Bolivarian countries of Latin America, the Islamic Republic of Iran and its allies in the Middle East, the Russian Federation with its state-run economy centered around oil and gas, all represent a kind of global axis of resistance to western capitalism. Despite their ideological diversity they all push a message of construction, social progress, and opposition to the unrestrained greed cherished by neoliberal economists. They are humanity's repudiation of the vandalism incarnated by the Atlanticist Pathology. Each of these countries is governed by a state which is hostile to the interests of rich and powerful corporations, and has a large base among the population. While in the western world, it commonly understood that "corporations control the government," the rising alternative on the global economy is pioneered by countries where the government controls the corporations in order to ensure continuous growth and innovation.

Venezuelan President Hugo Chavez took office in 1999 saying he was in favor of neither capitalism nor socialism, but that his *Bolivarian* movement, same after anti-colonial hero Simon Bolivar, represented doing whatever was best for Venezuela. However, in 2003 he announced that Venezuela would be taking the socialist road. Chavez was conscious of the fact that the kind of socialism emerging in the aftermath of the Cold War was different from the Soviet Union's model.

In 2005, Chavez told an audience at the World Social Forum: "We have to reinvent socialism. It can't be the kind of socialism that we saw in the Soviet Union, but it will emerge as we develop new systems that are built on cooperation, not competition....It is impossible, within the framework of the capitalist system to solve the grave problems of poverty of the majority of the world's population. We must transcend capitalism. But we cannot resort to state capitalism, which would be the same perversion of the Soviet Union. We must reclaim socialism as a thesis, a project and a path, but a new type of socialism, a humanist one, which puts humans and not machines or the state ahead of everything."

The Chavez government reconstructed the Venezuelan economy to be centered around the state-controlled oil company, similar to Putin's economic re-organization of Russia around the National Champions of oil and gas. This model of "petro-socialist" development had been perfected over the years, first put into practice by the Baathist Arab Socialists of Iraq and Syria, Gaddaffi's Islamic Socialist government in Libya, and the Islamic Republic of Iran.

As Venezuela presently faces the onslaught of destabilization and imposed shortages that began during the 2014 oil price drop, it is important to note what the Bolivarian government of Venezuela achieved prior to this crisis.

In 1998 when Chavez was elected, Venezuela had only 12 public universities, now it has 32. Between 1999 and 2009, poverty and unemployment in Venezuela were cut in half. In neighborhoods across the country, free healthcare is provided by Cuban doctors. The Bolivarian government oversaw the eradication of adult illiteracy in the country, with Cuban literacy volunteers imported to carry it out. Access to modern housing has greatly expanded with over a million modern housing units being constructed, and interest-free loans allowing millions of Venezuelans to build their own homes. It is because of these huge achievements that Nicolas Maduro and the United Socialist Party maintain a solid base with millions of loyal activists even amid the recent turmoil.

In 2006, Bolivia elected a socialist president, Evo Morales. He took office and began constructing roads across the country. Morales followed a path similar to Chavez and nationalized the natural gas and other resources of the country. He also brought in Cuban literacy and medical volunteers to provide services. In 2018, Bolivia experienced the highest rate of GDP growth of any country in South America, as the state-directed economy plowed forward, with Chinese investment aiding the process of expansion.

2006 was also the year that the Sandinistas, Marxist Christians who led the Nicaraguan 1979 revolution, were reelected to run the government. Their construction projects and social programs resulted in poverty being reduced in

Nicaragua by 30% from 2005 to 2014. Between 2007 and 2016, the GDP of Nicaragua has risen by 36% according to the Wall Street Journal. The Sandinista government created a network of Citizen Power Councils to enforce the goals of the revolution on a neighborhood level.

One of the most successful programs of Ortega's socialist government has been lending money to impoverished people in order to become micro-entrepreneurs and to form cooperatives. The World Happiness Index of the United Nations rated Nicaragua with the highest increase of happiness of any country in the world in 2016. The wave of new happiness was generated due to the flourishing economic opportunities many Nicaraguans were seeing due to socialist central planning.

The various incarnations of 21st century socialism, be they Chinese, Bolivarian, Islamic or Baathist serve as the primary source of optimism in the world. The global bloc, centered around the two Eurasian superpowers, preaches an ideology of construction and hope.

However, 21st century socialism very much reeks of the things that the *Synthetic Left* has labelled *fascist*. When reviewing Susan Sontag's words this becomes very obvious. In providing services for the most impoverished and mobilizing the entire country in a joint effort to improve conditions, the new socialism is most certainly working to build a "family of man." Young people in the socialist countries join the Young Pioneers and other groups that wear uniforms and are told they are part of the effort to build a better country: ("uniformly garbed and shown in swelling numbers" "the massing of groups of people"). The leaders, like Xi Jinping, Nicolas Maduro, Vladimir Putin and Ali

Seyyed Khamenei are seen as father-like figures, directing the country in its efforts for national rejuvenation: ("all-powerful hypnotic leader-figure or force" "orgiastic transactions between mighty forces and their puppets" "the will is staged publicly in the drama of the leader and chorus.")

In China, as Xi Jinping re-emphasizes the Marxist ideology and Communist aesthetics, increasingly elderly Chinese people have gathered to exercise together in public squares. Students also conduct joint exercises in front of their schools. Russia has Nashi summer camps for its high achieving youth, where they are taught to use their skills for the good of the nation. In Bolivarian countries, young people assemble in public parks for free martial arts classes, provided by the socialist government ("mass athletic demonstration, a choreographed display of bodies").

In China, Iran, Venezuela, Bolivia, and Russia, a spirit of selflessness is promoted. Those who give their lives to defend the revolutionary process are viewed as great heroes, and a spirit of "all for one" and "joint effort" is promoted ("the fetishism of courage, the dissolution of alienation in the ecstatic feelings of of community").

21st century socialism seems to be fulfilling the Marxist vision of a rationally-organized economy, marching toward the goal of great material abundance. The new socialist bloc has created societies in which production is no longer restrained by the irrationalism of greed and millions can be raised from poverty as the state, despite whatever problems generated by corruption and human fallibility, plans out economic activity. The socialist countries have neutralized the intellectual strata that played such a key role in dismantling the Soviet Union, and also learned to utilize the strengths of the market, to advance socialist planning.

The socialism of the 21st century is far more capable of producing consumer goods and unleashing human creativity, and does not face the stagnation and overall difficulties faced by the Eastern Bloc during the Cold War. The socialist countries are developing mechanisms for continued adjustment, so that their models of development do not become so rigid that they collapse as the USSR did. 21st century socialism is able to bend, so it does not break.

Since the Russian Revolution of 1917, socialism has taken impoverished countries and raised them up from poverty. Socialism has boosted science and the arts to a great degree, and has done a huge amount to advance all of humanity. At the dawn of the 20th century, Russia and China were both deeply impoverished, non-industrialized agrarian countries. Today, they are both superpowers. Cubans live far more comfortably than other people throughout the Caribbean. South America's Bolivarian countries have taken huge measures to construct infrastructure and eradicate poverty. Governing under the slogan *Not Capitalism but Islam*, the Islamic Republic of Iran has overseen a huge amount of economic development.

As these countries have risen from poverty with non-capitalist economies, the new socialism has effectively broken with much of the sentiments expressed by the revolutionary intelligentsia. In our age the revolutionary intelligentsia has largely been absorbed into the *Synthetic Left* of western countries and no longer strives to advance human progress, while socialism often presents itself in very conservative terms as a defender of stability and traditional cultures.

For those who see Marxism only as a method of deconstruction, the achievements of nations pulling together and striving for a global community of win-win cooperation can only be dismissed as "fascist." However, for those who view the question of historical progress in a scientific way, it must be understood that 21st century socialism stands as the modern day incarnation of the city-building tendency, facing an onslaught from the vandals who crave chaos and regression.

The Pending Gotterdammerung

Underlying the rising geopolitical tension is a big economic reality.

Karl Marx published his magnum opus in 1867. It was a very lengthy work of economic research called *Capital*. The text was intended as Volume 1 with other volumes published after his death. The pages of Marx's Capital explain the basics of how an economy based on profits works. Chapters describe profits, surplus value, commodities and how their value is derived, and other key Marxist concepts.

The climax of the text is Chapter 25 when Marx describes *The General Law of Capitalist Accumulation*. Marx describes how the capitalist is constantly looking to expand profits, so that these profits can be reinvested into expanding production, and making greater profits, to then be invested again. In the process of doing this, the capitalist aims to drive wages down, in order to maximize profits. The capitalist is also looking to hire as few workers as possible, further reducing costs and eliminating jobs with technology.

The result of what Marx described as workers competing with machines is a growing "reserve army of labor" i.e. unemployed workers whose labor is not being exploited for profits. Marx referred to the ever-growing mass of unemployed workers as the "reserve army of labor" because the more people that are unemployed, the lower the wages, as competition for jobs is more intensified.

As Marx had explained in his earlier book *The Poverty of Philosophy*: "From day to day it thus becomes clearer that the production relations in which the bourgeoisie moves have not a simple, uniform character, but a dual character; that in the selfsame relations in which wealth is produced, poverty is produced also; that in the selfsame relations in which there is a development of productive forces, there is also a force producing repression; that there relations produce bourgeois wealth, i.e., the wealth of the bourgeois class, only by continually annihilating the wealth of the individual members of this class and by producing an evergrowing proletariat."

The great physicist Albert Einstein was deeply inspired by Marx's explanation of the problems of capitalist economics. Einstein reiterated Marx's concepts in his own words in an essay called *Why Socialism?* published in 1949. Explaining Marx's analysis, Einstein wrote: "Production is carried on for profit, not for use. There is no provision that all those able and willing to work will always be in a position to find employment; an "army of unemployed" almost always exists. The worker is constantly in fear of losing his job. Since unemployed and poorly paid workers do not provide a profitable market, the production of consumers' goods is restricted, and great hardship is the consequence. Technological progress frequently results in more unemployment rather than in an easing of the burden of work for all. The profit motive, in conjunction with competition among capitalists, is responsible for an instability in the accumulation and utilization of capital which leads to increasingly severe depressions. Unlimited competition leads to a huge waste of labor, and to that crippling of the social consciousness of individuals."

In systems of the past, people became hungry due to food shortages. Only under the system of production for profit do people become hungry because too much food exists. In systems of the past, people were homeless due to shortages of housing, but in the aftermath of the 2008 financial crisis, spurned by the bursting of the *housing bubble*, millions of Americans lost their homes and many even became homeless because too much housing had been constructed, while the ability of the public to purchase it had vastly decreased.

A famous dialogue between a recently unemployed Polish coal miner and his son, published in 1930, illustrates the problem of capitalist production:

"Father, Why don't we light the stove? I am cold"
"We don't have coal, son"
"And why haven't we got coal?"
"Because there is too much coal."

The problem of overproduction, or "poverty amidst plenty," is a built-in failure of the capitalist system. It is something that endless efforts by capitalist governments, central bankers, fiat money printers, and others have never been able to resolve. As long as the means of production functions simply as "preliminary transformation into capital" growth will be restricted and cyclical crises will prevail.

However, the situation currently facing the global economy is of a distinctly different character. Artificial intelligence has taken the automation of labor to a new level, unforeseen by

Marx in 1867. In the modern era, the worker is not seeing his wages driven down by technology, and technology is not erasing a skilled trade or industrial position here and there. Rather, the defining change of our time is the worker being eliminated from production and even from the service sector. In essence, the computer revolution is almost eliminating the working class.

While Marx described workers in capitalism as being reduced from skilled craftsman to being merely appendages to machines, in the 21st century, machines are being stripped of their appendages. As Jack Ma, Chinese Communist Party member and tech billionaire put: "we made people like machines, now we make machines like people".

In the 21st Century apparatus of production, workers are not needed. Assembly line factory workers are being relegated to history books. Computers that are now armed with artificial intelligence are better at trading stocks, printing books, and doing almost any manufacturing or service task. As US Presidential Candidate Andrew Yang explained in an interview with the *New York Times*: "All you need is self-driving cars to destabilize society…we're going to have a million truck drivers out of work who are 94 percent male, with an average level of education of high school or one year of college. That one innovation will be enough to create riots in the street. And we're about to do the same thing to retail workers, call center workers, fast-food workers, insurance companies, accounting firms".

The global apparatus of production, centered around Wall Street and London, churns out products more efficiently than ever before, as millions and millions are cast out into poverty. Refugees pile into the United States from Latin America, from North Africa into Europe, and from Southeast Asia and the Pacific into the Middle East. The global reserve army of labor is growing and manifesting itself in a crisis of mass migration. The increasingly desperate masses of the global south manifest their poverty with the growth of terrorist groups and drug cartels.

The Arab Spring of 2011 was effectively hijacked and controlled by Washington's covert efforts, but the anger and desperation underlying it has not disappeared. The problem is global and the desperation is real.

The greatest crisis of overproduction in the history of capitalism is now unfolding. The "final conflict" is upon on us, and the Gotterdammerung is approaching for the vandal gods of finance and empire. The means of production can no longer be allowed to function in an irrational way. The need for the centers of economic power to be controlled by society is no longer a matter of making human life easier, but a matter of preserving humanity itself.

The Unfolding Low-Wage Police State

The symptoms of societal deconstruction in the United States go far beyond the usual examples highlighted in international media such as mass shootings, racial unrest, and political polarization. Across the United States, various municipalities are unpaving their roads. An article from wired.com published in June of 2016, describes the process in the state of capital of Vermont, which is currently taking place in towns across the United States: "Like many towns facing this recession, Montpelier has slashed its road budget. Meanwhile, several local bridges and retaining walls needed serious, urgent updates. "Asphalt's pretty expensive," says

Tom McArdle, the city's head of public works. By un-paving instead of repaving, Montpelier saved about $120,000—a big chunk for a city whose annual budget for street building and repairs was $1.3 million in 2009.... Transportation agencies in at least 27 states have unpaved roads, according to a new report from the National Highway Cooperative Highway Research program. They've done the bulk of that work in the past five years".

Water purification is also lacking across the United States. The infamous Flint water crisis of Michigan was only the most sensational example, but in many part of the country, drinking water is below sanitary standards. Power plants are crumbling, and public transportation systems are in complete disrepair. When New York City, the richest city on earth, was hit by Hurricane Sandy in 2012, the result was the entire city shutting down, and a major power plant on the Lower East Side of Manhattan exploding. Puerto Rico, a US territory was left without electricity for 11 months following a hurricane.

As low wage workers face the inevitability of being replaced by machines, their conditions become increasingly harsh. Howard Shultz, the billionaire owner of Starbucks, introduced his employees to slick innovation in exploitation known as a "Clopenings" in which employees are forced to work back to back day-long shifts with no time to sleep in between. The New York Times described how computer programs are utilized to manage the lives of employees in order to make them as profitable as possible: "Along with virtually every major retail and restaurant chain, Starbucks relies on software that choreographs workers in precise, intricate ballets, using sales patterns and other data to determine which of its 130,000 baristas are needed in its thousands of locations and exactly when. Big-box retailers or mall clothing chains are now capable of bringing in more hands in anticipation of a delivery truck pulling in or the weather changing, and sending workers home when real-time analyses show sales are slowing. Managers are often compensated based on the efficiency of their staffing".

But as miserable as the lives of food service and retail workers are becoming, they too are being phased out by technology. As Americans shop online, Main Street stores are closing down. The once buzzing suburban malls are fading into abandoned ghost towns.

As wages stagnate and the overall living standard of the United States declines, debt is rising. In 2018, the total amount of household debt in the USA reach $13.54 trillion. Student debt, the bill young people run up in order to pay for their education has reached $1.52 trillion. In June of 2018, *Forbes* magazine reported that over 44 million Americans have student debt, with the average amount owed being $38,390.

An escalation of authoritarian tendencies from the military and policing agencies seems to be underway in the hopes of controlling an increasingly impoverished and desperate US population. No-knock raids, in which police burst into the homes of people with guns drawn are a rising trend, as are video-recorded instances of police summarily executing people in their custody. The *Black Lives Matter* protests highlighted the real outrage about increasing numbers of people dying at the hands of largely unaccountable police officers, in some cases recorded on film. While the African-American community has felt especially hard hit, the trend of extra-judicial killings by police officers has not been restricted to any particular demographic in US society. The whole country faces a police state clamp down, accompanying a drop in living standards.

Surveillance culture, and the understanding that phone calls and computer activities are being monitored, seems to be a new reality as well. Instances of individuals being disappeared by the federal government without criminal charges are also on the rise.

The Chicago police were caught operating a *Black Site* at Homan Square where arrestees were disappeared for "interrogation" and torture before being taken to jail. An article from *The Guardian* published in February 2015 described the experience of one individual who was picked up and charged with terrorism, and later acquitted in court: "Brian Jacob Church was taken to Homan Square after police picked him up in 2012 on terrorism charges he beat at trial. He said police first photographed him for a biometrics database, took him down a long cinderblock hallway on a second floor, and handcuffed him to a bench bolted to the floor. He spent the next 17 hours there – approximately, as it was a windowless room and the lights were kept on overhead – while police attempted an interrogation he described as a fishing expedition".

The United States is, overall, dealing with a crisis of liberalism. The city-building tendency has been suppressed, and across all sectors the vandal mindset has been unleashed. The standard of living is dropping and basic societal functions become less-routine. The rising police state is merely a symptom of an overall process of societal decay.

The Psychology and Politics of Deconstruction

The curse placed on the United States in 2019 is pessimism. A sense of dread, doom, and hopelessness seems to hang over all of society. The right wing spins horror stories of immigrant invasions, terrorists, and a "politically correct" authoritarianism. The left tells of the coming ecological catastrophe, fascist hate mobs, police brutality, gun violence and unrestrained bigotry. As the US public becomes more politically engaged than ever before in recent years, almost every new political tendency presents a dark view of the future; a unique nightmare haunting its adherents, spurning them to action through fear.

Fear is a primitive instinct. It is the mindset of a mouse fleeing from a hungry cat or a rat leaping off of a sinking ship. In states of fear and panic people are subject to easy manipulation and their ability to think rationally is reduced. Politics based on fear can easily produce chaos and submission, but not rational construction.

While economic decline is the primary basis for the crisis in US society, the political landscape reacting to this situation has largely been shaped by cultural deconstruction. The political turmoil of 1968-1972, in which opposition to the Vietnam war shook college campuses and anti-racist rebellions took place across the urban centers had a lasting impact on US society. While US society remained well intact, the underlying mythology on which the USA was built was largely blown to bits. For millions, the United States ceased to be a *land of freedom of opportunity* and was instead an imperialist country founded on genocide and slavery.

The conservative strata, the *silent majority* first championed by Nixon and later by neocon Republicans held on to the belief that the USA was a *shining city on a hill* and *the greatest of all countries*. Leo Strauss and Irving Kristol carefully crafted a message of *my country right or wrong* that won elections. Rupert Murdoch adopted it for cable news. For a significant time period, most of the white middle class kept believing in this American mythology, despite the realities that the rest of the world and big chunks of US society had already observed. The religious right of Jerry Falwell and Pat Robertson promoted not just unquestioned belief in the Bible, but also unquestioned faith in the concept of *America* which became much harder to hold on to in a world of free-flowing information.

The Bush years marked the last hurrah, the final display of power from the *silent majority.* Amid the 2008 financial meltdown, conservatives gave up on *love it or leave it.* Libertarianism, paleoconservatism, and far-right populist concepts came to replace the mantra of *don't fix it if it ain't broke*. The Trump presidency with its talk of *Nationalism* and highlighting of voices such as Steve Bannon, signifies the conversion of the right wing and the death of the once-effective neoconservative messaging style.

Everyone in America seems to agree that the country is broke, yet most doubt that it can be fixed. The American political right seems to focus on the resentment of men against feminism, whites who feel that the concerns of minorities are given too much attention while their plight is ignored, and the belief that society's instability is the result of *Cultural Marxism*. While the *White Nationalist* and *Alt-Right* movements have certainly received a large amount of attention in recent years, their calls for a European ethno-state, amid attempts to rehabilitate the historical image of Adolf Hitler remain largely fringe and irrelevant. The *Alt-Right* has become the favored bogeyman of a liberal establishment that sees Trump's pseudo-populist appeal as potentially dangerous.

As capitalist societies enter crisis, bonapartism is a natural outgrowth. Figures like Trump and Sanders, who seek to build a mass movement and suppress sections of the ruling class in the hopes of liquidating the crisis, are likely to become more and more prevalent.

The *Anti-Fascism* of the Trump era very much follows in Susan Sontag's footsteps. The endless *Russiagate* mantra that Trump is an agent of Putin, as he escalates the new Cold War, almost mimics the conspiracy theories put forward by the John Birch Society during the 1960s. The broadcasts of Rachel Maddow portray Trump as dangerous because he questions US foreign policy narratives, while stirring up supporters portrayed as a mess of uneducated rabble. Most of the organized left has been pathetically swept up into a mobilization by the establishment against Trump, where it functions as a virtually unnoticeable speck.

Even beyond its relationship with the anti-populist mobilizations, the American left faces a strange moment of confusion. "Socialism" is now more popular than ever. Young Americans educated by professors who marched against the Vietnam War as youth, seem to agree that the USA is a country founded on racism and has engaged in genocidal wars. Talk of *white privilege* and *gender oppression* is everywhere and widely accepted by younger Americans.

Yet, the various Marxist-Leninist sects, most of which

have been championing these messages since the 1970s, remain smaller and more irrelevant than ever. Among those who have recently adopted leftists sentiments, a desire to take action is noticeably absent. Wings of the political establishment looking to counter the right have poured money into attempted creations of a wider social-democratic current, but this has happened reluctantly despite even a "nudge" from powerful forces.

The *Synthetic Left*, forged by the capitalist establishment, has stripped Marxism of all but its deconstructive aspect. With the essence of Marxism gone, leftism has degenerated, for some, into a youthful revenge fantasy of resentment and for most as merely a reason to feel hopeless, not a call to battle. While actual Marxism is about raising productive forces and allowing unlimited prosperity, the young socialists of today call to "abolish billionaires" in the hopes of depriving someone else of the material comfort they lack. *Call out culture* has made it almost a moral imperative for young people to take offense and unload their resentments and aggression on each other. Sticking to Susan Sontag's *anti-fascism* anything that reeks of fitness, courage or political effectiveness is declared to be *triggering*. All individuals who can manage to be perceived as victims are held in high esteem. In essence, strength is viewed with suspicion while weakness is celebrated.

As one watches crowds of young post-modern liberals tear down confederate monuments, it must be pointed out that they are not replacing them with statues of more honorable figures. The sentiment of the young leftists is that heroes and monuments themselves are the problem. Erecting any figure and movement of the past as an icon for reverence is *totalitarian* and *fascist*.

In carrying out these acts of vandalism, in the hopes of protecting Anne-Marie Slaughter's *open international system* from Trump's racism and pseudo-populism, young leftists are not so different from the crowds mobilized to tear down statues of Lenin across eastern Europe decades ago. Young leftists replace the racist mythology of the confederacy with an international order that says individualism is the highest good, and that collectivism is inherently *totalitarian* and dangerous.

Beyond politics, the trends of pessimism and aspiring to be a victim have spread to the psychology of many American youth. As the traditional discipline, loyalty, and family obligation of US society fades, the impulses and passions of younger Americans seem to be less restrained than ever. However, the meaning that once accompanied these passions of youth has been stripped away. The shallowness of pornography and casual hook-ups has replaced the beauty of romance. Accusing celebrities of racial insensitivity on social media has replaced the passion and solidarity felt by those who attended militant protests and actively promoted revolutionary ideology.

A generation of young Americans seem to find themselves universally asking the question: "Who am I? What does my life mean?" The United States political establishment once supplied answers to these questions, but those answers have been largely debunked. The *Synthetic Left*, spawned by sections of the ruling class itself, has effectively disproved *America*, capitalism, democracy, freedom and all the myths that once held US society together. However, true to its purpose, the *Synthetic Left* has not replaced these myths with any new purpose or ideology.

The *Atlanticist Pathology*, displayed in the demented culture that emerged along with the rise of British imperialism, has now manifested itself again in the United States. An economic order centered around plunder and destruction, dominance in global trade at the expense of overall development, has fomented a society-wide episode of mass insanity.

Young people stuck in cycles of short-term, low wage-jobs, living with and depending on their parents well into adulthood, are killing themselves at higher rates than the USA has seen in decades. Opioids are also claiming scores of lives. Alcohol-related deaths have also increased.

The mental-health industry has flourished with psychiatric medicine prescriptions higher than ever. Unlike the British empire that seemed to fixate on caning children into obedience, the *kinder and gentler* society in the USA relegates children who misbehave in school to being diagnosed and prescribed pills. The misbehaving or non-conforming school child, who was first diagnosed with ADD or ADHD and medicated as a preteen, soon finds themselves on antidepressants or antipsychotics as a teen. From there they enter adulthood condemned to a life increasing dosages and switching medications, all while whatever underlying tension or interpersonal difficulties driving their original childhood nonconformity or disobedience is never addressed.

Western society's primary vehicle for social and thought control in the 21st century seems to be social media. The users of Facebook, Twitter, and Instagram find themselves almost constantly craving signs of affirmation from their peers. While history has long been made by bold individuals who stood firm in the face of opposition, social media reduces users to a level of interpersonal weakness, where the need for more *likes* and *shares* drives a constant effort to conform and gain the approval of an ever-watching cyber-audience. Unlike George Orwell's dystopia, it is not government officials watching over us, monitoring our lives in order to punish any sign of non-conformity. Rather we watch over each other, granting the carrot of peer approval that we have learned to desperately crave and obediently conform in order to receive.

In addition to pushing conformity, social media has tragically become a vehicle for many young Americans who seem to crave sympathy. While being successful or displaying strength is often considered *triggering offensive* and *fascist* by the *Synthetic Left*, social media presents young people with the ability to display their weaknesses to the world, granting themselves the celebrated status of victimhood. In February of 2019, Instagram finally banned all images of self-mutilation, after a long-standing trend of teenagers and young adults cutting themselves and posting the photographs for attention.

While the British Empire unleashed the horror of serial killers, the staple criminal pathology of declining American capitalism seems to be the mass shooter. Young white men who are attracted to racial supremacism and hate, and tend to have anti-social personalities decide to end their lives in an orgy of death. They kill their classmates, and often random groups of strangers, in a hail of bullets, an explosion of long internalized rage. The young mass murderers hope to be immortalized, as news reporters summarize their manifestos on the airwaves and their life story is uploaded to Wikipedia.

Underlying the crisis facing western youth seems to be a horrific knowledge that cannot be escaped. Capitalism is a system where most human beings can only survive by selling their labor power. The result of automation and the computer revolution has been this system declaring millions of people, even within the most prosperous centers of western capitalism, to be expendable and useless. The youth, who kill or mutilate themselves, numb their pain with drugs, or wallow in other pessimistic escapes, all seem to be moaning "I am capable of something better than this. I have something to offer the world, but my society has refused to utilize me."

Human beings are collective creatures by nature. Even before civilization's dawn, we were tribal. Wanting to be part of something bigger than yourself and your own pleasure, being willing to sacrifice and work hard for a vision of improving the world around you; this is a natural, normal state of being. It is this very drive toward collective action and creativity that defines human beings and separates us from animals. However, the vandal mindset, spawned by excessive deconstruction and the liberal fixation on individualism, has robbed millions of people of fulfilling this basic human desire. As a result, western societies spiral into a greater state of instability amid economic decline.

One can contrast the suicidal, hopeless generation of western youth, who are full of potential that is seemingly *unwanted* by society with the youths of the Bolivarian countries, China, Iran, or Russia. Western media portrays the Bolivarian youth collectives, the Young Pioneers of China and Cuba, and Russia's Nashi Summer camps as ruthlessly "totalitarian." According to western media, nothing is worse than these youth programs, where impressionable young people are being *brainwashed* and *indoctrinated* by a *regime* that is *using them.* But yet, one must be forced to ask, is it better for young people to be *free* while stripped of any identity or purpose? Is it better to be cast into a state of permanent confusion than to be mobilized to build a better society for your countryfolk?

Is a society that deems the next generation as useless because no profits can be made from their labor really superior and *free* compared to a system that views each citizen as an asset, to be unleashed in order to build and to advance historical progress?

The Potential for American Rebirth

The presidential campaigns of Bernie Sanders, the elderly Vermont Senator who calls himself a *democratic socialist* has attracted a huge following among younger Americans. His message would seem quite normal for a politician in any other corner of the world, but to many Americans it is unique and bold.

Sanders' speaks to sold-out crowds of disproportionately young Americans bemoaning the crimes of *the billionaire class*. As he has explained: "Democratic socialism means that we must create an economy that works for all, not just the very wealthy. Democratic socialism means that we must reform a political system in America today which is not only grossly unfair but, in many respects, corrupt."

Sanders' message is miles away from Marxism. Sanders calls simply for European-style welfare-state reforms, such as free healthcare, free education, higher taxes on the wealthy, and better protections for workers on the job. However, this left-wing populism and class struggle rhetoric is new to American politics. The *Synthetic Left* moved away from such rhetoric long ago in favor of its pessimistic *privilege politics* and individualist anti-fascism. The right wing and center have long maintained unregulated capitalism as an ideal.

The importance of the Bernie Sanders movement is not found in what it advocates, but rather, in the conversation it creates. Rather than speaking of a "more perfect union" or "One America" as Obama and other liberals have long done, Sanders has reintroduced the seemingly forgotten notion of class against class.

He has identified the wealthiest people, the owners of the major centers of economic power, as having interests that are contrary to the rest of the country. This notion that he presents is the inescapable truth. As the United States has become deindustrialized and faces internal decay and impoverishment, the Wall Street and London monopolists have enriched themselves like never before. They are loyal, not to the country and the betterment of its population, but rather to their own profits, rooted in a global financial system.

The slogan that is most encouraging among the Sanders movement is "Not Me. Us." The slogan calls for unleashing some notion of a group or collectivist identity and joint effort. This message is particularly valuable in a society where the glorification of capitalism from the right-wing and the fixation with deconstruction from the *Synthetic Left* has eroded such essential sentiments. As Sanders' crowds chant "Not Me. Us." they are questioning the basic premise of liberalism, that individualism must be prioritized above all else.

The Sanders movement calls for more social programs and redistribution of wealth and has thus made itself a target of widespread right-wing criticism. Rightists portray the

Sanders movement as simply representing entitlement from a generation that is deemed lazy and unproductive. What would make the Sanders movement explosively powerful is if the sentiments of "Not me, us" could be harnessed into an energy for mass construction and mobilization to rebuild the country.

If the Sanders movement or elements like it were to go beyond simply calls for expanding social benefits, and instead toward calls for a state-directed rebirth of the economy, its power could be almost unstoppable.

The current pessimism is not coming from within the American people, but is imposed on them by a dying social system. The oil monopolists who fear new energy sources, see historical progress as a bad thing. Behind their talk of overpopulation, free markets, and the need for an open international system, is the real fear that the means of production and the world itself could slip away from them. History must be stopped in order to indefinitely extend their rule.

When one observes the youthful crowds rallying around Sanders, one can see that the potential for the city-building tendecy to reawaken itself on American shores is very real. The human energy seeking to build, create and forge societal unity that is very well alive in Eurasia, certainly exists within the American psyche, and has for a long time. Despite all the evils of settler colonialism and racism, the United States was long been identified around the world with a kind of pioneer desire to innovate and construct. It has only been the unique, 21st century incarnation of the *Atlanticist Pathology* that has eroded the "motor-mindedness" long identified with American culture. The spark of inner drive, and a "desire to go out and do something" has not vanished within the

American people. The classically American "go get 'em," live-wire mentality must be channeled into a collectivist endeavor for the country to be completely reborn on new, progressive and revolutionary foundations.

The model of win-win cooperation advanced by China and its Belt and Road initiative is the perfect answer to the *Atlanticist Pathology.* Connecting the world through trade and mutual development projects spells the end of countries being reduced to captive market and spheres of influence. The Asian Infrastructure Investment Bank, the Eurasian Economic Union, the Bolivarian Alternative for Latin America, and other joint-development operations centered around socialist countries, are more effective in creating a new world and smashing the old order than any other weapon.

These projects, seeking to restructure the global economy in a way that eliminates poverty, are the only realistic solution to the crisis of mass migration to western countries. The way to end the rise of terrorist groups and drug cartels is to shatter the old financial order based on holding back progress. Already we have seen the successes of the Eurasian alternative as within even the most underdeveloped, corrupt, and politically weak societies, they bring the most constructive and progressive elements forward.

The future of the United States ultimately mandates bringing the country into such efforts as much as possible. The more elements of the US economy that can be integrated into the Eurasian alternative, the greater potential will exist for the city-building tendency within the United States itself. Trump's calls for "economic nationalism" have turned into the opposite. Trump's tariffs are nothing more than leading the charge of Wall Street and London to barricade and siphon off the rising source of wealth and development that challenges their decaying system.

Just as Julius Caesar emerged to champion the tradition of Socrates, Confucius and Gilgamesh amid the plunder-based Roman Empire, forces that seek to build and not destroy will emerge within the United States. Such forces will see Russia, China, the Bolivarian Countries, Iran and other independent nations as potential allies rather than enemies or rivals.

An axis within US society that pushes for the rebirth of the country with central planning, and integrating it into the Eurasian alternative must be built.

As the factions within the ruling class of the United States pick constituencies among the population, and mobilize them to attack each other, the city-building tendency must not join such efforts.

The myth that one section of the American working class can gain only at the expense of another must be debunked. The crisis of US society cannot be cured by punishing or deranking one section of society in order to embolden and strengthen another. Such efforts to *whipsaw* the population are the basis of fascism and reactionary bonapartism. The crisis will not be solved with downgrading or shaming of those working families deemed to be historically privileged, or with enhancing the boot heels of repression used against those who have long been marginalized.

A line of march for leading all the people of the United States out poverty and toward something better, must be put forward. All of society must be mobilized against the monopolists and the *Atlanticist Pathology.*

To envision the city-building tendency taking power in the United States is to imagine the following:

· Imagine a government that immediately hired those unemployed or under utilized young people, and put them to work rebuilding the country. A generation of highly-skilled young people would no longer be wasted in the low-wage, short-term jobs of the vanishing service sector, but rather unleashed to build new schools and universities, high-speed rail systems, fuel-efficient energy sources, water treatment plants, public health facilities and other badly-needed infrastructure. Gainful employment, doing useful work should be considered both a right and an obligation of all citizens. A spirit of selflessness and patriotism must be promoted as a generation is put to work rebuilding the parts of the country that have fallen into decay.

· Imagine a government that seized control of the natural resources such oil, gas, timber, and coal and declared that they were the property of every person in the country. The public budget should be refilled with the revenue created by America's vast natural wealth. The proceeds should be spent in order to build a better life for the population, not to line the pockets of the rich.

· Imagine a government that seized control of banking and put the lending and printing of money into the hands of the state, not the Federal Reserve Bank or the private houses of finance. With control over the purse strings of the nation and a five year economic plan, drawn up by a brain trust of the greatest engineers and scientists, the state could directly oversee an overall recreation of US society. The state would finance great construction projects to make life and business easier for everyone in US society. The state would lend money to young people to become entrepreneurs and start new high tech firms. The state would provide start-up funding for worker cooperatives. The market would be allowed to flourish with rational leaders centrally planning it, and preventing the irrational greed of a few from destroying the hopes of the many.

· Imagine a government that treated every American citizen as being worthy of a decent life. Roosevelt's vision of an economic bill of rights, securing the right to housing, education, employment, and other basic needs, would be easily attained in the context of the state controlling the centers of economic power. A revolutionary government would work to secure a decent life for everyone in the country.

During the Cold War years, the Wall Street monopolists favored and backed authoritarian governments across the world to suppress the threat of communist revolution. However, in the new age of globalism and neoliberalism, the wreckers and vandals of international finance prefer weak, ineffective governments that merely sit back as their agenda of impoverishment unfolds.

Just as a parent who let their child go hungry or freeze in the cold would be charged with a crime, the government of the United States is guilty of criminal neglect. Rather than champion the people's interests against the forces of destruction, the government has allowed the predatory forces of monopolism to pray on the American people. With its hands off, neoliberal ideology, the political class of the United States has allowed the very people it is chartered to serve to be left destitute, hungry, and often feeling hopeless.

111

The curing of this overall state of societal decay can only come in the form of a government of action. A government of action would be one rooted in the understanding that it is the obligation of the state to improve living conditions and advance historical progress. The liberal notion that "the government is best which governs least" must be shattered and replaced with the conceptions of statecraft that built every great civilization and pioneered every great advance for the human species.

Socialism will come to the United States in a unique form that will be unlike anything seen in the Soviet Union, China, Cuba, Venezuela or anywhere else. Only the American people themselves are capable of rescuing the country from capitalism, and only a kind of socialism rooted in their own desires and hopes, intended to address their own problems and hardships, will ever be capable of rebuilding the United States. Socialism cannot and will not be the result of foreign subversion or a hostile takeover by geopolitical rivals. American socialism will be the result a homegrown upsurge of patriotism and internationalism. Just as the socialism that has allowed China to be reborn is labeled *Socialism with Chinese Characteristics,* it will be a *Socialism with American Characteristics* that rescue the United States from decline and societal decay.

A call must go out to those Americans whose will not just to live and survive, but to construct and create, is so strong that they cannot sit back any longer. Those who see the current situation as intolerable must begin the process of completely changing American politics.

For those who are like Socrates, Caesar, Copernicus, Lenin, and so many others, and who would seek to continue the city-building tradition in times of darkness, the moment of truth is now upon us. Those individuals who seek to push civilization toward a higher state of being, driven by an inner flame of creativity and boldness must now reveal themselves.

Time is running out.

PART ONE:
A PECULIAR PRESIDENCY

Trump vs. Bezos: Three Major Divisions in the Ruling Class

Jeff Bezos, considered to be the richest man on earth in terms of measurable wealth, and Donald Trump, arguably the most powerful man on earth as President of the United States, are figuratively at each other's throats. US media is abuzz with talk of genital photographs, blackmail allegations, sexual misconduct, and media bias. However, those who look deeper may see bigger differences and hidden rivalries at stake. Two hostile camps have emerged within the circles of American power.

Widespread Notions of a Shadowy Elite

The notion that wars, political unrest, and clashes within society are the result of disagreements among a shadowy elite is a theme that repeatedly surfaces in art, culture, and fringe political discourse in western countries.

Aleister Crowley, the early 20th-century occultist, was known for putting forward his concept of the "hidden church" that ruled the world. He presented his followers with the belief that shadowy societies and secret orders among the elite were behind the scenes, manipulating world events in order to serve their own ends. One of Crowley's novels, *Moonchild*, published in 1929, presented the First World War as resulting from a clash between different factions of witches and wizards who controlled various governments.

Crowley's occultist ramblings, most not presented as fiction, are easy to laugh at. To modern readers, they almost sound like a bizarre meeting between Alex Jones' broadcasts and J.K. Rowling's *Harry Potter* novels. However, Crowley's world view is pretty well echoed today in the various conspiracy theories that fill the internet.

In the early years of the 20th Century, many Anti-Communist Roman Catholics began asserting that the Bavarian Illuminati, which was discovered and suppressed by the church in the late 1700s, was still active. Adherents of this theory argued that the wealthiest and most powerful people were part of the anti-Christian secret society, and as part of it, were manipulating world events and fomenting chaos.

The former British athlete and sports commentator David Icke has gained a significant following preaching that a secret race of *reptilians* controls the world. The anti-Semitic conspiracy text *The Protocols of the Learned Elders of Zion* is still widely circulated in many parts of the world.

Materialist Analysis of Bourgeois Rivalries

The notion that some shadowy group of hidden rulers is manipulating world events, and that the conflicts and clashes in politics and geopolitics represent something deeper and more cryptic, is certainly a prevalent belief with many different narratives written to explain it.

In addition to all the various "conspiracy" narratives, there are some who have attempted to utilize political economy and historical materialism, rather than mystical legends, to develop a similar narrative. Karl Marx's pamphlet *The Eighteenth Brumaire of Louis Napoleon* describes a fight among the rich and powerful in France in the midst of an economic crisis. Marx describes Louis Napoleon's *Party of Order* that seized power in 1851 as representing the finance capitalists and farmers of France, and suppressing the industrial capitalists while enacting swift economic reforms, in the hopes of restoring order and holding off a revolution.

In 1935, Georgi Dimitrov oriented the Communist International to make strategic alliances with "democratic" capitalists against a global fascist conspiracy, which he described as "most reactionary, most chauvinistic and most imperialist elements of finance capital." The "popular front" strategy of the global Communist movement was based on a division among the capitalists of the world between "democratic bourgeois" and "fascist bourgeois."

Carl Oglesby the 1960s radical penned a similar narrative during the 1970s, hoping to explain divisions among the American ruling elite. His text, widely circulated in leftist and progressive circles was called *The Yankee and Cowboy War*, and attempted to explain the Vietnam War, the Assassination of John F. Kennedy, and the Watergate Scandal in a context of clashing economic interests.

When one examines Jeff Bezos and Donald Trump's disagreement, and the forces that line up behind one or the other of the powerful men, one can see three primary divides among the circles of power in the United States. The first is a divide between the allies of Saudi Arabia and the allies of the Muslim Brotherhood.

Division #1: Saudi Wahabbis vs. The Muslim Brotherhood

Jeff Bezos has spoken up and said Saudi Arabia is possibly involved in efforts to embarrass him. He points out that the Washington Post, which he owns, has been harshly critical of Saudi Arabia for killing Jamal Khashoggi. He also has emphasized the ties of Donald Trump and the Saudi Monarchy to *The National Enquirer*.

It is true that in recent years, the *Washington Post*, long an outpost of apologism for US-backed autocracies, suddenly became more critical of the Saudi monarchy. Meanwhile, Donald Trump, who bashed Saudi Arabia on the campaign trail, has become a sharp defender of the Saudi monarchy.

And while Trump has doubled down on supporting the Saudi Kingdom, US relations with Erdogan's government in Turkey have also declined. Meanwhile, Trump has echoed Saudi Arabia's allegations against the monarchy of Qatar.

It is no secret to anyone that Saudi Arabia is a fountainhead of "Wahabbism," an interpretation of the Islamic faith that mandates an autocratic government and a strict interpretation of the Koran. The Kingdom of Saudi Arabia intentionally funds and promotes religious figures and institutions described as Wahabbis or Salafis, sometimes called Deobandis in India and Pakistan, that promote this version of Islam.

The Wahabbi networks of the Saudis have long been a source of revenue for Pentagon military contractors, and vehicle for waging proxy wars. Zbigniew Brzezinski arranged for the USA to support a young Saudi named Osama Bin Laden, who was the wealthy heir of a construction firm. Bin

117

Laden purchased huge amounts of weapons from the United States, and with CIA assistance, built a Wahabbi army in Afghanistan to fight against the Soviet Union and topple the People's Democratic Republic.

More recently, in Syria and Libya, the Saudis have purchased US-made weapons and mobilized their Wahabbi networks to work against the independent socialist governments. In both Syria and Libya, Wahabbi factions control a large amount of territory. It should be noted that the ISIL terrorists emerged from within the larger, Saudi-backed Wahabbi milieu.

Another Islamic faction that has worked with US intelligence in the Middle East, is clearly at odds with Saudi Arabia. The Muslim Brotherhood was founded in Egypt in 1928 as a group of small business owners who saw western ideas, Marxism, and nationalism as the greatest dangers to the religious traditions of the Arab World. When Gamal Abdul Nasser took power and began moving Egypt toward Arab Socialism, the US government began covertly funding and supporting the Muslim Brotherhood to work against him. With the funding and assistance of US intelligence, the Muslim Brotherhood spread across the Middle East. It fed rural and poor Arabs and used them as foot soldiers against Baathism and Marxism.

The Muslim Brotherhood is illegal in Saudi Arabia and considered to be a terrorist organization. The Muslim Brotherhood opposes Wahabbism, rejects the notion of an absolute monarchy, and favors free markets and elected governments.

The monarchy of Qatar is the primary funder of the Muslim

Brotherhood, and its media, *Al-Jazeera*, promotes an editorial perspective that is in line with the Qatari monarchy and the Muslim Brotherhood's perspective. Erdogan, the Turkish President, is seen as a close ally of the Muslim Brotherhood, and his government also echoes a similar worldview. During Obama's presidency, Qatari media, Saudi funded Wahabi preachers, the Muslim Brotherhood, and US foreign policy all marched in lockstep. They targeted Syria and Libya despite their disagreements with each other.

But now, it seems that the Wahabbis and the Muslim Brotherhood are clashing. Jeff Bezos, the *Washington Post*, and the Democratic Party seem to be sympathetic to Qatar and the Muslim Brotherhood. Trump seems to be favoring the Saudi monarchy and Wahabbism.

Division #2: The Pentagon vs. Intel Agencies

Why do some factions of the US business and state elite favor the Saudis while others favor the Brotherhood? This can be explained in the context of an ongoing feud between the intelligence agencies and the US military.

The US military apparatus and the hundreds of billions of dollars spent on it are a huge subsidy to the economy. Arms exports by weapons manufacturers are also a huge money maker. The term "military Keynesianism" has been used to describe the astronomical military spending, which functions as a government stimulus which the US economy could not do without. The many corporations involved in weapons manufacturing and export see a global arms race, the escalation of conflicts around the world, and the image of the USA as a mighty, war-like power, armed to the teeth, as in their financial interest. Trump has been very friendly to such

119

forces, describing himself as being eager to sell weapons, and using the slogan "Peace Through Strength" on the campaign trail.

However, the intel agencies of the United States tend to favor a different foreign policy strategy. Intel agencies, staffed with graduates of Harvard and Yale, have carefully studied the art of "soft power." They seek to present the United States as a friendly world power that rarely meddles in other nations affairs. The CIA also works to present the United States as overcoming racism, embracing Islam and other cultures, and becoming a more benevolent country, disproving the propaganda of its detractors. The Intel agencies have mastered the art of manipulating global conflicts from behind the scenes, utilizing proxy forces, and crafting public opinion to fit US foreign policy narratives.

But now, as Trump insults the Muslims of the world, and openly dismisses concerns about Saudi atrocities, the Muslim Brotherhood sees itself increasingly at odds with the White House. Not surprisingly, Qatar and Turkey are clashing with Saudi Arabia.

Trump speaks of the importance of weapons sales to Saudi Arabia, pandering to the Pentagon and its suppliers. Meanwhile, Jeff Bezos ties to US intelligence agencies are not secret at all. Amazon has designed software and cloud services for intelligence agencies.

But beyond Bezo's direct connections, the various Silicon Valley monopolies owe their very existence to funding and assistance from American intelligence agencies. It was a strategic move to counter the Soviet Union during the late cold war that clearly paid off for the United States.

The weapon manufacturers, who make loads and loads of money selling military hardware to Saudi Arabia, favor a very different strategy around the world than the Central Intelligence Agency, that has spent years cultivating the Muslim Brotherhood as a useful proxy force. The two sections of the American state apparatus seem to be tied to opposite sides of the Trump/Bezos disagreement.

Division #3: The Rich vs. The Ultra-Rich

However, another longstanding clash among the elite is also at play. This is the fight between the rich and the ultra-rich.

Jeff Bezos is the richest man in the world, according to some calculations. Bezos fits in with a crowd of people in the United States that could accurately be called "the Ultra-rich." Family names like Morgan, Carnegie, Dupont, Mellon, Rothschild, and Rockefeller make up a special class of untouchable entrenched power that goes back generations.

The United States has over one million millionaires and many billionaires, but most of them are not in this select group. The Rockefeller family of Standard Oil, Chase Bank, the Council on Foreign Relations, and a score of powerful think tanks and lobbies have far more influence than a typical millionaire or billionaire could even dream of.

The Rockefeller family have been the primary financial backers of Planned Parenthood, abortion, birth control, experimental art, and the legalization of pornography. The Rockefellers funded and promoted the Kinsey Report during the 1950s, widely circulated social research that results in a more tolerant attitude toward homosexuality and the sexual revolution of the 1960s. The Rockefellers are tied in closely with the US Intelligence Agencies. The Council on Foreign Relations is primarily funded by Exxon-Mobil, the direct descendant of John D. Rockefeller's Standard Oil. Art projects sponsored by the CIA's "Congress for Cultural Freedom" program of the 1950s and 60s often also received grants and promotion from Rockefeller foundations.

Representing this stratum of ruling families, Warren Buffet famously said "tax me more" after the financial crisis, arguing that Keynesian welfare state solutions should be explored. Why do the richest of the rich favor more leftwing economic policies? Because they can afford it. Higher taxes will barely dent their astronomical piles of wealth, and they can easily skate the tax collectors with their elaborate networks of foundations and trusts to conceal their vast, often incalculable wealth. It should be no surprise that *Foreign Affairs*, the publication of the Rockefellers touted the "Social Democratic Future" of the USA in 2014.

But, among the wider circles of wealth and power in the United States, there is huge resentment against the ultra-rich. The "fracking cowboys" of the oil and gas market resent the near-monopoly status of the big four supermajor oil companies, tied to Wall Street banks. The owners of retail giants resent Jeff Bezos pushing them off the market with online shopping. Trump has openly complained about alleged special treatment for Amazon from the US postal service.

These lower levels of the rich, these "cockroach capitalists" favor a more libertarian economic approach. They tend to truly believe the economic theories that say capitalism can create a market utopia, and they tend to be less convinced of the need for social welfare programs and regulation to hold off the threat of unrest.

Betsy Devos, the Education Secretary of the Trump administration is a wealthy woman. But what is the source of her wealth? She is the air to the fortune created by Amway, the multi-level marketing corporation widely decried as a pyramid scheme. The fact that a fundamentalist Christian associated with the selling of Tupperware is allowed to run US Department of Education, not some carefully trained and cultivated Harvard graduate with the blessing of the Rockefellers and Duponts, has got to be a point of contention between Trump's coalition of "new money" and the old establishment of ultra-rich families.

In 2004, the liberal radio commentator Garrison Keillor accurately articulated the sentiments among the ultra-rich, describing the Republican Party as: "the party of hairy-backed swamp developers and corporate shills, faith-based economists, fundamentalist bullies with Bibles, Christians of convenience, freelance racists, misanthropic frat boys, shrieking midgets of AM radio, tax cheats, nihilists in golf pants, brownshirts in pinstripes, sweatshop tycoons, hacks, fakirs, aggressive dorks, Lamborghini libertarians…"

Trump represents the fracking companies, the hotel and restaurant chains, Sheldon Adelson's Nevada based empire, sports team owners, and other wealthy people who have been locked out of "the club" that traditionally runs the US government. The fact that Donald Trump enacted such dramatic reforms in the Federal Prison System should not be deeply shocking either, as it seems that so many of the wealthy people who have gone to Federal Prison for financial crimes are among his backers. Trump represents the lower levels of American capital. Trump stands with the Wall Street execs who cannot buy their way out when charged for insider trading or tax fraud.

Donald Trump is himself, a real-estate mogul, was able

to rise in prestige among the wealthy by manipulating the media and "fighting dirty" in struggles for valuable New York City property. His presidency, almost universally opposed in mainstream media during the campaign, represents an upsurge among the rich against ultra-rich figures like Jeff Bezos.

"Friends After Six" No More

Ronald Reagan is known for constantly reminding other American politicians "We are all friends after six o'clock." And in his time, this was mostly true. Disagreements on policy and strategy were secondary. The enemy was Soviet Communism, the goal was US hegemony, and the sources of financial backing for major political figures were often identical. The stakes in American politics were not very high, and the significant political debates were often overcompensating in complexity for what they were lacking in substance.

However, in recent years, it seems pretty clear that America's political leaders are not "friends after six" anymore. Astute scholars of American history will recall incidents like the caning of Charles Sumner when southern racist Congressman Preston Brooks violently attacked an anti-slavery colleague on the floor of the US House of Representatives in 1856.

Disagreements among the ruling elite and Bonapartist maneuvers by different factions to suppress the other seem to be a defining aspect of America in 2019.

Originally published in New Eastern Outlook

RECALLING NIXON IN THE TRUMP-ERA: THE GEOPOLITICS OF IMPEACHMENT

Throughout Trump's presidency, the memory of Nixon has been invoked by both opponents and supporters of "The Donald." Richard Nixon stands out as the only President in U.S. history to have resigned, and not completed his term in office.

During Trump's presidential campaign, Trump used Nixon's famous catch-phrases, referring to the "silent majority" and calling himself a "law and order" candidate. Roger Stone, who worked for the Nixon administration's Office of Economic Opportunity, was notably on board with the Trump campaign. Meanwhile, outspoken Trump opponent Meryl Streep starred in the recently released film *The Post* dramatizing the *Washington Post*'s legal battle against the Nixon administration. Rachel Maddow and other liberal voices have compared allegations against Trump to the revelations surrounding the infamous Watergate Scandal.

Calls to impeach Donald Trump are widespread among the Democratic Party's representation in Congress. While most leftists echo the calls to impeach Trump, they seem to miss the real motivation and driving force behind them. Amid their confusion, they also continue to invoke a misinterpretation of the events surrounding Nixon's resignation.

Mobilizing The "Hard Hats" and "Silent Majority"

Richard Nixon took office as the U.S. was losing the war in Vietnam, and Marxism-Leninism was spreading across the planet. This was a time when even some western countries appeared to be moving toward socialist revolution. In 1968,

the year Nixon was elected, France was rocked by a massive
communist led uprising. In April of 1968, following the
murder of Martin Luther King Jr., almost every major city in
the United States went up in flames of rebellion.

African-Americans were not alone. Among urban white
intellectuals and college students, unrest grew and protests
escalated. The Democratic National Convention in 1968
was surrounded by a bloodbath as leftist anti-war protesters
were brutalized by the police. New York City's Columbia
University was shut down by a mass student strike.

Nixon, a long-time Republican congressman whose
trademark was anti-communism and contempt for
mainstream media, moved into the spotlight. Nixon's
rhetoric gradually evolved throughout the 1968 campaign.
He adopted much of the rhetorical style of George Wallace,
the racist southern Democrat who was running as a third-
party candidate in the race. Nixon discovered that Wallace's
narrative about "the good people" and "the silent majority"
while castigating hippies and anti-war activists, was a big
crowd-pleaser.

Nixon presented himself as a strongman who would bring
the United States back to order, ending the domestic turmoil.
He promised "an honorable end" to the Vietnam War, and
"law and order" i.e. an end to the mass protests and violence.

In Marxist terms, Bonapartism is defined as one section of
the capitalist ruling class violently suppressing other sections
in the hopes of resolving turmoil. Nixon was an American
Bonapartist, if ever. Like Louis Bonaparte in 1851, Nixon
took office representing a certain section of America's rich
and powerful. Like the French authoritarian Marx described

in his famous pamphlet *The Eighteenth Brumaire of Louis Napoleon* the faction supporting Nixon hoped he could restore order by suppressing a lot of very powerful and influential people.

Nixon had a base of supporters who were often described as "hard hats" i.e. unionized construction workers. Nixon had huge support from within the International Brotherhood of Teamsters, one of the largest labor unions in the country. On May 8th, 1970, New York City witnessed the "Hard Hat Riots" in which union construction workers who supported Nixon were mobilized to attack anti-war protesters in New York City.

While the Kennedy and Johnson administrations had tried to restrain and control the FBI's COINTELPRO program used to suppress leftists and civil rights organizers, Nixon granted J. Edgar Hoover a free hand to suppress Black nationalism and leftist activism.

Swift Global Maneuvers and Domestic Reforms

With the hard-hats, the FBI, and the Pentagon brass, along with majority of public opinion supporting him, Nixon made dramatic moves. He, first, escalated the Vietnam War, expanding into Cambodia and launching a massive bombing of northern Vietnam. When this failed, Nixon withdrew U.S. troops from the country.

Nixon followed the strategic plan of Henry Kissinger, and began to court China as an ally against the Soviet Union. He enabled the People's Republic of China to join the United Nations as permanent member of the Security Council. Nixon enacted the "One China" policy, recognizing Taiwan as part of China.

These dramatic moves would have been impossible under any other President and were openly opposed by many within Nixon's own Republican Party. The "China Lobby" and the John Birch Society rallied against him with billboards denouncing Mao Zedong and falsely claiming China was responsible for the global heroin trade.

Nixon's olive branch was embraced by the Gang of Four, an ultra-leftist clique within the Chinese Communist Party that was influential in the final years of Mao's life. With "The Theory of Three Worlds" China presented the United States as an ally against what they called "Soviet Social Imperialism." In Angola, Ethiopia, Chile, Cambodia, and many other parts of the world, Communists who took direction from China aligned with the United States in the name of fighting the Soviet Union which they dubbed "the main danger to the people of the world."

At home, Nixon's administration passed a constitutional amendment lowering the voting age from 21 to 18, in the hopes of bringing alienated young people back into the political process. Nixon also created the Environmental Protection Agency and signed a number of anti-pollution laws.

The Occupation Safety Health Administration (OSHA) was created in order to enforce laws designed to protect employees on the job. Nixon also enacted the first affirmative action policies in federal hiring, enabling a higher level of representation for African-Americans and Latinos in government jobs.

The Nixon Shocks – "We're All Keynesians Now!"

Milton Friedman, the neoliberal economist who called for mass deregulation and shrinking of the government's role in the economy was an adviser to Nixon's Presidential campaign. During the first years of Nixon's Presidency, Friedman played a key role in crafting economic policies. The result was an economic downturn.

Nixon then boldly expelled Milton Friedman and the Chicago School Economists from the White House. Nixon famously said, "We are all Keynesians now!" in 1971, and enacted his famous "Nixon Shocks" removing the gold standard as backing for the US dollar, imposing a 90-day freeze on all prices and wages, and a 10% import surcharge.

The moves infuriated advocates of neoliberalism and were denounced widely in the pages of *National Review* magazine. Friedman, along with Ayn Rand and other widely promoted free right-wing intellectuals at the time, espoused an economic philosophy of "survival of the fittest." They argued that the state should not intervene, but simply "let the economy take care of itself." Many libertarians went as far saying that those without economic opportunity should be allowed to die off as inferior. The words of Friedman, Rand and Hayek often invoked memories of the Nazis, who utilized rhetoric about "useless eaters" to justify the extermination of disabled people.

The Ford Foundation and the Rockefeller Family, while funding cultural leftist and anti-racist activism, also widely promoted libertarian economics during the 1970s. The Rockefellers financed and promoted various lectures and TV programs promoting Milton Friedman's concept of "Free to

Choose," unregulated capitalism. Media mogul Ted Turner launched a billboard campaign promoting Ayn Rand's philosophy. Famously, at the Ford Hall Forum, sponsored by the Ford Foundation in 1972, Ayn Rand proclaimed that the slaughter of the Native Americans was justified.

Nixon's purge of Friedman from his administration was not merely symbolic. Facing a serious economic downturn, Nixon utilized huge amounts of government spending, spending $25.2 billion to stimulate the economy in 1972. Nixon went as far to openly propose a plan to provide a universal basic income of $1,600 (the equivalent of $10,000 present day) to every American family of four. Congress blocked Nixon's proposal for a Family Assistance Plan in 1969. He continued to push the idea even in his 1971 State of the Union Address saying "So let us place a floor under the income of every family with children in America-and without those demeaning, soul-stifling affronts to human dignity that so blight the lives of welfare children today."

Nixon also made of point being blatantly supportive of organized labor. He was endorsed by many labor unions in his campaigns. He famously commuted the sentence of Jimmy Hoffa, the strongman leader of the International Brotherhood of Teamsters, and released him from Federal Prison.

Protecting "Archie Bunker" To Wield Political Power

At the time of Nixon's Presidency, a TV comedy program called *All in the Family* became quite popular. The program portrayed an elderly, conservative, racist construction worker named *Archie Bunker*, who has ongoing political arguments with his liberal, college-educated son-in-law *Meathead*.

Nixon interpreted the TV program as an attack on him and his supporters, and discussed the program with his advisers. Nixon found the program's support for LGBT rights to be particularly repugnant. Speaking with his spiritual adviser, Rev. Billy Graham, he used anti-Semitic language to describe what he viewed as a conspiracy against him in the media.

In March of 1974, roughly six months before Richard Nixon resigned, a nationally broadcast cartoon TV special *Free to Be You Me* urged children to reject traditional gender roles. Hollywood actors seemed unanimous in their denunciations of Nixon as a "fascist." While Nixon spoke for average Americans in expressing fears about drug use and promiscuity, Hollywood and Broadway musicals presented LSD, Marijuana and premarital sex as "cool" and "hip" recreational activities. Though Nixon's cultural conservatism represented solid majority opinion, the media was dominated by voices who saw him and the middle America he represented as "up tight" and "square." The reason Nixon kicked Milton Friedman out of the White House is simple. In order to maintain his base of support among "Hard Hats" Nixon could not allow the US economy to be looted. In order for Nixon to carry out his dramatic Bonapartist program, it was necessary for a strata of white workers in the United States to have a comfortable life, and be economically satisfied. If Nixon's "Silent Majority" were to become hungry and unemployed, they would no longer support him.

While Nixon was happy to unleash Milton Friedman against the people of Chile in 1973 following the military coup, Nixon would not unleash the nightmare of neoliberalism on America's middle class.

Once the domestic political crisis of 1968-1972 had been resolved, and protests and rebellions were infrequent, the

Rockefellers and Ford Foundation unleashed an all-out attack on Richard Nixon, the strongman who was increasingly working to control the economy and protect his working class base from Wall Street greed.

The *Washington Post*, the *New York Times*, and other publications with a history of cooperation with the CIA and the intelligence community, worked to paint Nixon as a tyrant. College students, middle class liberals, African-Americans, and many other liberal strata were mobilized in a call to bring down a "dictator." Angela Davis and the Communist Party saw Nixon as dangerous because of his strategic use of China as an ally against the Soviet Union and his policies of domestic political repression. The Soviet aligned Communists worked with the Democratic Party in calls for Nixon's ousting. Though China was friendly to the Nixon White House, the Revolutionary Union (now the Revolutionary Communist Party), a Maoist communist group with roots in Students for a Democratic Society, staged massive rallies in Washington DC calling to "Throw the Bum Out."

While the widespread New Communist Movement of the 1970s often invoked the industrial working class and memories of 1930s populist struggles, it was effectively duped and manipulated by some of the richest and most powerful people. Nixon was not removed for his racism or his crimes against the people of Vietnam. The push to remove Nixon from office came from the Rockefeller Family, the intelligence community, the Ford Foundation, and the Chicago School of Economics. Nixon was right-wing, but his Bonapartism often stood in the way of Wall Street profits. With the domestic crisis of the late 1960s done and over with, there was no need for the billionaire elite to tolerate a

"strongman" in the White House who could and did tell them
"no."

The crimes that led to Nixon's resignation were wiretapping
his political opponents to gain information during the 1972
election, keeping an "enemies list" of people disloyal to the
administration, and other activities that amount to probably
standard foul play in Washington's ongoing power struggles.

Whistleblower Edward Snowden revealed that millions
of Americans are currently being wiretapped by the US
National Security Agency for reasons that are not available
to the public. The FISA court, established in 1978 to oversee
wiretaps is described as a "rubberstamp," almost never
declining a warrant. Official records show that from 1979 to
2014, 34,000 wiretaps were approved by the FISA court, with
only 11, less than 0.03% being denied.

Opening the Door to Neoliberalism

Bringing down Nixon opened the door to Milton Friedman
and neoliberal fanatics. The new President, Gerald Ford, the
only President never elected as Vice President or President,
appointed Alan Greenspan to his board of economic advisors.
Greenspan brought his mentor, Ayn Rand to the White House
to watch him be sworn in. Greenspan also directed the
Council on Foreign Relations from 1982 to 1988, overseeing
the expansion of international trade agreements. Greenspan
became chairman of the Federal Reserve Bank from 1987
to 2006, and was probably the most influential figure in US
economic policy.

The fall of Nixon was a pivotal moment in the process of
transforming the once prosperous American heartland into the

"rustbelt," plagued by opioids, low wages, and suicide. The forces that brought down Nixon, while embracing social and cultural liberalism, had no need to protect the living standards of the "Archie Bunkers" and "Hard Hats." Jobs were shipped overseas, lending was deregulated, and public budgets were gutted.

Following Nixon's demise, both the Democratic and Republican parties gradually embraced the economic theories of Adam Smith, Milton Friedman and Ayn Rand. Pat Buchanan and other advocates of protectionism were driven from the Republican Party. Eventually, Bill Clinton's Democratic Leadership Council emerged to purge the Democratic Party of all who advocated Rooseveltian policies.

The bitterness associated with Trump supporters in places like Michigan, Ohio, Pennsylvania, and Wisconsin is rooted in decades of policies that Nixon refused to enact. The downfall of Nixon was a pivotal moment in opening the doors of neoliberalism and the destruction of the American middle class.

Donald Trump emerged within the Republican Party as a repudiation of its established leadership. During the debates, Trump accused George W. Bush of lying about weapons of mass destruction and called the Iraq War a disaster. Trump openly advocated for friendlier relations with Russia, and questioned U.S. support for arming terrorists to overthrow the Syrian government. Trump talked of economic protectionism and accused the Republican leadership of abandoning the working class. Trump talked of rebuilding the infrastructure of the United States, and reorienting the economic policies of the U.S. government in order to the put the interests of the population above those of multinational corporations and international bankers.

Things that could have been said by left-wing filmmaker Michael Moore in 2004 were said by right-wing populist candidate Donald Trump in 2016. It should be no surprise, that many of those who had supported the Bernie Sanders during the democratic primaries, voted for Trump in the final election.

Trump's rhetoric broke with the neoliberal consensus, and challenged the idea that the government should "let the economy take care of itself." Furthermore, Trump stated that the U.S. was done "toppling regimes." He openly admitted that US military involvement in Iraq and Libya had resulted in strengthening terrorism and instability.

Many Americans object to Donald Trump's scapegoating of immigrants and calling for a crackdown on undocumented workers. Many Americans object to Donald Trump's bigoted words against Islam. Many Americans object to Trump's support of torture, and his backing of the police amid a wave of documented brutality. However, these progressive sentiments among many Americans are not the real driving force behind those calling for Trump's impeachment. The opposition to Trump, which echoes from CNN, MSNBC, John McCain, and the Democratic National Committee has entirely different motives.

Attacking Trump From Above

The focus of Bob Meuller's investigation is the allegation that Trump somehow "colluded" with Russia during the Presidential campaign. The allegation hurled in the media is that Trump is not enthusiastic enough about overthrowing the Syrian government and is too enthusiastic about the possibility of restoring friendship between Russia and the United States.

Furthermore, many "free trade" Republicans are unhappy that Donald Trump canceled the Trans-Pacific Partnership and is renegotiating aspects of the North American Free Trade Agreement.

Trump, like Nixon, appealed to the grievances of many white working class people, who are far more economically destitute than they were during Nixon's era. He promised to rebuild infrastructure, and end foreign wars and international trade deals.

Currently, Trump has enacted free-market policies, cutting social spending and regulations. However, Trump continues to hold big rallies around the country, rallying a base of working-class supporters. In a crisis situation, these forces could be pushed into motion in order to carry out a different agenda.

The same forces that maneuvered to bring down Richard Nixon, undoubtedly see Donald Trump as a threat and are actively discussing the idea of removing him. Trump has done a great deal to appease these forces, including de-regulating Wall Street and bombing Syria. However, the media campaign against Trump and the wave of fresh accusations has not ceased.

Trump, like Nixon, could potentially be a barrier in the way of those who want one, global, free-trade, low wage economy, and war to enforce it. For this reason, he faces a wave of opposition, not from those suffering due to the crisis of American capitalism or his problematic policies, but from some of the highest and most powerful forces within the existing power structure.

Originally published in New Eastern Outlook

INF Treaty Withdrawal: Does Trump Believe THE Reagan Mythology?

As Trump dramatically pulls out of the Intermediate Range Nuclear Forces (INF) Treaty, while sending John Bolton to Moscow to negotiate a new agreement regarding the production of nuclear weapons, it appears that false narratives about the Cold War's conclusion could be influencing White House foreign policy.

It is clear that Trump seeks to present himself as a new Reagan to the elderly, red state, FOX news audience. Trump's slogan "Make America Great Again" was intentionally lifted from Reagan's war-chest of campaign slogans, presented as "Let's Make America Great Again" in 1980. Now, it looks as if Trump is "escalating the arms race" in order "defeat the Russians," further fulfilling his image as the new "gipper."

On FOX News, Right-Wing Talk Radio, and other Republican-aligned sections of US media, Ronald Reagan is treated as an immortal hero and icon. The religious and military obsessed neoconservative right-wing has canonized him to the point that one almost expects to see graphics of Reagan adjusted to include halos, or to see FOX news anchors cross themselves after uttering his name. Endless radio and TV segments in the right-wing media sphere have been dedicated to memorializing the man who held the US Presidency from 1981 to 1989.

The mythology perpetuated about the Reagan Presidency is that, while cowardly democrats had negotiated with the Soviet leaders and called for de-escalating the arms race, Reagan escalated the drive to build nuclear weapons. Reagan's escalation of the arms race is said to have forced the Soviets to increase military spending, causing economic problems in the USSR. The heroic POTUS is said to have beat his chest with thunderous "tear down that wall" speeches, blasted the USSR as an "evil empire," and eventually forced the Communists to surrender through his sheer strength, boldness, and refusal to compromise.

The problem is that the Republican narrative regarding the Cold War is largely inaccurate. While pressure to increase military spending certainly played a role in placing economic pressure on the Soviet Union, the USSR was destroyed by a political, not fiscal crisis. The political crisis that destroyed the USSR was mainly influenced by liberal soft-power policies from the US government not militarism and threats.

Manipulating Discontent & Alienation

After the Russian Revolution of 1917, the Soviet Union had three legal political parties. The Bolsheviks were joined by the Left Mensheviks and the Left Socialist Revolutionaries in a coalition government dedicated to building socialism. However, those who were truly loyal to the new government joined the party of Lenin, and the two opposition parties became a collection of naysayers and conspirators. After a member of the Left Socialist Revolutionary Party shot Vladimir Lenin, and the Left Mensheviks participated in a series of armed actions against the Bolsheviks, the two opposition parties were outlawed.

In 1921, Lenin passed the famous "Resolution on Party Unity" that banned factions within the Communist Party, in the hopes of creating the iron-clad discipline needed by a government facing economic blockade and military encirclement.

The Stalin era was known for vast improvements in living conditions and industrialization of the country. The program of "Socialism in one country" carried out with Five Year Economic Plans, resulted in making the USSR a world industrial superpower, while creating the military strength needed to eventually defeat the Nazi invasion and liberate Eastern Europe. However, the Stalin-era was also known for the "great terror" in which many people were sent to gulags or executed, and panic about foreign subversion was widespread. At the famous "Moscow Trials" from 1936 to 1938, a number of top Soviet officials were convicted of conspiracy against the government.

The Soviet public was sent the message that being outspoken or involved in political affairs was dangerous business. In the field of economic development, Stalin tended to favor a kind of technocratic pragmatism, bringing in foreign capitalists to help set up state industries, and generously rewarding those who labored most productively with his "Stakhonovism" movement.

Decades later in the 1980s, Soviet leadership was at a generational turning point. The founders of the Soviet Union were dying off. Leonid Brezhnev and Yuri Andropov were both small children when the Bolsheviks had taken power in 1917, and they represented the last of the old guard of political figures who rose to power during the Stalin era. The Soviet government was now made of people who had grown up in a depoliticized, pragmatic atmosphere in which political debate was stifled. With *Perestroika* and *Glasnost*, the Soviet Communist Party was visibly watering down its ideology and liberalizing its economy, with a significant portion of the leadership no longer believing in Marxism.

Brzezinski's Soft Power Schemes

In this atmosphere of de-politicization within the USSR, the Democratic Party and the US Central Intelligence Agency increasingly attempted to present the Soviet public with a friendlier image of the USA. Liberal cities established "sister city" relations with Soviet cities. A joint Soviet-American TV children's special *Free to be...a Family* aired in 1988 on ABC and Soviet State television. The program featured *The Muppets* and sought to send a message that Soviet children and American children had similar hopes and fears. These "good will" efforts intended to present the USA as a benevolent, liberal country. As Soviet Communist rhetoric was being watered down, this soft power strategy did far more in setting the stage for the fall of the USSR than Reagan's aggressive moves. A large sector of the Soviet public was mistakenly convinced that US leaders were trustworthy and somehow wanted to help them.

The Ford Foundation and various Rockefeller-linked outfits funded an army of liberal, Hollywood-admiring, counterculture "activists", who studied texts like Marilyn Ferguson's *The Aquarian Conspiracy* and held pacifist anti-nuclear rallies. These groups sent friendly delegations to the USSR and established ties with dissident intellectuals.

This fit in with the overall strategy developed by US intelligence during the Cold War. In the decades following World War II, the US Central Intelligence Agency was involved in fomenting and escalating a series of episodes of unrest across Eastern Europe. In Hungary in 1956 and in Czechoslovakia in 1968,the CIA worked to enflame dissent and tension, pushing anti-Russian factions within these governments and forcing the Soviet Union to intervene.

Zbeignew Brzezinski, a Polish-American who eventually rose to the rank of National Security Advisor under US President Jimmy Carter, perfected the art of fomenting episodes of chaos. Brzezinski knew specifically how to target intellectuals and young people. A strata of educated young people, often the children of Communist Party bureaucrats, felt stifled by the Eastern bloc governments. These young dissidents tended to be turned off by doctrinaire anti-communism. While they denounced the Marxist-Leninist governments of Eastern Europe, they often spoke of "Democratic Socialism," "Participatory Democracy" and idealistically clung to a vision of a less authoritarian anti-capitalism while subtly receiving CIA support. George Soros, now hated by conservatives for his Democratic Party ties, helped to bank roll various liberal, anti-communist movements across Eastern Europe.

To these young people, the USA was the homeland of *Beatles* music, blue jeans, and other luxuries forbidden by the Soviet-aligned governments. In the delusional narrative covertly spoon-fed to young Eastern European intellectuals, overthrowing the Marxist-Leninist parties would mean maintaining the guaranteed jobs, healthcare and education, while adding the ability to "express yourself" in art and music and to purchase the shiny consumer products abundantly available in western countries.

Hardline rhetoric from conservatives like Ronald Reagan tended to strengthen the Soviet government. In order for the young intellectuals in awe of western liberal culture to be effectively manipulated, they had to believe they were not fighting to restore capitalism or aligning with the Pentagon. The illusion was that this was a movement of "free thinkers" from both the USA and the Eastern Bloc who were "coming together" to remove the barracks-like conditions branded as "Stalinism" as part some universal, pacifist, spiritual awakening.

In the referendum of 1991, the majority voted overwhelmingly to keep the Soviet Union. After the fall of governments in Poland, Czechoslovakia, Romania, and many other countries, the populations voted for the Communist Parties. In 1993, Russia had a constitutional crisis as the US-aligned President, Boris Yeltsin, suppressed the elected parliament made of Communists, who overwhelmingly had public support.

Among factory workers and farmers, the socialist system and the Communist Parties associated with it had support. The support for Communism had been lost among college professors, artists, teachers, and within the ruling parties themselves. The ideology and will to continue standing up to pressure among the Communist Parties leadership was also eroded by an atmosphere of pragmatism and liberalism.

The fall of the Soviet Union and the Eastern Bloc was not a military defeat or even an economic defeat, but an ideological one. When military coups and efforts from the top dismantled the Marxist-Leninist governments, a significant sector of intellectuals and young people supported it, and the though the majority of the population wanted to maintain socialism, after years of being depoliticized they did not have the will to fight for it.

The result of the fall of the Soviet Union and the Eastern Bloc was utter catastrophe. Mass unemployment and malnutrition accompanied the rise of sex trafficking, heroin addiction, and organized crime. The term "economic genocide" was used by different analysts to describe how state industries were sold off and millions were cast in desperate poverty. The fantasy that these societies would all become disneyland playgrounds dotted with consumer goods never materialized. Capitalism brought mass poverty and suffering, and many countries in Eastern Europe have never recovered from the downfall of socialism.

Trade Wars and Sanctions Will Not Hurt Xi and Putin

Unlike Eurasia's leaders from the 20th Century, Vladimir Putin in Russia and Xi Jinping in China are not espousing a desire to spread Communist revolution across the planet. Putin speaks a language of Russian nationalism and populism, and simply wants to strengthen his country economically. Xi Jinping emphasizes the need for "win-win cooperation" and has repeatedly made clear that the Chinese Communist Party is not interested in exporting its political system or ideology.

Both Vladimir Putin and Xi Jinping maintain their popular support due to actual achievements in terms of improving people's lives. From 1999 to 2006, Putin's economic reforms restored the Russian economy, drastically increased living standards, and ended the crisis that followed the fall of the USSR. Xi Jinping is seen as carrying on the legacy of Mao Zedong and Deng Xiaoping and the ironclad leadership that transformed China into the second largest economy on earth, lifting 800 million people from poverty.

The huge amount of sanctions and pressure placed on Russia in 2014 following the Ukraine crisis did not weaken Putin. In fact, it made Putin's public support stronger. Russians felt that the USA and NATO were threatening them, and saw Putin as defending them from hostile moves.

Meanwhile, Xi Jinping is not becoming less popular due to the confrontational economic moves of the White House. Contrarily, Xi Jinping's reputation as "the big boss" who will not be pushed around is being solidified.

The fact is that Cold War escalations did not really weaken or destroy the Soviet Union. The Soviet Union was defeated by soft power manipulations and internal political decay, aided by a "Mr. Nice Guy" image of the United States as the land of material plenty and intellectual freedom. Trump's announcements regarding the INF Treaty and his continued tariff escalations with China are most likely not going to, in any way, weaken the governments of Russia and China. If anything, Putin and Xi are likely to become more popular in the face of a prolonged "New Cold War" scenario. Their image as strong leaders protecting the country from a hostile and aggressive west will increase.

Like much of the Trump White House's maneuverings, one wonders if the intent is really to win on the global stage. Does Trump really believe the FOX news narrative about Ronald Reagan's victory?

Or are Trump's international moves simply performance art, appealing to a constituency of people who actually buy in to the bombastic propaganda narrative of Cold War history?

Originally published in New Eastern Outlook

TRUMP AGAINST THE PENTAGON? POSSIBLE SHIFTING OF WHITE HOUSE ALLIANCES

The line from James Mattis that seemed to stand out the most was "Because you have the right to have a Secretary of Defense whose views are better aligned with yours on these and other subjects, I believe it is right for me to step down from my position."

Mattis spent the prior paragraphs of his resignation letter describing the threats of terrorism, the importance of US military alliances, and the perceived danger of Russia and China. He then dropped the subtly worded bombshell sentence, indicating that Trump did not share these views which are considered to be the standard perspective of the global situation by US mainstream media.

The Mattis resignation coincided with the announced withdrawal of US troops from Syria and Afghanistan. Mattis is reported to have disagreed with the President's decision. Shortly after the resignation, Trump visited US troops in Iraq and infuriated the military by signing "Make America Great Again" hats and announcing, falsely, that he had increased the troop's pay by 10%.

The mainstream of American politics went into overdrive denouncing Trump for "giving a huge gift to Putin" and "abandoning the women" of Afghanistan. US Senator Lindsey Graham said "The only reason they're not dancing in the aisles in Tehran and ISIS camps is they don't believe in dancing." Those who are familiar with contemporary US history should realize that Trump seems to be in an increasingly dangerous position as he has apparently earned the scorn of the Pentagon brass.

The struggle between the elected President as "commander-in-chief" of the US military and its uniformed brass is quite longstanding. Abraham Lincoln famously fired General George McLellan with the historic rebuff "If General McClellan does not want to use the Army, I would like to borrow it for a time." Truman fired General Douglas Macarthur for threatening to drop atomic bombs on China without Presidential authorization.

The Pentagon and the Presidency

John F. Kennedy's assassination can be widely interpreted in the context of a rivalry between the intelligence community and the Pentagon. Kennedy refused to send in the US military into Cuba after the failure of the Bay of Pigs invasion by exiled anti-Communists. Kennedy refused to escalate the Vietnam War and increasingly argued that the best way to defeat Communism was with a foreign policy of good will and charity. After Kennedy's assassination his successor, Lyndon Johnson, did indeed escalate the Vietnam War, and eventually resigned as the war became unpopular.

While Jimmy Carter's presidency is remembered as an era of Peace, it was also an era in which the intelligence agencies had the upper hand. With the United States public still traumatized by the Vietnam War, Carter presented a liberal, nearly pacifist image. However, Carter called openly himself a student of Zbeignew Brzezinski, the mastermind anti-communist who worked with the CIA to foment protest among the eastern bloc intellegensia and pioneered the use of Wahabbi terrorists as proxy fighters in Afghanistan.

Carter was loved by Langley, but hated in the Pentagon. The US Senate blocked Carter from ratifying the Strategic

Arms Limitation Talks 2 agreement of 1979, with retired Generals and military linked voices in the media denouncing him as "soft." Carter was also accused of having "lost" Iran after the victory of the 1979 Islamic Revolution.

The Pentagon loathed Carter's soft-power approach and seemed almost unanimously behind Ronald Reagan who trounced him in the 1980 election. Reagan raised military spending. According to the Washington Post: "Reagan came along and brought.... an infusion of money. Defense spending hit a peak of $456.5 billion in 1987 (in projected 2005 dollars), compared with $325.1 billion in 1980 and $339.6 million in 1981, according to the Center for Strategic and Budgetary Assessments. Most of the increase was for procurement and research and development programs. The procurement budget leapt to $147.3 billion from $71.2 billion in 1980."

Trump: On The Outs With Both Intel & the Generals?

The mutual distrust between Trump and the intelligence agencies has been apparent from early on. The media largely credits intel agencies with the steady stream of leaks. Trump's speech to the CIA shortly after taking office was described by *New Yorker* magazine as a "vainglorious affront."

Trump echoed the Pentagon's mantra of "Peace Through Strength" on the campaign trail. He raised military spending, and even let the Pentagon utilize the largest non-nuclear explosive device, the infamous MOAB, in Afghanistan. Trump arranged for Saudi Arabia to increase its purchases from US military contractors.

In the old feud between intel agencies and the Pentagon,

Trump seemed solidly with the Pentagon. But in December, a series of bizarre tweets criticizing US military spending were apparently foreshadowing the withdrawal of forces from Syria and Afghanistan. With Mattis out, and Trump's Iraqi holiday visit widely criticized, it now appears Trump is on the outs with the US military.

One particular passage from Mattis resignation letter is striking:

"It is clear that China and Russia, for example, want to shape a world consistent with their authoritarian model – gaining veto authority over other nations' economic, diplomatic, and security decisions – to promote their own interests at the expense of their neighbors, America and our allies. That is why we must use all the tools of American power to provide for the common defense."

This statement is loaded with hypocrisy and projection. Russia and China are rather loose and free societies compared to many US-aligned regimes such as Saudi Arabia or South Korea. Meanwhile, both Russia and China have been working to develop and eradicate poverty in neighboring countries. The Eurasian Economic Union and the One Belt, One Road initiative have involved massive spending by Russia and China to stabilize and raise living standards in nearby countries, not "promote their own interests" at their "expense."

However, the structure of Mattis' letter seems to indicate on some level that Trump does not agree with his assessment, and perhaps has another view of Russia and China and their role in the world.

This raises many questions, not just about what kind of conversations are taking place behind closed doors within the White House, but what the future of the current administration will be. After all, the US military and those who manufacture its weapons and tools are an extremely powerful constituency.

Originally published in New Eastern Outlook

Blasphemy From The White House: What is Behind Trump's Big Mouth?

Under the new US administration, the ruling order of the country has not drastically changed. Domestically, the rising power of policing agencies alongside cuts in social spending has not ceased. Internationally, the USA still stands with western Europe against the bloc of independently developing countries centered around Russia, China and Iran.

While trends in actual policy remain roughly the same, one thing has certainly been altered. While the international order of western liberalism and globalist capitalism remains intact, statements hostile to it and contrary to its values continue to flow from the White House.

On an almost daily basis, statements that are completely contrary to the narrative of the "international liberal order" flow from the mouth of the commander-in-chief. The examples are numerous.

While the narrative of neoliberalism presents Russian President Vladimir Putin as a bloodthirsty tyrant, unlike figures in the "civilized" and "democratic" western nations, Trump thundered back "Do you think this country is so innocent?" when questioned about Putin being a "killer."

While the voices of global capitalism insist that Kim Jong-Un is a mentally unstable, unintelligent, delusional, paranoid lunatic, Donald Trump has called Kim a "smart cookie" and said he is open to meeting him.

Trump said that Obama had utilized the surveillance apparatus of the USA to "wiretap" him during the election.

The US media responded angrily insisting that the federal government always follows due process and standard procedures and that such an occurrence just could not have happened.

"Blasphemy" in the 21st Century

While Trump's statements are absolutely contrary to the narrative and worldview of the prevailing international order, they have not translated into any concrete changes. If anything, Trump has escalated the policy trends of his predecessors. Trump did what Obama proved ultimately unwilling to do, and directly struck the Syrian Arab Republic with cruise missiles. Trump now threatens war against North Korea, and has escalated the anti-Iranian and pro-Israeli tone of US leadership. Furthermore, Trump cuts social programs and spending much more vigorously than his opponents, and has positioned himself as an ally of the policing agencies against those who protest them.

The crime that Trump is continuously castigated for is a 21st century version of "blasphemy," a crime that people were often executed for during medieval times. Merriam-Webster's dictionary defines "Blasphemy" as "irreverence toward something considered sacred or inviolable."

During the age of feudalism, the political and economic order depended on the absolute obedience of society to authority. Nobles claimed to have the authority of God, the "divine right" to rule over serfs and peasants. The church, based in Rome, led by the Pope, was considered to have infallibility in defining and articulating God's wishes, the basis the state.

To utter statements that were contrary to that of the Church was to call into question the entire order of society. To deny the existence of God or to question the theology of Rome was one of the most wicked and harshly punishable crimes.

Galileo Galilei was famously forced to recant his belief that the earth was not the center of the universe, as this simple astronomical fact put the entire social order in danger.

Much like Galileo's belief in that the earth was not the center of the universe, Trump's heretical statements are pretty much true, driving the mainstream media to harshly castigate him for making them.

Dangerously True Words

Trump's response to the allegations about Putin: "do you really think this country is so innocent?" should be obviously agreeable to any student of American history. The USA was founded with the slaughter of Native Americans and the exploitation of African slaves. Since the end of the Second World War, the United States has worked to topple numerous independent governments, while backing many bloodthirsty and repressive regimes that were friendly to Wall Street and London. Within US borders many dissidents such as Martin Luther King Jr., Joe Hill, and Chelsea Manning have faced the wrath of the state.

There's nothing untrue about questioning the innocence of the United States in response to the accusation that a foreign leader is a "killer." However, such a statement is blasphemous. The US government and the international system orbiting it depend on the mythology that the USA is a benevolent democratic power that goes around liberating oppressed people from "dictators."

Trump's statement that Kim Jong-Un is a "smart cookie" does not defy logic. The entire world objects to the DPRK's continued proliferation of nuclear weapons. The DPRK faces crushing economic sanctions, as well as a huge hostile military presence in the southern part of the Korean Peninsula. The Korean territory controlled by the DPRK is mainly mountainous, with very little arable land, making food self-sufficiency quite difficult to maintain.

Yet, despite all of this, the Korean Workers Party holds on to power, and the centrally planned socialist economy, based on the principles of "Juche" remains fully intact. Under these most hostile circumstances, not only does the DPRK not collapse, but it has launched satellites into space, and continues to conduct missile and nuclear tests, flying against the wishes of highly powerful enemies.

Whether one approves of him or not, why would a leader capable of presiding over such activities, under such hostile circumstances, not be considered a "smart cookie?" Such ability certainly demonstrates prowess of leadership.

Furthermore, Trump's suspicion that Obama or the NSA may have abused powers of surveillance against him, while still unproven, is not completely incredible. The response of the media, citing the elaborate procedures and legal protections of US citizens seems to ignore the fact that US officials violate such rules all the time.

For many years a police officer in the Chicago Police Department tortured people in order to extract confessions from them. Jon Burge was eventually caught and punished for his activities, but for years he was carrying them out on a routine basis. Many individuals were convicted of crimes and sent to prison based on confessions extracted with electrical shocks and other illegal methods. The fact that Burge's actions were illegal and violates standard procedure did not prevent them from occurring.

During the 1950s and 60s, the FBI launched a program called COINTELPRO designed to silence political dissidents. The program involved surveillance, infiltration, and active disruption and repression of many political activists groups. The COINTELPRO program not only targeted the US Communist Party, but also pacifist groups, civil rights organizations, and many others which opposed the status quo in the USA by only peaceful means. The program obviously violated constitutional protections of free speech and assembly, but it continued for many years.

To think that authorities in the United States always respect the right to privacy and civil liberties of the population, and would never abuse their power is absurd. Edward Snowden revealed a widespread apparatus of surveillance in the USA. Is claiming that this apparatus may have targeted Trump really such a big stretch?

"God Save The King"

Trumps willingness to stray from the standard narrative and make statements against the status quo probably caused many of his supporters to believe that his Presidency would lead to a complete re-shuffling of America's domestic politics and foreign policy. This obviously appears not to be the case.

So, if not serving as the basis of policy, what purpose do Trump's routine "blasphemous" statements really serve?

Perhaps the answer can be found by once again looking back into the medieval social order known as feudalism.

During the time of feudalism, nobles ruled over serfs and peasants with almost complete and absolute power. Peasants could be tortured, killed, starve, or otherwise repressed at their convenience. Concepts like 'the rule of law' and 'human rights' had not yet emerged.

However, there was an entity that did occasionally protect peasants and serfs from the extreme violations reigned down on them by the land owning aristocrats. This was the King. The King was part of the aristocracy who did not have a small principality of his own to rule over, but instead ruled over all the nobles as the head of state. The King often served the purpose of disciplining and restraining the nobles, on behalf of the peasants.

Peasants often sang 'God Save The King' and viewed the King as the one who was on their side against the local landowning noble, their direct oppressor.

By holding back the landlords, the King served the purpose of keeping the feudal order intact. Peasants were far less likely to revolt against the system that claimed divine authority, if it appeared that there was at least one figure within the feudal structure, who worked on their behalf.

By occasionally demanding that the nobles provide services or show acts of kindness to peasants, and reprimanding them for particularly outrageous acts, the King presented the illusion that the system of feudalism wasn't all bad. The problem wasn't the system, it was just those bad nobles who were selfish. The peasants could be reassured by the fact that despite the outrages of their local day to day oppressor, there was a good man at the top who occasionally stepped in to protect them.

Containing an Explosion?

Trump's blasphemous statements against the liberal order may serve the same purpose as the King's repression of nobles. With the increased accessibility of information, millions of people are aware that the USA is not innocent of repression and murder; that the standard narrative about the DPRK and other demonized countries is not correct; or that policing agencies and federal officials often abuse their power for selfish reasons.

Such rising sentiments, inflamed by the accessibility of information and the economic crisis, have fed protests, rising dissent and the growth of alternative political forces on the far-left and the far-right.

By saying what he says, Trump is reassuring the increasingly critical and cynical population that there is someone who agrees with them on the inside. While the rise of the low wage police state continues, Americans get poorer, civil liberties disappear, and international tensions escalate, those Americans who are displeased can feel reassured by the fact the most powerful man in the country sounds like he might possibly agree with them.

Trump's blasphemous words, while in no way backed up with policy changes, may actually serve to reinforce the status quo he contradicts. As long as those who agree with his cynicism feel like they can be heard and that someone as powerful as the President agrees with them, they will be less likely to actually work toward challenging the powers they despise. It appears that in a world based on myths, where an increasing number of people realize that they are surrounded by falsehoods, a loud mouth in the most powerful seat, who routinely blasphemes against the standard narrative, can be essential to maintaining order and preventing a social explosion.

Originally published in New Eastern Outlook

PART TWO:
CAPITALISM IN CRISIS

GREENSPAN WAVES HIS FIST AFTER WALL STREET SHAKES

As Americans brace for an economic downturn, adherents of free market ideology are busily assuring everyone that their ideas must be not be questioned.

Just two days after the Stock Market dropped on October 10th, the front page of the *Wall Street Journal*'s Weekend Review featured an article entitled *How to Fix the Great American Growth Machine*. The piece repeated a series of neoliberal clichés, and contained some obvious logical holes.

The article pointed toward the unregulated nature of US railroad construction in 1800s as an example of American free market superiority, ignoring the many who died in the process. The construction of railways connecting North America's coasts involved the displacement and genocide millions of Native Americans. It also involved many Irish, African-American, and Chinese people being worked to death. The racist expression "You don't have a Chinamen's chance" referred the semi-slave conditions that Chinese Americans faced when laying rails in western states.

The article hailed the period of 1865 to 1900 as an ideal time in US history due to lack of government interference with business. The article ignored how frequently the US stock market fell into crises during this time, with "panics" frequently leading to bank failures, mass unemployment, and widespread societal turmoil. The article also ignored in the appraisal of this supposedly glorious era, that it was the time, not just of robber barons and widespread government corruption, but also of child laborers and sweat shop factory conditions.

The article went on to say that the problems of the US economy were due to "entitlements" such as food stamps, social security, and Medicare. The article explicitly called for overturning the Dodd-Frank regulations passed by the Obama administration in the aftermath of the 2007-2008 catastrophes.

The article was written by none other than Alan Greenspan, along with co-author Adrian Wooldridge. Alan Greenspan was named by *Time* magazine as one of the people most responsible for the financial crash of 2008. Greenspan even admitted before congress that his "mistakes" had played a key role in the fall of Lehman Brothers and the "housing bubble" bursting.

Alan Greenspan: The Protégé of a Psychopath

Greenspan, who now lives out a comfortable retirement between lavishly paid speaking engagements, spent the prime of his life inside the circles of power. Greenspan was Chairman of the Federal Reserve Bank from 1987 to 2006. He also directed the most important foreign policy think tank of the United States known as the Council on Foreign Relations from 1982 to 1988.

Greenspan has never been elected to public office. But as an un-elected advisor, economic manager, and crafter of foreign policy, he was arguably one of the most powerful people in the United States and the world.

Greenspan's background is not ambiguous or secretive. He was very openly the protégé of the novelist and "philosopher" Ayn Rand. When Greenspan was first appointed to a government position by US President Gerald Ford, his controversial mentor even came with him to take the oath in the oval office.

Ayn Rand is widely understood to be a psychopath who rejected common notions of morality. Rand immigrated to the United States from the Soviet Union, after her family's property was redistributed following the Bolshevik revolution. She received a free education in the Soviet Union, getting a degree in cinematography. She then fled the country with a fraudulent visa, moving first to Chicago and later to Hollywood.

According to the 2009 biography *Goddess of the Market* written by Jennifer Burns, Rand openly swooned over William Hickman, a Chicago man who strangled his wife to death and refused to show remorse for it in court. Rand collected newspaper clippings of Hickman and decorated her bedroom with his photograph.

As Rand became a well-known writer, her novels also celebrated the mentality of violent criminals. Her novel *The Fountainhead* portrays a non-conforming architect, Howard Roark, who rebels against social norms. At one point, the protagonist character breaks into the apartment of a woman and rapes her. Rand's narration portrays this as a heroic act of "a great man" asserting his will.

Rand entitled a collection of her essays *The Virtue of Selfishness*. Rand argued that compassion and empathy were signs of weakness, and altruism was the greatest evil. She was an atheist who denied the existence of God, and proclaimed that religion should be rejected because it promoted compassion, solidarity, and collective thinking.

Rand became very wealthy by employing psychologist Nathaniel Branden to build an extensive cult of admirers who paid lots of money to attend her lectures. Media mogul, Ted Turner purchased a series of billboards containing slogans from Rand's novel *Atlas Shrugged*, hoping to popularize her ideology of selfishness. One of Ayn Rand's greatest admirers was Anton Levay, the founder of the Church of Satan. Levay frequently quoted Rand to his followers in explaining why all notions of morality should be abandoned and replaced with unrestrained selfishness.

Alan Greenspan was one of Rand's most loyal followers, giving economic lectures alongside her. Greenspan lived in the same apartment building and frequently went to Jazz Clubs with Rand up until her death in 1982. Greenspan co-authored a collection of essays along with Ayn Rand entitled *Capitalism: The Unknown Ideal*. In the various essays written by Rand, Greenspan, and other members of her inner circle, the texts assert that big business is the most persecuted minority, that taxation is theft, and that "true capitalism" can only be achieved in a futuristic society where greed is unrestrained and humans have been cured of their drive toward solidarity and cooperation.

The Road to Disaster

In the conclusion of Greenspan's October 12th article, the US public is advised "unless the USA changes its course its economy will continue to flag…" The article urges austerity cuts, de-regulation, while warning of the danger of "populism."

The notion that the USA must "change course" and redirect toward the Greenspan/Rand vision is tragically laughable. Greenspan speaks as if he is a marginal figure, "a voice crying out in the wilderness" advocating a radical shift in policy.

However, the USA has been well on Greenspan's course of neoliberal austerity policies since the 1970s. Greenspan himself directed the Council on Foreign Relations and the US Federal Reserve Bank. These are arguably the most powerful unelected positions in the country. The writings of Greenspan's mentor Ayn Rand are required reading in business schools across the country, with Republican Congressional leader Paul Ryan claiming them as his greatest source of inspiration.

Of all countries in the industrialized world, the United States is by far the most "free market." Every other industrialized country provides healthcare to its citizens, but the USA continues to leave medical care in the hands of profit-hungry insurance and pharmaceutical corporations. The USA does not provide free education to its population either, with a massive "student debt" curse hanging over the heads of millions of young people as bankers make profits and the price of education continues to rise.

Greenspan calls for cuts in public spending, but across
the country, basic services are already being widely eroded
as local governments drown in debt. Municipalities across
the USA have actually begun un-paving the roads, replacing
paved roads with dirt roads in order to save money. The US
postal service continues to face a crisis of funding, while
Trump talks of privatizing it. Many bridges across the USA
are not secure, and much of the US drinking water is not
properly purified.

As the US falls into disrepair amid an orgy of capitalist
profits, Greenspan and his ilk purport that somehow the USA
is providing too many services ('hand outs') to the population.
As the standard of living decreases, infrastructure decays, and
the country falls into great disrepair, somehow the problem is
too much spending.

The current libertarian fanfare claiming that the USA is
"socialist" or "communist" parallels a similar barrage of
desperate, defensive propaganda, preceding and following the
2008 crisis. As the US economy crashed due to deregulation
and an erosion of the standard of living and spending power
of the public, the Tea Party mobilized to proclaim that
somehow "Marxism" was too blame. The fear was that as
Americans become more desperate, the widely inculcated
ideas of the Cold War era, equating "Americanism" with
unbridled greed and selfishness will be eroded. These fears
are once again asserting themselves, as the financial sector
braces for another downturn, following the October 10th
episode.

The specter of populism has the likes of Greenspan fearing
the rise of figures like Huey Long or Franklin Roosevelt, who
utilized the government to take dramatic action and improve

the lives of working people.

For 40 to 50 years, the policies advocated by Greenspan, Rand, Milton Friedman, and others have been implemented in the United States. However, the fact is that one simply cannot create economic growth by cutting spending and impoverishing people. Letting the population fall into deeper debt and insecurity simply does not result in an economic boom, contrary to what the Chicago School textbooks claim.

The USA certainly needs to change course if its economy is going to improve, but changing course will mean rejecting neoliberal fantasies, and asserting that the government has an obligation to build infrastructure, control the economy, and not let the country decay. As President Roosevelt famously proclaimed in order to justify his dramatic economic moves: "An American government must not allow Americans to starve."

Originally published in New Eastern Outlook.

POPE FRANCIS & BEIJING: THE GEOPOLITICS OF
THE VATICAN

The Roman Catholic Church and the Peoples Republic of China are set to sign an agreement, which would formally end the hostilities between these two entities. The Chinese government will formally acknowledge the Pope as the leader of the Catholic Church in China. In exchange, the Pope will reinstate ex-communicated Bishops selected by the Communist Party to lead Catholics on the Chinese mainland. In this context, it is worth reviewing the shifts and evolutions of Catholicism in global politics.

Opposing Capitalism and Marxism

Surprising as it may be to many Republicans in the United States, the Roman Catholic Church officially opposes capitalism. In fact, clerical anti-capitalism predates Marxism by centuries. As the merchant class was emerging in Europe, Catholic theology tended to uphold the "natural order" represented in the feudal hierarchy. The church saw the marketplace as a sinful mess of greed and anarchy. Gutenberg's printing press, which led to the translation and widespread publication of the Bible, and eventually the Protestant Reformation, is seen as the opening shot act in the struggle resulting in the eventual rise of liberal democratic nation-states and the market. Papal proclamations that shifted regulations on money-lending laid the foundations for modern finance. For example, the roots of the titanic institution known as Bank of America can be traced back to early Italian bankers, who emerged as the church loosened its restrictions on Usury.

While Catholic anti-capitalism, which emphasizes morality and obedience over "economic freedom," has been longstanding, the ideology of Marxism is something Rome has always opposed. Catholicism views Marxism as godlessly fomenting revolts against legitimate "God given" authority. Furthermore, Marxist economic determinism is perceived as undermining the moral responsibility of individuals for their actions.

As Marxism proliferated throughout Europe, most especially after the Russian Revolution, it was not uncommon for Roman Catholic Anti-Communists to invoke a supposed "Jewish origin" of Marxism while condemning it. Many Catholics also espoused the belief that Marxism was linked to the Bavarian illuminati, which the Church had suppressed in the 1780s. Rome never formally endorsed any conspiracy theory about the origins of Marxism, but among politicized Catholics, such beliefs were certainly widespread.

In the 1920s and 30s as the political current known as Fascism emerged, the Roman Catholic community was a primary recruiting ground. The Vatican's status as an independent state was arranged by the originator of the word "fascism" himself, Benito Mussolini. Prior to the Second World War, the Soviet Union was condemned by the Catholic Church as an atheistic autocracy, and the duty of all Roman Catholics was to work against the global communist movement. Catholics were rallied to support General Francisco Franco in his Civil War against the Spanish Republic.

"Kill A Commie for Christ"

In the United States, rural and southern communities were the primary base of rightwing politics, and bigotry against Catholics was prevalent among conservatives. The Ku Klux

Klan hated Roman Catholics, going as far as to stage a national rally in opposition to "Columbus Day." Prohibition on alcohol was passed as conservative protestants perceived the Catholic tolerance for social drinking as a threat to American values. Hostility from conservatives resulted in most Catholics, many of whom were recent immigrants living in urban centers, occupying the liberal end of the political spectrum. Anti-Catholic sentiments against Democrat Al Smith were key in securing the victory of Herbert Hoover in the 1928 Presidential election.

However, a Catholic oriented brand of far-right politics in the United States eventually emerged in the 1930s. Father Charles Coughlin of Michigan, the infamous "Radio Priest" known for his Pro-Hitler and Anti-Semitic Sermons became a national political figure. Unlike the Ku Klux Klan and other far-rightists of the time, Coughlin's fascist rhetoric spoke against "international bankers" and condemned capitalism, while at the same time opposing the labor movement and the Roosevelt administration as an example of "Godless Communism." When the Second World War broke out in 1939, the Vatican ordered Coughlin to cease his radio broadcasts.

As the Cold War began, the Soviet Union considered the Roman Catholic Church to be one of its primary enemies and vice-versa. Communist publications frequently referred to the Catholic Church as "fascist" and accused it of complicity in the Holocaust. Urban Catholic Democrats such as the Kennedy family were supporters of the House Un-American Activities Committee as McCarthyism set in. The Catholic Trade Union associations worked to ban Communists from working in Auto-plants and Steel mills. Catholic high school students, bearing placards that said "Kill a Commie for

Christ" were mobilized to violently attack the May 1st parade in New York City in 1948.

As the USA and Europe marched in lockstep against the Soviet Union during the 1950s, the Catholic Church was in an anti-communist frenzy. Across post-war Europe, Church attendance significantly declined, but those who remained practicing Catholics were not only opposed to Communists, but also to Social-Democracy. The Vatican's flock generally embraced "Christian Democratic" political parties, perceiving even the anti-Soviet Social-Democratic parties as being tainted by Marxist materialism.

Vietnam, Central America & Nuclear Weapons

The geopolitics of Catholicism began to shift in the 1960s. The Second Vatican Pastoral Council convened in October of 1962. The event is seen as pivotal in the modern history of the Catholic Church. The council published a document proclaiming "any act of war aimed indiscriminately at the destruction of entire cities… is a crime against God and man himself. It merits unequivocal and unhesitating condemnation." This was widely interpreted as a condemnation of the bombing campaigns conducted by the US military during the Second World War and the Korean War.

A minority of Catholic clergy in the United States protested the Vietnam War from the beginning. Father Daniel Berrigan, a Catholic Priest, was even briefly placed on the FBI's most wanted list for his role in destroying draft records as an act of protest. By the early 1970s, it seemed that the Church was no longer espousing the fanatical anti-Sovietism that had previously defined it and many Catholics were vocally opposing the Vietnam War. As Evangelical Christians emerged as a significant axis within US politics following the upheavals of the Vietnam-era, the Catholic Church did not echo their hysterical fears of the Soviet Union.

In the 1980s, divisions between the Vatican and Washington seemed the most stark in Central America. The Sandinista government that took power in 1979 in Nicaragua embraced the Catholic Church, and priests openly held governmental offices. "Liberation Theology" that put forward a socialist interpretation of the Bible became very popular in Central and South America, and many Catholic clergy openly declared support for it.

As Guatemala, El Salvador, and other countries were swept up in Civil War, the United States aligned itself with armed anti-communist fanatics dubbed "Contras." The Contras and the right-wing of Latin America embraced evangelical protestant teachings from the United States, and saw free market capitalism as biblically mandated. Reverend Jerry Falwell, a key political figure in the United States who formed the "Moral Majority," spent a large amount of time south of the US border, rallying Spanish speaking crowds against Marxism. As Civil Wars raged across Central and South America in the 1980s, Catholic clergy were slaughtered in a number of different massacres and assassinations.

During the 1980s, West Germany, Italy, and France were becoming more friendly to the Soviet Union, and distancing themselves from Ronald Reagan and his escalation of the arm's race. The Catholic Church was well represented among the crowds that condemned both nuclear weapons and nuclear power in a widespread protest movement across the western world. Dennis Kucinich of Cleveland led anti-Nuclear protests in Ohio, citing his Catholic faith as motivation, and was eventually elected to the US Congress. While opposing the arms race and being critical of US foreign policy, Pope John Paul II generally embraced anti-Soviet protests and "color revolutions" across eastern Europe. The most famous example was the "Solidarity" movement of Catholic dock workers in Poland. As the Eastern bloc and eventually the Soviet Union itself fell, the Catholic Church was very vocally aligned with the overthrow of Marxist-Leninist governments, which resulted in economic catastrophe as the state run economies were dismantled. In 1998, Pope John Paul II visited Cuba. Anti-Communists and right-wingers in the United States were furious, accusing the Vatican of granting legitimacy to Fidel Castro. However, the move was widely praised in Europe, where the US economic blockade of Cuba was perceived as irrational.

The Left Turn of Pope Francis

In 2016, Pope Francis made headlines around the world when he began emphasizing opposition to capitalism. Pope Francis was clear that he did not support Marxism, or any Marxist interpretation of Liberation Theology, but he continued to emphasize opposition to income inequality with rhetoric similar to US Presidential Candidate Bernie Sanders. Pope Francis has maintained the Catholic opposition to abortion and gay marriage, but has gone as far as meeting with groups of gay activists and repeatedly declaring that homosexuals are welcome in the Church.

This apparent left turn from Pope Francis paralleled a similar shift among anti-Communists in Latin America. While those who opposed the governments of Hugo Chavez, Nicolas Maduro, Evo Morales, and other Marxists in Latin

America had generally defended capitalism and free markets, the right wing of South and Central America shifted its rhetoric at approximately the same time. Henrique Caprilles of Venezuela and other anti-Communists began saying they were also advocates of "socialism" but favored friendly relations with the United States, and opposed the "extremism" of the Bolivarian governments. While Pope Francis puts forward criticism of capitalism, he has loudly condemned the government of Venezuela.

Pope Francis has also made harsh criticisms of the "new right" in Europe and Trump administration in the United States. The Vatican officially condemned the US policy of separating of immigrant families and calls for refugees to be welcomed in Europe.

The new friendliness between the Vatican and Beijing, and Pope Francis' criticism of Trump, fits in with increasing division between the USA and Western Europe. The Obama administration seemed to work hard for unity within NATO. The Trump administration seems to be far less accommodating to the western European countries. As Trump puts tariffs on China, countries throughout western Europe seem to be embracing the Belt and Road Initiative and having increasingly friendly ties to Beijing. Following a pattern of contemporary Catholicism, the Vatican seems to follow Western Europe in embracing or opposing US foreign policy.

The NATO countries in Europe seem to focus on opposing Russia, while continuing to do business with China. This seems to be the opposite of Trump's policy of escalating a trade war with China while deflecting accusations that he "colluded" with Russia in the 2016 elections. As distance between the United States and Europe expands, it can be expected that the Vatican will be more critical of US foreign policy. However, as Britain exits the European Union, and Germany and other EU countries assert their right to import Russian natural gas, new shifts are certainly possible.

It is worth noting that while the Vatican appears to be on the verge of pivotal agreement with the Chinese Communist-led government, the Church in Vietnam continues to be viewed as a source of opposition. As Vietnam continues to be critical of China, it has been positioning itself closer to the United States, even hosting US naval vessels. Meanwhile, the Vatican continues to condemn Vietnam and accuse the Communist Party of repressing the Catholic minority, which represents only 7% of the population.

What is clear is that the geopolitical positions of the Vatican are not stagnant, and tend to evolve and shift based on circumstances. At the same time, the role of the Catholic Church in societies around the world seems to also be shifting, creating room for even more dramatic adjustments and surprises. Yet, sexual abuse scandals continue to plague the Vatican, regardless of its geopolitical turns.

Originally published in New Eastern Outlook

GANGSTER ECONOMICS AGAINST HUAWEI & NORDSTREAM 2

Many Americans base their entire view of the world, and their understanding of the relationship of the United States to other countries, on the contents of a college-level "Economics 101" course. They view the world market as a land of "free competition" in which different countries and international corporations "compete." They then believe that consumers, communities and countries "vote with their dollars" rewarding the best products and services.

In this delusional fantasy, championed by figures like as George Soros and Anne-Marie Slaughter as an ideal "Open International Market," the United States and western countries occupy their dominant position, simply because they are the best. The products and services offered by western financial institutions and international corporations are simply superior to those found anywhere else. This delusional fantasy goes on to present the western financial elite as somehow mentoring and assisting the world, by helping it "develop" and perhaps someday be more like the superior west.

The "Energy Dominance" Scheme

Those who argue that this western narrative is false have no greater confirmation than the recent actions of the US government. The response to Nordstream 2 pipeline and the recent crackdown on Huawei technologies confirms that the US government has no interest in free competition among international corporations.

Nordstream 2 is a natural gas pipeline that is currently

under construction, scheduled to be completed later this
year. It will enable Russia's state-run energy corporations
to sell natural gas to countries inside the European Union.
The people in various EU countries favor the construction
of Nordstream 2, because it will expand and ad greater
convenience to their access of Russian natural gas.

However, in the United States, the Trump administration
is joined by Democratic Party "resistance" leaders in
demanding that the people of Germany and other European
nations not purchase gas from Russia. They foolishly demand
that the European community purchase gas from the United
States, and import it across the Atlantic Ocean.

It is simple common sense to know that importing natural
gas from across the planet will be far more expensive for
central Europe than simply pumping it over the border from
Russia. However, in a shrill atmosphere of hysteria, invoking
all kinds of unrelated issues and allegations against the
Russian government, the US political establishment is talking
of sanctions and other means of coercing the European public
into buying their gas.

While US leaders invoke human rights-based criticism
of the Russian government, the hypocrisy is obvious. The
Kingdom of Saudi Arabia, a brutal autocracy that beheads
and tortures, remains a top business partner of the United
States in both the energy and weapons markets. The brutal
murder of journalist Jamal Khashoggi has not changed this
relationship, which Trump openly defended on a purely
financial basis.

The goal of making money for American energy
corporations and weakening Russian energy corporations,

their competitors, is not even carefully concealed. The White House openly speaks of "Energy Dominance" as the basis for its policy, and speaks of how protecting the profits US-based oil and gas firms is its blatant intention.

The Anti-China Smartphone War

Are the Germans, Belgians, and other European people's not free to "vote with their dollars" and chose where to purchase their oil and gas? Apparently, the "open international system" is not so open when geopolitical rivals of Wall Street monopolists are involved.

The same rhetoric and methods are being used to try and strong arm countries around the world, and demand that they do not purchase Huawei telecommunications technology from China. Huawei is the largest telecommunications manufacturer in the world. It is an integral part of the market-socialist model developed by Deng Xiaoping and now adjusted and advanced by Xi Jinping.

Huawei phones have longer battery life, better cameras, and more durable, longer lasting hardware than American made phones. All across the world, in places like India, Latin America, and various African countries, the public has selected to buy these cheaper and higher quality phones. The profits of Apple have recently dropped as Huawei's products have become the choice of more and more consumers around the globe and within China.

However, US leaders are demanding that people around the world do not "vote with their dollars" and pick the superior phone. If the free market logic were to apply, US leaders would simply urge American manufacturers to be more competitive. Instead, US leaders continue to demand that countries like Poland and Bulgaria stop doing business with Huawei technologies.

Within the United States, Americans have been prevented from "voting with their dollars" and purchasing the P20, a cutting edge new phone released by the Chinese manufacturer. A whole list of Chinese smartphones are now banned as a supposed national security risk.

US leaders allege that smartphones manufactured by Chinese corporations are a threat to national security because these entities have ties to the Chinese military and government. This claim is rather hypocritical as Apple, AT&T, Verizon, and other American telecommunications companies have not even bothered to conceal their relationship with the US intelligence agencies.

US phones are no more a "military" or "intelligence" threat than Chinese phones are. To expect the Chinese Communist Party, which essentially created Huawei Technologies, to not maintain a relationship with this telecom giant is a ridicules demand.

Not Gentlemanly Business but Gangsterism

More than the "free competition" and "open international system" they advocate, American leaders, seem to be embracing the economic philosophy of Mafia gangsters. Much like criminals operating a protection racquet, US leaders claim that certain countries around the world are their "turf." They demand that their competitors be locked out, and scramble to impose "consequences" on those who would get in their way.

US leaders are themselves discrediting the very ideology they have spread across the world. They are revealing that in truth, "free competition" is a delusion and that governments tend to rig things in favor of their wealthy paymasters and do their bidding. The mantra of "free competition" has been utilized to restrain developing countries and potential competitors, but US leaders are happy to disregard it and protect the global "turf" of the Wall Street and Silicon Valley monopolies.

The truth is that the richest of the rich in the United States did not acquire their wealth by mere personal sacrifice and brilliance, and the western world did not acquire its place in the world through gentlemanly business practices.

In the 21st Century, countries across the world have rejected these free market delusions and utilized their own governments to construct state-controlled economies to eliminate poverty and raise living standards. Huawei, like Russia's Gazprom and Rosneft, are the result of economic innovations, in which post-Cold War governments took action to control the economy on behalf of the population.

Unlike so many of the working class people in western countries, the populations of Russia and China have not been left behind in the process of building up these super-corporations. As the two Eurasian superpowers emerged in the 20th century, not due to free markets, but due to socialist central planning, millions were lifted from poverty.

Originally published in New Eastern Outlook

PETRO-SOCIALISM IN SCOTLAND? OIL, GAS AND INDEPENDENCE

As the Brexit process moves forward, calls for a second Scottish Independence Referendum are picking up steam. The SNP is calling for a second referendum, paving the way for Scotland to leave the United Kingdom, and remain in the EU.

Imagine the people of a country, faced with increasingly difficult economic circumstances, organizing a mass movement and declaring independence. Then, imagine a new government that puts the country's natural resources under state control and sells them on the international markets, and uses the proceeds to build infrastructure and subsidize the construction of a vibrant domestic economy.

This is a scenario that has played out many times throughout the 20th and 21st centuries. The struggle for domestic control over oil profits has been central in a very high percentage of the revolutions and geopolitical confrontations of modern times. The "Yes" movement in Scotland fits in with a global pattern related to energy and the global capitalist market.

Oil Politics in Our Epoch

The central question of the 1917 Bolsheviks Revolution was whether or not Russia would continue fighting in the First World War. It wasn't just a question of whether Russia's soldiers would keep fighting the Germans, but also a question of whether the Baku oil fields of Azerbajjin, controlled by the Czarist government, would continue fueling the war machines of allied countries. In the Russian Civil War that follow the October Revolution, the British military was sent to Azerbaijan to seize back the oil fields belonging to the Rothschild family. Thousands died as the Bolsheviks and the British empire battled over decisive, petroleum-rich territories.

Following the Second World War, "Patriotic officers" and Arab Nationalists across the Middle East revolted against western puppet governments. The Baath Arab Socialist movement that took power in Iraq and Syria argued that the oil of the Middle East should be used to improve the lives of the people as they moved to create a unified state. The 1979 revolution in Iran resulted in the creation an economy described by Imam Khomeni as "not capitalism, but Islam," with state-controlled oil subsidizing all kinds of social programs.

The Bolivarian movement came to power in Caracas in 1999 on a platform of opposing both capitalism and socialism. In 2003, after defeating a coup attempt, Hugo Chavez announced his intention of building "21st Century Socialism." Venezuela's state oil company was reorganized, and a huge state apparatus was created. The Bolivarian movement, calling for domestic control of the economy of Latin America, soon spread to Bolivia, Ecuador, and Nicaragua.

Even 100 years after the Russian Revolution, control of natural resources remains essential to Russia's geopolitical position. Putin's political strength is based on his rebooting of the Russian economy, utilizing Gazprom and Rosneft, two state-controlled energy corporations. The United States and Britain are vocally infuriated by the "Nordstream 2" pipeline, a program which will increase Russia's economic presence in the European Union as an energy supplier.

Even within the United States, oil has been central in political conflicts. Back in the 1930s, Huey Long, the famous and infamous Governor and Senator, built bridges, hospitals and provided education by heavily taxing the extraction and refining of Louisiana's oil. Huey Long became a national figure with his "Share Our Wealth" movement before being gunned down on the steps of the State Capitol Building.

More recently, under the Obama administration, when oil prices dramatically fell in 2014, it became no secret that the "fracking cowboys" aligned with the Republican Party were screaming in pain. However, the four super major oil companies, much cozier with the Democratic Party, saw their monopolistic position enhanced. In Obama's final State of the Union address in January of 2016, he joked about how cheap gasoline was, getting massive applause and laughter from the democratic side of the isle. Just two months later, conservative fracking tycoon Aubrey McClendon died after driving his car into a wall at high speeds, an apparent suicide after being financially ruined.

Scottish Nationalism vs. Austerity

The 2014 Independence Referendum in Scotland was much closer than observers expected. Independence and nationalism had occupied the position of a fringe issue in Scotland, but in the lead-up to the 2014 vote, it emerged to become a mainstream view, especially among millennials.

The 2014 vote was not a referendum on cultural independence, or preserving the traditions of Scottish people. The issue was economics. Scotland has long been a stronghold of socialism in Britain, and the "Yes Scotland" movement has become a vehicle for opposing cuts in social spending.

The Scottish National Party (SNP) with 35 out of the 59
Scottish seats in the UK parliament, has continued to wave
a banner against austerity. Scotland continues to provide
free education for University students, as well as assistance
to low-income mothers. In four Scottish cities, Fife, North
Ayrshire, Edinborough and Glasgow, the SNP controlled-local
government is providing a universal basic income.

The SNP platform does not only contain anti-austerity
planks, but also an item that scares big energy corporations
more than anything. The 2017 SNP conference explicitly
called for "creating a not for profit oil company for Scotland."

This comes in the context of British Petroleum, the Wall
Street and London energy giant, declaring that it will double
oil and gas production in North Sea by 2020. In January of
2018, Mark Thomas of BP declared: "We expect to double
production to 200,000 barrels per day by 2020 and keep
producing beyond 2050."

However, if Scotland becomes independent, and the
SNP's call for a state-run "not for profit" oil company comes
into existence, it might not be London bankers who enrich
themselves with North Sea oil and gas. Scottish independence
could lead the country down the petro-socialist road. A
welfare state and domestic economy could be subsidized with
energy revenue, controlled by the government.

As calls for a new referendum escalate amid the Brexit
process, it can be predicted that the allies of super major
energy giants and the titanic banking entities wedded to them,
will continue to oppose independence for Scotland.

Meanwhile, it can also be predicted that the global bloc of opposition, the forces that urge the USA to stop meddling in Venezuela's affairs, the forces that understand the importance of China's Belt and Road program of infrastructure investment, the voices that recognize the right of EU countries to import natural gas from Russia; the entities disturbed by the hostile threats against Iran; they will favor Scotland's right to break away, not simply in terms of politics, but most especially in terms of economics.

Originally published in New Eastern Outlook

THE POLITICS OF KOREAN STEEL

Import quotas have long been out of fashion among U.S. leaders in the age of free trade and globalization. However, on April 30th, the White House announced that the United States has now revived the practice, with South Korea being the first country subject to this harsh economic measure. The deal reached between the Trump administration and the administration of Moon Jae-In involves a quota of 2.63 million tons of steel from South Korea per year.

South Korea is the third largest foreign supplier of steel to the United States. The new quota is set at roughly 70% of the average import number for the past 3 years. The *Wall Street Journal*, noting the devastating impact of the new quota, reported that "nine out of 54 categories of South Korean steel exports to the U.S. have already had their annual quota filled."

Why does South Korea have a steel industry?

The steel industry of South Korea was the result of a number of geopolitical maneuvers throughout the Cold War. Following the Korean War, the Soviet Union poured huge amounts of resources into industrializing and developing the Democratic People's Republic of Korea (DPRK) in the northern part of the peninsula. Technicians from the Soviet Union helped the DPRK to begin exploiting the coal from its mountainous regions.

The steel industry of North Korea is considered to be one of the greatest accomplishment of the Korean Workers Party. *The Blast Furnace* (1950), the fourth film ever produced in North Korea, documents the birth of its domestic steel industry with Soviet and Chinese assistance. There are paintings of Kim Il Sung visiting the country's first steel mills still being displayed in North Korea.

Between 1953 and 1956, North Korea tripled its gross domestic product. According to the BBC: "The mass mobilisation of the population, along with Soviet and Chinese technical assistance and financial aid, resulted in annual economic growth rates estimated to have reached 20%, even 30%, in the years following the devastating 1950-53 Korean war." During the 1950s and 60s, not only was illiteracy wiped out in North Korea but universal housing and education was established.

Meanwhile, during the same period of the 50s and 60s, poverty and malnutrition persisted in South Korea. Many working class Koreans sympathized with their northern countryfolk. Despite the execution and torture of many leftists, including the infamous massacre in response to the uprising on Jeju Island, strikes and protests were abundant. In 1960, leftist students and activists staged what was coined the "April 19th Movement" and forced the U.S.-backed dictator, Syngman Rhee to step down.

In 1961, a top military officer named Park Chung Hee formed the Military Revolutionary Committee and ultimately seized power in a military coup. Park, unlike the previous military dictator, Syngman Rhee, depended on the loyalty of a solid base among the population and worked hard to maintain it.

In 1965, Park restored diplomatic relations between South Korea and its former colonizer, Japan. Park then arranged for Japan to finance the construction of a steel industry in South

Korea. Park Tae-Joon was assigned the task of creating what would eventually become one of the largest steel corporations in the world, POSCO. The Import-Export Bank of Japan provided a loan of $54 million to enable South Korea to build the corporation. The Japanese government provided an additional $119 million. Diplomats from the United States were key in arranging the economic deals that gave birth to the steel industry of South Korea.

Stabilizing the Park Regime

The deal to create the South Korean Steel Industry was arranged because the continued unrest and protests were seen as a threat to the entire region. The bonapartist Park regime had promised to bring stability by creating a strata of well-paid Koreans who opposed communism and supported the United States. In order for the Park regime to remain intact, a significant portion of the population needed to be loyal to it. This required economic development.

Throughout the developing world, various US aligned dictators were granted loans in order to develop domestic industries. The soon massive steel industry of South Korea mirrored similar development projects in Singapore, Iran, Chile, and Argentina. The Kennedy and Johnson administrations viewed this as a means to prevent revolutions and keep the various highly authoritarian, anti-communist regimes intact.

The policy of building up and industrializing aligned regimes was a staple of Cold War liberalism in the United States and was actively favored by the intelligence wing of US politics. Kennedy famously said, "Those who make peaceful revolution impossible make violent revolution inevitable." Kennedy created the Peace Corps, a humanitarian organization, which also actively coordinates and collects information for the CIA.

The military regime in South Korea committed horrendous violations of human rights in addition to its economic successes. During the 1970s and 80s, the South Korean government had a policy of arresting "vagrant children" i.e. orphans and holding them in prison camps. Thousands of children died in custody after fatal beatings. The children held in the camps were also subject to routine rape, lack of adequate food, and torture.

The policy of rounding up vagrant children fit into the Park regime's policy of building up an urban middle class, while "purifying" the cities of unwanted elements. Thousands of dissidents were also tortured, held in prison camps, or extrajudicially killed by the military regime.

Neocons Move Against the Iron Silk Road

Following the domestic political crisis of 1968-1972, Cold War liberals of the Kennedy ilk began to fall out of favor in Washington. Richard Nixon's presidency was seen as a pivotal moment in the birth of Neo-conservatism, a new brand of right-wing leadership and geopolitical strategy for the United States.

In 1973, Nixon oversaw the economic demolition of Chile. Socialist President Salvador Allende, was toppled in a bloody, military coup. Like South Korea, the United States had previously enabled Chile to develop a large industrial middle class. With the rise of the Pinochet dictatorship, Milton Friedman and Chicago School economists destroyed the Chilean middle class and domestic industries. The middle class in Argentina was subject to a similar demolition following the 1976 coup against populist, Isabel Peron.

The US-Japanese policy of building up a strong economy in South Korea as a way of holding back Communism came to an end in the 1980s. Without active US support and subsidization, the economy of South Korea worsened. Amid the economic downturn, protests and strikes erupted and in 1987, the military regime was brought down by the June Democracy Movement.

The fall of the Soviet Union resulted in catastrophe in North Korea and a crisis of malnutrition. In the midst of this crisis, a liberal administration in South Korea enacted the famous "Sunshine Policy" of reconciliation with North Korea. Even fanatical anti-Communist Reverend Sun Myung Moon met with Kim Il Sung, in this very optimistic atmosphere.

Plans were made for the Iron Silk Road or the Trans Asian Railway that would connect South Korea and North Korea to Russia, China and western Europe. The Trans Asian Railway would have enabled North Korea to join the world economy, import needed food and petroleum, and export more of its steel and coal. It would have also enabled the steel industry of South Korea to export more diversely, and not be so closely tied to the United States. During the same period, the Clinton administration agreed to provide heating gas and food relief to North Korea in exchange for the country not proliferating nuclear weapons.

The infamous "Axis of Evil" speech given by George W. Bush in 2002 ultimately terminated the bright hopes of the 1990s. The US Congress had already refused to fund the agreement North Korea had reached with the Clinton administration. The Iron Silk Road was put on hold, and right-wing political factions moved ahead in South Korean politics. North Korea withdrew from the Nuclear Non-Proliferation Treaty and tested its first nuclear weapons in 2006.

Moon's "Economic Map" Memory Stick

Although the U.S. abandoned its policy of building up the South Korean economy during the 1990s, South Korea's economic ties with another country have expanded. China, now the second largest economy in the world, is closely tied to both North and South Korea, and favors peaceful reconciliation between the two countries.

Park Geun-hye, the daughter of the military dictator was elected President in 2012, and aligned herself with the Neoconservative faction in Washington. President Park presided over austerity cuts in public spending and installed the Terminal High Altitude Air Defense (THAAD) Missile System in coordination with the US military. This strike enabling missile system involves radars monitoring not just North Korea, but also Russia and China.

After the first parts of the THAAD system were unloaded, China responded with swift economic moves against South Korea. Shortly afterwards, Park was impeached for corruption, and the liberal President Moon Jae-In was elected to take her place.

At the recent meeting between Moon Jae-In and Kim Jong-Un, the south Korean leader handed the DPRK's President a USB flash drive. On this flash drive was a proposal for the economic development of North Korea.

According to the *New York Times*, "In charts and video clips, Mr. Moon's memory stick laid out a "new economic map for the Korean Peninsula," including new railways and power plants for the impoverished North, should Mr. Kim abandon his nuclear weapons, according to South Korean officials." Such a plan, if implemented, would result in an expansion of steel exports from both North and South Korea.

It seems the vision of the Iron Silk Road, and the policies of the Cold War liberals, as well as China's vision of "One Belt, One Road" connecting countries and creating peace through economic development has resurfaced in recent Korean negotiations.

However, the neoconservative faction that openly favors crushing other nations' economic development in order to maintain U.S. economic dominance seems to have the upper hand in Washington, DC. The recent decision to punish the South Korean steel industry, which was created for specific geopolitical reasons, breeds many questions about what could result from the upcoming meeting between Trump and Kim Jong-Un.

Originally published in New Eastern Outlook

GREAT WARS: PASSÉ FOR THE USA?

While militarism is prevalent across US society, the idea of a new, big confrontation between superpowers seems quite unrealistic for contemporary America.

Our grandparents told us stories of the Second World War. All four of my own had participated in some capacity. The Second World War was not a "regime change" operation carried out under the guise of humanitarianism. The Second World War was a battlefield clash between two global alliances that sought to destroy each other. The war involved mass mobilizations of the population. In order to achieve victory, the Soviet Union, the United States and Britain were forced to put society under the most ironclad discipline.

In the USA, children collected scrap metal and watched the skies for Japanese planes. The population had "meatless Tuesdays" prioritizing agricultural products for the front-lines. The automakers put commercial cars on hold and manufactured military vehicles instead. Japanese-Americans were interned in prison camps. The Trotskyite Communists who opposed the war, along with fascist sympathizers like the German-American Bund, were locked in prison or detained by federal authorities, and every able bodied young man was required to join the military. The entire country was mobilized for victory, and victory was achieved.

Would such a thing be possible today?

No war since the the Second World War has been anything like it, despite the fact that US leaders constantly invoke it. World War Two analogies are almost a trade-mark staple of neoconservatism. George H.W. Bush compared Saddam Hussein to Hitler while inciting the US public to support "Operation Desert Storm." Cable News endlessly brought up the Second World War when his son, George W. Bush, invaded Iraq. Reagan's invasion of Grenada, Clinton's bombing of Serbia, the NATO intervention in Libya, and continued US support for extremists in Syria, all have come with rhetoric invoking World War Two.

Yet none of these countries are military superpowers trying to take over the world. By 1939 the Nazis had turned their country into a military powerhouse ready to roll across "Fortress Europe" and crush millions of lives. They had a plan for world conquest. Comparing Iraq, Libya, Afghanistan, Serbia, Grenada, or Panama to the Third Reich is almost laughable. These anti-imperialist governments across the developing world wanted to sell oil on the international markets and build infrastructure. They may have clashed with their neighbors, but world domination was not on their agenda.

Vietnam Syndrome, Kicked?

None of these wars were declared by the US Congress under the constitutional procedure. They were "operations" "police actions" or "interventions" ordered by the executive branch, and perhaps approved in a congressional resolution. But these were not "wars" in the full on, legal sense. Everyday Americans were asked to put up yellow ribbons and "support our troops" bumper stickers, but aside from that, American civilians were left to live a normal life, as they watched TV reporters "embedded" in order to repeat the Pentagon narrative.

The US government learned the hard way after World War Two that "big wars" were just not going to work anymore. Toward the end of Korean War of 1950-1953, the population seemed to be losing enthusiasm. The anti-communist fanaticism that accompanied this war faded, and by 1954, Joe McCarthy had fallen out of favor with the US public.

The political crisis sparked by the Vietnam War still haunts the memory of the US public. Young people burned their draft cards. Soldiers shot their officers. By the time the USA withdrew, insubordination was widespread among the military itself. Peace marches were massive, and public opinion was completely opposed to further military involvement. Urban rebellions shook the Black community, and violent protests rocked the college campuses.

The wars in Vietnam and Korea, with military conscription and significant US casualties may have been experiments with "big war" tactics, but they both flopped. Korea ended in a "stalemate" armistice, with a US Army General actually being captured in the process. When China decided to get involved, and MccArthur's threats of nuclear attack didn't deter them, the USA began to sweat. Vietnam was a military defeat for the United States, with the National Liberation Front effectively unifying the country and giving birth to the Socialist Republic of Vietnam.

After sending US forces to Kuwait to push out Iraqis, George H.W. Bush declared: "by God, we've kicked the Vietnam syndrome once and for all." The phrase "Vietnam Syndrome" referred to the US public's lack of enthusiasm for war following the 1970s.

Despite Bush's claim that Vietnam Syndrome has been

"kicked," the US public doesn't seem enthusiastic about wars at this point, and observers have noted that the country hasn't clashed directly with a rival superpower since 1945. While the United States has the largest military budget in the world, the governments it has selected for attack are all in a much lower weight class.

USA Faces Internal Problems

Now, as US leaders beat the drums against the two Eurasian Superpowers, an unacknowledged truth hides behind the threats and heated words. Russia and China are both highly disciplined, well organized societies. The population marches behind the government and the military in order to achieve its goals even in peace time. Both countries have economies that are centered around the state.

Meanwhile, in the United States, different agendas seem to be everywhere. Political and regional divisions are getting deeper. Different wings of the "deep state" seem to be at each other's throats with different agendas and goals.

Furthermore, the idea of putting the millions of millennial and "Generation Z" youth into uniforms and on to the battlefields is somewhat laughable. These generations are loaded with cynicism, mistrust, and many of them have a real distance from the ugly realities of violence in their every day life.

Schoolchildren in the USA are no longer even permitted to defend themselves in schoolyard scuffles, but required to passively accept the blows of assailants while calling for help from police or teachers. In most American schools if a child so much as raises a fist in self-defense, he can expect the same punishment as his attacker.

In the new police state that is unfolding, Americans are increasingly taught to be passive, non-confrontational and obedient. Police in uniforms, security cameras, and employers watch their every move. "Abusive" or "insensitive" language on social media can result in academic or workplace penalties. As authoritarianism increases in US society, so does a kind of "touchy feely" niceness that doesn't breed good soldiers.

The US military already relies on a large number of "green card soldiers" i.e. non-citizen immigrants who fight in order to earn legal status in the country. Much like the Saudi military, which is not exactly winning in Yemen, the US military is increasingly made up of people from other countries, bribed to fight our wars on our behalf.

Perhaps it is the huge leap in the US standard of living that followed the Second World War, which made the public less enthusiastic about military conflicts. Wealth comes with comfort, and those who live comfortable lives tend to be far less willing to march off into battle.

Or perhaps it is the fact that the country which called itself "the sole remaining superpower" has stretched its economic tentacles all across the planet. When the US economy is the central part of a huge, global market, with so many different corporations, with so many different short term interests, it is pretty hard for the state declare a single enemy and unify the country to direct its energy toward a single goal.

Regardless, it is safe to say that a new "great war" in which the USA faces off with "someone its own size" isn't quite realistic in 2018. However, short, quick "regime change" wars against third world nationalists seem to still be in fashion. Yet, the increasing power of Russia and China on the global stage has made it a lot more difficult.

Originally Published in United World International

"Too Much Coal" – Grabbing Energy Markets with Geopolitics

After a two year slump, coal, iron, and everything related to mining is seeing a boom. Entities on the New York Stock Exchange linked to the extraction of minerals from the earth are seeing their profits go up. Like most things in the global economy, this dramatic shift cannot be separated from geopolitical events. The boom on the energy markets is directly linked to confrontation between the USA and China, related to the crisis in the Korean peninsula.

Too Much Coal

In 1930, a coal miner in Poland famously explained the economic crisis to his son with an unforgettable dialogue:

"Father, Why don't we light the stove? I am cold"
"We don't have coal, son"
"And why haven't we got coal?"
"Because there is too much coal."

The father had been laid off from his job as a coal miner, due to the abundance of coal created by advances in mining technology. Because he was unemployed, he could not afford coal to heat his home. The coal miner and his son were without heat, not due to a lack of coal, but because there is "too much coal."

This is the problem of the capitalist mode of production. Abundance creates poverty. Overproduction leads to economic ruin.

The problem plaguing the energy markets, not just coal, but also oil and natural gas, has been a problem of abundance. The development of hydraulic fracking has drastically increased the amount of oil and natural gas on the markets, driving the price down.

In 1949, China had no steel mills, and its coal mining was very limited. Today, 50% of the world's steel is produced in China. As "Socialism with Chinese Characteristics" blossoms, 700 million people have been raised from poverty. As China's independent economy grows, numerous mountain ranges are now being opened up for mineral extraction. The expansion of China's coal mining, as well as aluminum and steel production have also driven prices down, and cut into the profits of Wall Street mining and metal investors.

However, the trend has suddenly been reversed. The price of coal is now rising, with the metal markets not far behind. Why? The USA has opened up the attack on China's industries, using North Korea as a cover.

Coal and Food in North Korea

One of the biggest problems that North Korea has faced is its lack of arable land. The Democratic People's Republic of Korea is located in the mountainous parts of the Korean Peninsula, and it has long struggled to maintain food independence. The DPRK's agricultural system is one of the most complex in the world, with fields on the sides of mountains, and all kinds of complexly engineered methods of growing food in terrain that is far from ideal for agricultural production.

In the 1990s, when the Soviet Union fell, the DPRK was

197

unable to purchase petroleum on the international markets. This brought the country's food production system to a grinding halt. Millions of people starved to death during what the Korean people refer to as the "arduous march." The Korean Workers Party blames the sanctions from the United States, and the hostile military threat in the south, for the humanitarian crisis.

While the DPRK may not have much arable land, it has lots of coal. The sanctions imposed on the DPRK have worked to prevent the DPRK from selling its coal on the international markets. By preventing the DPRK from selling coal, the USA is preventing the DPRK from using the proceeds to feed its population, develop its infrastructure, or further improve the living standards of its population.

The hope of US leaders is that enough economic misery can be piled onto the Korean people, they will lose faith in the Korean Workers Party, and this independent government and economy can be eliminated.

It should be obvious that such a plan will not lead to peace. The more isolated and threatened the DPRK is, the more it will develop its military capabilities, including nuclear weapons in the hopes of defending itself.

Poverty and war are directly linked. The most unstable parts of the world are usually the most impoverished. Drug gangs and terrorist groups tend to set up shop in places where people are desperate to survive.

Furthermore, countries that are doing business with each other, and are economically linked, are far less likely to go to war. The road to peace is not through impoverishing the Korean people, while conducting provocative military exercises in the south.

A Real Peace Plan – The "Iron Silk Road"

The plan for peace in Korea championed by China and agreed on by the United Nations is called the "Iron Silk Road" or the "Trans-Asian Railway Agreement." The idea is to create a train system in southern Korea that would extend into North Korea, through China, through Russia, and into Europe. This would integrate North and South Korea, as well as isolated parts of Siberia, to the world economy, and allow for industrial development and economic cooperation.

Despite the agreement for the "Iron Silk Road" being put into force in 2009, the project remains very much on hold in the Korean Peninsula, as threats of war and nuclear tensions hold back development.

Wall Street has an obvious motivation for stopping the "Iron Silk Road" which would result in a lot more of the DPRK and China's coal being placed on international markets, accessible through the new railway line.

Targeting China's Mines & Steel Mills

US leaders currently allege that North Korea makes $1 billion per year from selling its coal to China. China disputes this figure, but regardless, an income of $1 billion for a country of over 25 million people shouldn't be a real source of outrage. Most countries with a similar population size have a much larger domestic income.

US leaders have put sanctions on numerous entities in China, alleging that they somehow cooperate with North Korea's coal industry. US leader say they are determined to stop North Korea from making money by selling its coal, alleging that the money will be used for nuclear proliferation.

Indeed, almost all the entities in China, which are accused of collaborating with North Korea and are subject to US sanctions, are somehow linked to China's booming mine and metal markets. These entities have had their assets in the USA frozen. They have been prevented from utilizing US banks for their transactions. Millions of dollars have essentially been stolen, and huge barriers have been put in place in order to prevent these corporations from working on the international markets.

No trial ever took place. These Chinese entities never had an opportunity to defend themselves, or challenge the claims made against them by US leaders. A decree was issued by the state department, declaring them guilty of doing business with North Korea, and simultaneously punishing them for it by seizing their property and blocking their transactions.

This unilateral attack on China's vital industries constitutes economic warfare, and China's leaders have responded with justifiable anger.

China's state controlled steel manufacturing apparatus currently produces half of the steel in the entire world. 60% of steel production involves metallurgic "coking coal" in its production. Crippling China's steel industry and China's coal mines has a much wider effect than anything related to North Korea. North Korea serves as a convenient excuse to weaken China's state controlled industries.

The High Cost of Wall Street "Energy Dominance"

Now, not surprisingly, Wall Street mining corporations are

seeing their profits increase in the aftermath of the sanctions. Due to sanctions harming its domestic coal operations, China now has to import more coal from the USA.

Trump's White House has called for "energy dominance," a goal that it seems to be pursuing by means of geopolitical confrontation. The efforts to push China and North Korea out of coal markets, mirror US efforts to push Russia off the oil and natural gas markets. The new sanctions on Russia work to undermine the Nordstream 2 natural gas pipeline, and force Germany and other EU companies to purchase natural gas from the USA instead of Russia.

Tim Ryan, a US Congressman from Ohio, blatantly stated that the new sanctions on Russia were a market grab, saying verbatim: "We must continue to focus on how we can get our gas to allies in Europe." The European Union currently gets 38% of its natural gas from Russia, but the USA is looking to erode this.

The western monopolists in Wall Street and London have no room for any competitors. The development of independent countries cuts into their profits. US confrontations with independent countries are not about ideology or human rights.

Whether they be the Communists of the DPRK and China, or the Orthodox Christian Russian Nationalists in Moscow, or the Bolivarian Socialists in Latin America, or the Islamic Revolutionaries of Iran, all independent countries which break free, start to develop, and begin selling resources on the international markets are opposed by Wall Street, London, Washington, and the Pentagon.

The "energy dominance" and wealth of western corporations comes at a high price. This "dominance" can only be maintained by keeping the world poor.

Originally Published in New Eastern Outlook

Mark Zuckerberg's Dilemma: Eventually Silicon Valley Will Fall

The Silicon Valley monopolist Mark Zuckerberg, who controls the social media empire known as "Facebook" finds himself in an increasingly tough spot. Certain forces within the western political establishment want him to exercise his power more ruthlessly, but he realizes this could lead to his ultimate downfall.

The printing press, first invented by Koreans, was cultivated in Europe for the purpose of maintaining the feudal order, primarily through its ideological vehicle, the Roman Catholic Church. Johannes Gutenberg's printing press was used to print Bibles and indulgences. The new invention made the system in which Kings and Nobles ruled and owned the land based on divine right more functional.

For a brief period, the printing press remained in the hands of the Catholic Church. But it was only a matter of time before this monopoly was broken. Critics of the Catholic Church and the rising mercantile class soon got access to this technology and utilized it to oppose the feudal order. Soon, translations of the Bible were circulated, screeds criticizing the Vatican were distributed, and the Protestant Reformation swept through Europe. This began a long process that ultimately resulted in the overthrow of feudalism, and the rise of industrial capitalism in the western world, along with the liberal democratic political system.

To use stereotypically Marxian phraseology, by developing the printing press, the Catholic Church had "laid the seeds of its own destruction." It is unlikely, however, that the

Catholic officials who encouraged Gutenberg were aware of the ultimately suicidal implications of their actions. However, Mark Zuckerberg and other social media giants are most likely well aware of the historical precipice on which they are sitting. This self-awareness causes them to become increasingly nervous and inconsistent.

Who Invented The Internet?

Politician Al Gore was widely mocked for the phrase "I took the initiative and created the internet" which he stated during a TV interview, often misreported as "I invented the internet." He was, however, referring to the fact that Silicon Valley emerged from strategic decisions made by the US intelligence community and political leaders during the Cold War. Huge covert efforts by the US government enabled California and corporations like IBM and Apple to sit at the center of the tech boom, and as a result, hold the purse and puppeteer's strings in the post-Cold War "New World Order" that brought us the internet. The "social media" revolution that followed a few decades later, seemed to very much serve the interests of Wall Street and London in its early years.

In 2011, Jared Andrew Cohen played the role of a coordinator, ensuring that the Pentagon, Wall Street, and the Tech Monopolies all marched in lockstep to shake-up the Middle East. Cohen is the CEO of Jigsaw, previously known as "Google Ideas." He is also a member of the key US Foreign Policy think tank, the Council on Foreign Relations, paid for by Exxon-Mobil and the Ford Foundation. He served as a personal advisor to both Condoleezza Rice and Hillary Clinton.

Cohen is quite open about the fact that he has used the

internet and social media to foment unrest in countries that stand in the way of Wall Street and London. The New Yorker described his rise to prominence saying: "During the peak of the protests in Iran, Jared Cohen, a young staffer at the State Department who worked for Slaughter, contacted officials at Twitter and asked the company not to perform a planned upgrade that would have shut down the service temporarily in Iran, where protesters were using it to get information to the international media."

Cohen's boss at the time, Anne-Marie Slaughter, has also been quite open about her contempt for "Populism" and the need to utilize social media to create an "open international system" and an "open market," and in 2011, the tech elite and State Department seemed to do so quite effectively.

Slick social media propaganda presented the events as glorious uprisings of the people, demanding democracy and freedom. In the "Arab Spring" wave of unrest, the Muslim Brotherhood temporarily seized control of Egypt and Tunisia. Libya, the African country with the highest life expectancy, led by the socialist revolutionary Moammar Gadhafi, was reduced to rubble and chaos because of a NATO bombing campaign as well as a wave of social media deception. The Syrian Arab Republic, a stronghold of Arab Nationalism and anti-Zionism, was swept into civil war in a similar manner. Western liberals cheered for the "revolutions" that flashed across their iPhones in Guevara-esque propaganda.

The crowds of Libyans who fought to defend their homelands from being reduced to chaos were mostly ignored by the media, as were the radical Islamist and non-democratic goals of those who led the US-backed uprisings. The protests demanding democracy in Bahrain were crushed by a brutal

Saudi invasion, with western audiences almost completely unaware it took place. CNN refused to air the single documentary it had created on Bahrain, though its coverage of Egypt, Tunisia, Libya and Syria seemed to be nonstop 24/7. As the Shia community within the Wall Street oil plantation and weapons client Saudi Arabia demanded its rights, the social media machine did not celebrate its protests but looked the other way as torture and other human rights violations were used to crush it.

Social media effectively enabled the US government to stage and manipulate uprisings, maneuver their allies in the Muslim Brotherhood into power, topple the Socialist government of Libya, and foment a bloody civil war in Syria. The press celebrated the social media revolution for this achievement in glowing manifestos of tech optimism and globalist revolutionary fervor.

The Ruling Class Demands Censorship

But fast forward to 2019, the language of America's intellectuals is no longer about "free information" or paving the way to a glorious "open international system". Now there is talk of "bots" "Russian trolls" and "hackers." Mark Zuckerberg has been dragged before Congressional committees and interrogated about why he allows certain "offensive" views to be tolerated on Facebook. Articles in the *Wall Street Journal* castigate youtube for allowing "conspiracy" videos to be prevalent. Zuckerberg faces a more scandalous reputation in the United Kingdom after revelations about his relationship with the firm known as Cambridge Analytica. Protests and calls for people to "delete facebook" have resounded and been pushed by mainstream media.

Meanwhile, Facebook has engaged in a new level of censorship, in the face of pressure. Rachel Blevins, an RT reporter, had her Facebook page shut down. "In The Now," a Facebook page with millions of subscribers was blocked after CNN had attacked it for being tied to Russia.

Sections of the political establishment seem to be demanding that Mark Zuckerberg use his power to shut down speech they deem to be harmful, specifically speech that undermines the narratives of US foreign policy. And while Facebook has certainly done this on multiple occasions, certain powerful voices perceive some reluctance in this censorship and are quite angry about it.

But the reality is, if Facebook becomes too strict and heavy-handed, those seeking alternative views will go elsewhere. This result would be far more damaging to both Zuckerberg and the political establishment in the long term.

Silicon Valley Will Fall

Mark Zuckerberg is like the Catholic Church when it held control over the printing press. He holds a monopoly over a powerful information technology vehicle. However, unlike the Catholic Church, Zuckerberg is strategically allowing those he would deem to be heretics to use his apparatus, in the hopes they won't develop social networks of their own, that are completely beyond his control.

Zuckerberg is keeping his grip loose in the hopes of not losing his monopoly. Zuckerberg may hate those who challenge US foreign policy, but he would very much prefer they state their views on Facebook than on another social network. If Zuckerberg tightens his grip too much, alternatives to Facebook will emerge to satisfy those who want to challenge the status quo.

Much has been written about Mark Zuckerberg's apparent admiration for Caesar Augustus, the relative of Julius Caesar who became Emperor after the fall of the Roman Republic. Zuckerberg is said to admire the fact that Augustus launched 200 years of "Pax Romana" in which no wars took place because Rome's power was so massive that none could challenge it throughout the empire.

Zuckerberg may see himself as a modern-day Augustus, presiding over a global information empire, and carefully mediating and giving a platform to debate in a way that doesn't allow any powerful rival to emerge.

But one must ask, isn't it just a matter of time? Eventually, Facebook, along with twitter, youtube, and other platforms will lose their monopoly. The Catholic Church could not have controlled all the printing presses forever. Soon this new technology went over to their opponents.

Mark Zuckerberg's situation, where he tries to maintain a monopoly while flexing his muscles in particular strategic circumstances, is only temporary. The whole world knows that eventually Silicon Valley will fall, and alternative voices and platforms will contend for the ability to set the discourse.

Originally published in New Eastern Outlook

PART THREE:
THE MIDDLE EASTERN THEATER

SALMAN'S SHAKE-UP: SAUDI MANEUVERS ARE BAD FOR THE AMERICAN PEOPLE

The Ritz Carlton Hotel in downtown Riyadh is now serving as a temporary prison, holding some of the 201 people that have been detained on the orders of Crown Prince Muhammad Bin Salman. 1800 bank accounts have been frozen.

The drama is escalating on the international front as well. The Saudis are blaming Iran for a recent missile attack from Yemen. The Prime Minister of Lebanon has resigned from his post, while in Riyahd, and echoes Saudi rhetoric against Hezbollah. The price of oil is rising again, the highest its been in two years, approaching $58 per barrel.

What's going on? Something is clearly boiling below the surface on the Arabian Peninsula. How can we interpret these chaotic moves?

Middle-Men for Wall Street & London

Why does the Kingdom of Saudi Arabia exist? Did it simply arise naturally? Does the mindset of the people living in the region simply long for this Wahabbi autocracy? This is what certain forces would like us to believe. But the reality is that the rise of the House of Saud, and the prolonged life of this absolute monarchy that beheads and tortures, is closely linked to forces outside the region, namely, western oil bankers.

The British empire discovered in their efforts to dominate the region that Ibn Saud, known as Abdulaziz in the Arab world, was a great middle man. In 1915, a "friendship and cooperation" pact was signed with this autocratic ruler, and the British supplied him with huge amounts of weapons. It was mainly due to British military and financial support that Ibn Saud was able to beat down all his rivals, and dominate the Peninsula. In 1938, oil was discovered, and the third Saudi state, established due to British intervention, became even more valuable to its western backers.

In 1944, the oil bankers of the United States moved in on the game. While British Petroleum and HSBC have kept a finger in Riyahd, it was the Rockefeller's Standard Oil, predecessor of today's Exxon-Mobil, along with other American petro-billionaires who became the primary purchasers of Saudi crude.

At this point Saudi Arabia is a top purchaser of US military hardware, and has the fourth largest army on earth. The Kingdom sits at the center of a network of "gulf states" with similar political and economic models. In the United Arab Emirates, Bahrain, Kuwait, Oman, and other oil states in the region, an autocratic monarchy presides over an un-developed country. These countries have oil fields controlled by American and British corporations and purchase large amounts of US weapons.

In 1973, the USA experienced fuel shortages caused by the OPEC boycott. Americans were told that US involvement in the Middle East was necessary in order to keep the oil flowing in.

The 1979 Iranian Revolution, toppling a brutal US backed dictator, shook the region. The Shia workers of the Saudi oil fields, a religious minority in the Kingdom, took inspiration and began fighting for their rights. The USA supported the Saudi King in crushing this mass uprising demanding democracy. A prominent figure in the Reagan administration later announced that the USA would intervene to protect the monarchy "if there should be anything that resembled an internal revolution in Saudi Arabia."

Locking Down For War?

Among those recently arrested are some big players in Saudi power circles, such as Prince Miteb bin Abdullah, previously the head of the National Guard. Al Waleed bin Talal, a big player on Wall Street, who owns big shares of Citigroup, Microsoft, Four Seasons Holdings Inc., and Apple Inc. has also been arrested.

Prince Mohammed Bin Salman, the son of the King, seems to be the director of this sweeping crackdown, not on dissidents, but within the ruling family itself. Bin Salman has been pushing for reform in Saudi Arabia's economy, arguing that it should move away from being completely oil-centric. He has also recently announced huge cuts in public spending.

The old policy of "rule by consensus" among the royal family seems be long gone. Now, even members of the ruling family will have no choice but to march behind the King. And

211

where are King Salman and his son leading them? It appears that they are looking for a wider war.

Already, Saudi Arabia is bombarding its southern neighbor, Yemen. The people of Yemen have asserted their independence in a popular revolution. Saudi cruise missiles and invading mercenaries are fighting to crush the Supreme Political Council. Thousands are already dead, and malnutrition is affecting millions, as the Saudis desperately seek to reinstall Mansour Hadi, their handpicked ruler.

Saudi Arabia is backing extremists in Syria as they seek to topple the Syrian government. The anti-government fighters in Syria have used chemical weapons, according to Carla Del Ponte and other UN officials, and have slaughtered Christians and other religious minorities. The Saudis have also sent troops into Bahrain in order to crush the popular uprisings demanding democracy. Now, they are echoing Israeli officials and rallying against the government of Lebanon.

US 'Energy Independence' & The Saudi Existential Crisis

In 1991, when Iraqi forces moved against the Saudi-aligned Kuwaiti autocracy, the USA swung into action. Americans were reminded of the OPEC boycott, and told that we had no choice but to protect the Saudi and Kuwaiti regimes, in order to secure the flow of oil. Democrats raised the idea of "energy independence" as the road to peace. "If only we didn't need their oil," liberals and environmentalists told us, "then we could leave the middle east alone."

Yet, in 2017, the USA has already established energy independence. Hydraulic Fracking, a method of extracting oil and natural gas from the shale below the soil, has made the US a top domestic oil producer. With the American oil sector in the hands of competing capitalists hungry for profits, deeply irrational things are taking place, as usual. The US still imports Middle Eastern, African, and Latin American oil, while exporting its own oil around the world, with the 1975 oil export ban lifted.

US meddling in the Middle East has not decreased due to "energy independence," but it has increased. With a greater abundance on the market, American oil companies are even more desperate to remove competitors. The drive to move against countries like Iran, Venezuela, and Russia, with state run oil companies that function as competitors, is even stronger.

However, the position of Saudi Arabia in this global drive for monopoly is no longer what it once was. The USA doesn't need Saudi oil the way it once did, and while it has no desire to see competitors sweep up the Saudi oil fields, the "sweet spot" the Saudis once occupied as irreplaceable suppliers, is slipping away. They are no longer sacred cows in American foreign policy.

Donald Trump openly criticized Saudi Arabia during his Presidential campaign, winning lots of applause and no real condemnation for it. The redacted pages from the 9/11 commission report, documenting the links of the Saudi government to the hijackers, have been released to the public.

Saudi Arabia is now facing an existential crisis. The Kingdom must prove its value to those who prop it up in Wall Street, London, and Washington. While it no longer has the same economic value, the regime in Riyadh is now working to prove its worth in military terms.

More Chaos, Not America's Interest

The main target of Saudi Arabia's saber-rattling rhetoric is the Islamic Republic of Iran. After the 1979 Islamic Revolution, Iran established a political order based on the principles of "War of Poverty Against Wealth" and "Not Capitalism But Islam." Iran's economy is centrally planned, with state controlled oil as its lynchpin. Iran is aligned with various anti-imperialist forces throughout the region who call themselves "the Axis of Resistance."

Saudi Arabia presents the conflict in the region as a war between Sunni and Shia. In reality, the targets of Saudi attack are the forces demanding independence and economic development. They are not religiously sectarian, or even unified. The majority of the fighters in the Syrian Arab Army are Sunnis, not Shias like the Iranian leadership. The Zaidi Shias in the Ansar Allah (Houthi) organization in Yemen, are a small minority in the country. Most of the Yemenis fighting against the Saudi onslaught are not Shia either. Hezbollah in Lebanon is a Shia organization, but it sits at the center of a united front, aligning with secular anti-imperialists, nationalists, christians and communists in a political bloc opposing Israel and the United States.

If Saudi Arabia escalates its actions against forces asserting independence throughout the region, this will likely result in more chaos. Syria, Libya and Yemen are already in turmoil due to Saudi meddling, in cooperation with the United States. Iraq and Afghanistan have been in chaos ever since their governments were toppled by US-led invasions.

Iran has never attacked the United States. Neither has the Syrian Arab Republic. The people of Yemen, the people of

Bahrain and Lebanon, pose no threat to the American people. In fact, Hezbollah and the Islamic Revolutionary Guards of Iran are battling the ISIS terrorists every day in Syria, alongside the Syrian Arab Army.

Wall Street certainly sees more chaos in the region as beneficial. For the billionaire elite that runs the USA, further chaos in the Middle East means lots of weapons sales, and the destruction of independent governments that function as competitors on the oil markets. But for average Americans, the prospects of further instability in the Middle East only means more danger from terrorism, and more tax money wasted on foreign wars.

Polls show that average Americans want less foreign involvement, and have a low opinion of the Saudi autocracy. Only 36 percent of Americans consider Saudi Arabia to be a friend or ally. However, US leaders seem to be accountable elsewhere. The gap of interests, between those of the American people, and the profit hungry oil-banking elite are growing bigger each day.

Originally Published in New Eastern Outlook

AMERICAN DEEP STATE FLOPS IN IRAN

The Islamic Republic of Iran is probably even stronger than it was prior to December 28th, 2017. On that date, the international media announced that protests were taking place across Iran. The White House, the US State Department, and the American media all swung into action, celebrating the protests and demonizing the Iranian government. It was all over within a few days, and despite an emergency UN Security Council meeting, it was pretty clear that no "Iranian Spring" was in the works. Unlike the "revolutions" in Libya and Syria, Washington's efforts to foment unrest were unable to shake the country.

Seizing A Moment To Create Unrest

In reality, the initial protests which sparked the instability were convened by supporters of the government. The issue raised by crowds on the streets of Mashhad was bank defrauding of the public. The protests expanded into a general display of outrage at cuts in social programs and financial de-regulation.

President Rouhani is associated with Iran's Reformist Movement. The current Iranian President is more socially liberal than many of his colleagues and favors a more free market approach to the economy. He has made the P5+1 negotiations, the JCPOA, and the hope that lifting sanctions will strengthen the Iranian economy, a central plank of his political identity. Many of the young people who had protested in 2009, celebrated when Rouhani first took office in 2013.

Rouhani has positioned himself as a voice of "change" and

toning down the country's Islamic revolutionary ideology. Many of the figures in Iranian politics who call themselves "principalists" (labelled "hardliners" by their detractors) consider Rouhani to be a "moderate" and argue that his policies have undermined the Islamic Revolution. The initial protesters saw Rouhani as a sellout and moderate. Those who protested in Mashhad were not calling for the Islamic Republic to toppled, but rather for its principles of "Not Capitalism But Islam" and "War of Poverty Against Wealth" to be reinforced.

However, with reports of unrest breaking out, all the "usual suspects" who dislike the Iranian government and are promoted and supported by the United States, immediately swung into action. The wealthy "westernized youth" of northern Tehran, who frequent underground dance parties and have a delusional perception of the United States, were out in the streets near Tehran University, breaking windows and burning cars. Elsewhere, crowds of Iranians calling for the return of the autocratic pre-1979 monarchy, chanted "Reza Shah! Reza Shah!" The terrorist organization known as the Mujahadeen E-Khalq (MEK), a violent sect that worked with Saddam Hussein and calls itself "Islamo-Marxists" sent its supporters out as well, to unfurl banners of their leader in exile, Maryam Rajavi, and escalate the level of bloodshed.

A Strategic Response from the Islamic Republic

The initial protests were suddenly forgotten, as a Washington's bizarre coalition of anti-government forces based in wealthy neighborhoods stole the spotlight. The isolated anti-government minority had very little support among the population at large as it was screaming out racism, calls for an autocratic monarchy, and the extremist rhetoric of MEK. The protesters became more violent, burning police stations and escalating calls for support from the USA, as it became clear that the population would not join their attempted putsch.

Following the standard "color revolution" playbook, the US media presented the protesters are "human rights activists," ignoring their actual grievances and stated goals. As the protests faded, the US media continued to make them its central focus.

The response of the Islamic Republic to the protests demonstrated a level of strategic brilliance in the age of social media. Rouhani declared:

"People are absolutely free to criticize the government and protest but their protests should be in such a way as to improve the situation in the country and their life…. Criticism is different from violence and damaging public properties…. Resolving the problems is not easy and would take time. The government and people should help each other to resolve the issues…"

The words of Rouhani reassured those in his Reformist camp that their concerns were being addressed, and they did not need to become desperate and join with the violence of US-supported anti-government extremists. Meanwhile, the Revolutionary Guards and the Principalist movement swiftly organized huge, peaceful, and disciplined rallies of their own, supporting the Islamic Republic, and emphasizing its anti-capitalist goals. Not surprisingly, images of these pro-government rallies were used in western media, misrepresented as anti-government protests.

Trump Panders to Pahlavist Racism

Tweeting in response to the protests, Trump accused the Islamic Republic of "squandering of the nation's wealth to fund terrorism abroad." He echoed earlier rhetoric from his UN speech: "Oppressive regimes cannot endure forever, and the day will come when the Iranian people will face a choice. Will they continue down the path of poverty, bloodshed, and terror? Or will the Iranian people return to the nation's proud roots as a center of civilization, culture, and wealth where their people can be happy and prosperous once again? The Iranian regime's support for terror is in stark contrast to the recent commitments of many of its neighbors to fight terrorism and halt its financing."

This rhetoric is clearly aimed at nationalists and supporters of Iran's deposed monarchy. The common grievance of this constituency among wealthy Iranians is that the Islamic Republic is wasting its resources by supporting people they deem to be racially inferior, both inside and outside of Iran's borders. The Islamic Republic's constitution forbids racism, but the belief that Persians are ethnically superior to Arabs, Kurds, Africans, and others was a central tenant of Pahlavi ideology. These racist and supremacist beliefs remain popular among wealthy people in country's private sector.

However, even serious Iranian Nationalists don't really buy Trump's argument. What Trump characterizes as "support for terrorism" and "squandering the nation's wealth" is really Iran's efforts to stabilize the region. In Iraq, Iran supports Shia forces that are fighting ISIS and trying to hold the country together. In Syria, Iran supports the secular Syrian government in fighting a wave Al-Queda linked extremists. Hezbollah has also played a key role in helping to drive ISIS out of Syria. Iran's role in the region is not defined by some fanatical desire to spread terrorism, but rather by an effort to secure itself and keep the region from becoming even more chaotic.

Saudi Arabia, Israel, and the United States, seem to have a different agenda in the Middle East, and have been working to support uprisings and "regime change" against governments they dislike. The result has been the strengthening of terrorism and a mass refugee crisis.

Iran already faces a large amount of terrorism and drug smuggling on its Afghan border, and Iran's military support for forces in Syria and Iraq makes rational sense to anyone in the country who wants a better life, regardless of their ideology. Even the staunchest Iranian nationalist, who may be loaded with deep contempt for the Arab people, can understand that if Syria or Iraq become the site of greater bloodshed, Iranians will be far less safe. Trump's argument simply doesn't hold up.

The Failure of a Confused Deep State

The reality is that unlike Barack Obama, who many Iranians admired for his perceived intellect and familiarity with Islam, Donald Trump is widely hated in Iran. As a wealthy CEO known for his use of obscenities and obsession with money, Trump is almost a caricature of what Khomeni established the Islamic Republic to oppose. On the recent annual "Day to Oppose the Global Arrogance of the United States" the people of Iran rallied against Trump, and made friendly appeals to the American people. Slogans included "Down with US regime, long live US people."

Donald Trump's loud support for the Iranian protesters did not ultimately help them. If anything, it discredited them to the Iranian public, along with the statements of another hated figure, Benjamin Netanyahu. Rouhani rebuked Trump's support for the protesters, saying: "This man in America who is sympathizing today with our people has forgotten that he called the Iranian nation terrorists a few months ago. This man who is against the Iranian nation to his core has no right to sympathize with Iranians."

Many in the CIA and other US intelligence agencies, who have mastered the craft of trying to wage "soft power" covert operations to serve US hegemony, were most likely urging Trump to tone down his support for the protesters. It appears that Trump wasn't really trying to help the Iranian protesters with his words, but was pandering to a specific constituency among his supporters, namely figures like Sheldon Adelson, and other allies of the Israeli Likud Party. Trump may very well have known he wasn't doing the Iranian protesters any favors by cheering them on, but he continued to cheer them on loudly, for his own domestic political reasons.

Recent maneuvers from the White House, such as recognition of Jerusalem, indicate almost a desperation to prove Trump's loyalty to Israel. As Trump is constantly called "fascist" and accused of being anti-Semitic or Hitleresque, held in absolute contempt by CNN and most mainstream American TV networks, his efforts to hold on to key allies like the Likud Party and the Christian Zionists have increased. Trump's excessive rhetoric against Iran isn't exactly strategic, but it is what a key group among his supporters really likes to hear.

US Ambassador Nikki Haley called an emergency
meeting of the UN Security Council to discuss the protests
in Iran. Haley utilized the meeting to make a lengthy speech
denouncing the Iranian government. It seemed rather apparent
that behind her words was an attempt to win the approval
of Iran's enemies, specifically those in Tel Aviv. Voices
throughout the chamber criticized the meeting, and even
usual US allies like France chimed in to subtly denounce US
meddling in Iran's affairs.

As the crisis ended, a false news story began to circulate
throughout US media. Reports that former Iranian President
Mahmoud Ahmadinejad had been arrested for inciting
protests circulated throughout western media. This story was
confirmed to be completely false, first by Ahmadinejad's
lawyers, then by his sons. A few days after the protests ended,
Ahmadinejad held a public event with Kurdish activists. Yet,
no retraction was ever published and long after the story was
disproven, it continued circulate across the internet.

No Repeat of 2009

While many forces behind the scenes in the US government
are looking to roll back the rising power of Russia,
China, Iran and other independent countries, the Trump
administration seems to be constantly pandering to specific
minority factions among the rich and powerful in the United
States. These groups have specific short terms interests, and
unlike the banking elite and the intelligence community, are
not thinking about long term strategy or geopolitics.

With Obama as President, the unrest following Iran's 2009
election was prolonged and had the potential to do a great
deal of damage to the country's political order. Obama was

strategic in his words, as the international media and the US deep state worked to promote the anti-government forces and manipulate frustrated sections of the Iranian population. At the time, forces in the USA that are now aligned with the current administration denounced Obama for not being louder in support of Iranian protesters back in 2009, saying he "spat in their face."

In the first weeks of 2018, with a new administration, the White House operated in a quite different manner than in 2009, and the results were far different. While Trump and Haley roared in support of the protesters, the efforts of US backed, anti-government forces in Iran completely flopped. Stability was restored in a matter of days, with the Revolutionary Guards crushing the isolated, violent oppositionists amid massive pro-government counter demonstrations.

It is very likely that the Principalist Faction, the so-called "hardliners" often demonized in US media, will become the ultimate victors as the unrest originated in response to Rouhani's market oriented policies. The incident ultimately illustrates that Rouhani's JCPOA has not made the USA any less determined to overturn the revolution, a point the Principalists have long been raising.

In the first month of the 2018, it is pretty clear that the high level of disunity and conflicting interests in Washington DC resulted in an epic geopolitical failure for the United States. Botched efforts to destabilize the country have ultimately strengthened the Islamic Republic of Iran.

Originally Published in New Eastern Outlook

THE TRUTH ABOUT SYRIA

In April of 2016, President Barack Obama announced that 250 U.S. special operations troops were being deployed to Syria. Unlike the Russian and Iranian forces aiding anti-terrorism efforts in the country, the U.S. military personnel have entered Syria against the wishes of the internationally recognized government.

In terms of international law, the United States has invaded Syria, a sovereign country and United Nations member state. This is the not the first time, though — Arizona Sen. John Mccain crossed into Syria without a visa to meet with anti-government fighters in 2013.

While the new U.S. boots on the ground have officially been dispatched for the purpose of fighting Daesh (an Arabic acronym for the organization known in the West as ISIS or ISIL), they will most likely be working to achieve one of the Pentagon's longstanding foreign policy goals: violently overthrowing the Syrian government.

As the terrorism of Daesh and other extremists grows more intense, and as millions of Syrians have become refugees, the heavy costs of the U.S. government's "regime change" operation in Syria should come into question.

Education, health care and national rebirth

The independent nationalist Syrian government, now being targeted by Western foreign policy, was born in the struggle against colonialism. It took decades of great sacrifice from the people of Syria to break the country free from foreign domination — first by the French empire and later from puppet leaders. For the last several decades, Syria has been a strong, self-reliant country in the oil-rich Middle East region. It has also been relatively peaceful.

Since winning its independence, Syria's Baathist leadership has done a great deal to improve the living standards of the population. Between 1970 and 2009, the life expectancy in Syria increased by 17 years. During this time period infant mortality dropped dramatically from 132 deaths per 1,000 live births to only 17.9. According to an article published by the Avicenna Journal of Medicine, these notable changes in access to public health came as a result of the Syrian government's efforts to bring medical care to the country's rural areas.

A 1987 country study of Syria, published by the U.S. Library of Congress, describes huge achievements in the field of education. During the 1980s, for the first time in Syria's history, the country achieved "full primary school enrollment of males" with 85 percent of females also enrolled in primary school. In 1981, 42 percent of Syria's adult population was illiterate. By 1991, illiteracy in Syria had been wiped out by a mass literacy campaign led by the government.

The name of the main political party in Syria is the "Baath Arab Socialist Party." The Arabic word "Baath" literally translates to "Rebirth" or "Resurrection." In terms of living standards, the Baathist Party has lived up to its name, forging an entirely new country with an independent, tightly planned and regulated economy. The Library of Congress' Country Study described the vast construction in Syria during the 1980s: "Massive expenditures for development of irrigation, electricity, water, road building projects, and the expansion of health services and education to rural areas contributed to prosperity."

Compared to Saudi-dominated Yemen, many parts of
Africa, and other corners of the globe that have never
established economic and political independence, the
achievements of the Syrian Arab Republic look very
attractive. Despite over half a century of investment from
Shell Oil and other Western corporations, the CIA World
Factbook reports that only about 60 percent of Nigerians
are literate, and access to housing and medical care is very
limited. In U.S.-dominated Guatemala, roughly 18 percent of
the population is illiterate, and poverty is rampant across the
countryside, according to the CIA World Factbook.

What the Western colonizers failed to achieve during
centuries of domination, the independent Syrian government
achieved rapidly with help from the Soviet Union and other
anti-imperialist countries. The Soviet Union provided Syria
with a $100 million loan to build the Tabqa dam on the
Euphrates River, which was "considered to be the backbone
of all economic and social development in Syria." Nine-
hundred Soviet technicians worked on the infrastructure
project which brought electricity to many parts of the country.
The dam also enabled irrigation throughout the Syrian
countryside.

More recently, China has set up many joint ventures with
Syrian energy corporations. According to a report from the
Jamestown Foundation, in 2007 China had already invested
"hundreds of millions of dollars" in Syria in efforts to
"modernize the country's aging oil and gas infrastructure."

These huge gains for the Syrian population should not be
dismissed and written off, as Western commentators routinely
do when repeating their narrative of "Assad the Dictator." For
people who have always had access to education and medical

care, it is to trivialize such achievements. But for the millions of Syrians, especially in rural areas, who lived in extreme poverty just a few decades ago, things like access to running water, education, electricity, medical care, and university education represent a huge change for the better.

Like almost every other regime in the crosshairs of U.S. foreign policy, Syria has a strong, domestically-controlled economy. Syria is not a "client state" like the Gulf state autocracies surrounding it, and it has often functioned in defiance of the U.S. and Israel. It is this, not altruistic concerns about human rights, that motivate Western attacks on the country.

Syria needs reform, not terrorism

In 2012, Syria ratified a new constitution in response to the protests during the Arab Spring. In compliance with the new constitution, Syria held a contested election in 2014, with international observers from 14 countries.

One thing that distinguishes Syria from Saudi Arabia, Qatar, Bahrain, and various other U.S.-aligned regimes throughout the region is religious freedom. In Syria, Sunnis, Christians, Alawites, Druze, Jews, and other religious groups are permitted to practice their religious faith freely. The government is secular, and respects the rights of the Sunni Muslim majority as well as religious minorities.

In addition to religious freedom, Syria openly tolerates the existence of two strong Marxist-Leninist parties. The Syrian Communist Party and the Syrian Communist Party (Bakdash) openly operate as part of the anti-imperialist coalition supporting the Baath Arab Socialist Party. Communists lead trade unions and community organizations in Damascus and other parts of the country.

Though Syrian President Bashar Assad is an Alawite, his wife, Asma, is Sunni like the majority of the country. Historically, the biggest opponents of the Syrian government have been supporters of the Muslim brotherhood, with a bloody episode taking place in 1982. Hoping to heal the longstanding tension, President Assad has made many gestures of solidarity toward the Sunni community in recent years. He has made a point of engaging in religious practices not commonly done by Alawites, such as praying in mosques and studying the Quran.

Shortly after fighting began in 2011, the Syrian government granted autonomy to Kurdish regions and transferred political authority to leftist Kurdish nationalist organizations.

Syria's political system is certainly in need of reform and modernization, and representatives of the Syrian government such as U.N. Ambassador Bashar Al-Jaafari readily admit this. However, the civil war which has raged across Syria for the last five years, is not about reform, democratization or modernization.

The BBC published a "guide to Syrian rebels" in 2013. Among them are not only the infamous "Islamic State" organization, which now horrifies the world, but also the Nusra Front, previously known as Al-Qaida in Syria. Other organizations with names like the "Islamic Front," the "Islamic Liberation Front," and the "Ahfad al-Rasoul Brigades" are also listed.

While Western media presents the Syrian civil war as a

"battle for democracy" led by "revolutionaries," the primary goal of almost every insurgent organization is creating a Sunni caliphate — one that does not actually suit Sunnis though, but rather a perverted politicized version of Sunnism created by Saudi Arabia to ideologically control that region. The unifying religious perspective of the Syrian "rebels" is the interpretation of Sunni Islam practiced and promoted by Saudi Arabia, known as Wahhabism.

Foreign fighters, chemical weapons and child soldiers

A large number of the insurgents are not Syrian. Impoverished people from throughout the Middle East have been recruited to fight against the Syrian government. Facilities in Bahrain train recruits to kill, and send them to Syria.

Terrorist training facilities exist in many other U.S.-aligned Gulf states. Foreign fighters from as far away as Malaysia and the Philippines have been found among the ranks of the foreign Wahhabi insurgents that are trying to depose the Syrian government.

The flow of violent insurgents into Syria is not accidental. It has been directly facilitated by the U.S. and its allies. The CIA has spent billions of dollars on training camps in Jordan for anti-government fighters.

The U.S.-aligned regimes of Turkey and Saudi Arabia are openly supporting the Nusra Front, the Al-Qaida-linked organization that has already killed tens of thousands of innocent people in Syria. Gen. David Petraeus has called for the U.S. to join these efforts and begin sending arms directly to the Nusra Front.

The Israeli government has made a point of aiding the Wahhabi extremists by providing them medical care in the occupied Golan Heights. Israel has also made a point of targeting allies of the Syrian government with airstrikes.

While Western media has highlighted allegations that the Syrian government has used chemical weapons, Carla Del Ponte from the United Nations confirmed that the foreign-backed insurgents have long been been using sarin nerve gas and other chemical weapons.

As the insurgents make life unlivable in Syria, kidnapping for ransom, bombing schools and hospitals, beheading people, torturing people, they do it with thousands of child soldiers among their ranks. Impoverished children from across the Arab world have been recruited to work toward violently overthrowing the Syrian government, according to UNICEF.

Between 50 and 72 percent of the population lives in areas controlled by the Syrian government. Meanwhile, even USAID confirmed that the turnout in Syria's 2014 elections was more than 70 percent.

While the barrage of foreign fighters and extremists, aligned with a minority of the population and armed by Western powers and their allies, is committed to bringing down the Syrian government, the Syrian people clearly disagree. The fact that the Syrian government remains strongly intact after a five-year onslaught shows that the country is dedicated to preserving its independence. Time magazine and other mainstream media outlets have even been forced to admit that President Assad is unlikely to be deposed.

How can the war end?

As foreign fighters have flowed into Syria, hundreds of thousands of people have died over the last five years, and Western media continues to blame the Syrian government for the conflict. However, the war would have been a very short one if not for the foreign support given to the extremists.

As an independent country with a centrally planned economy, Syria has serves as an example to the world. It has proven that without neoliberalism and Western economic domination, it is possible to improve living conditions and develop independently. The Syrian government has made huge sacrifices to aid the Palestinian people and their resistance against Israel, and this has been a contributing factor to Syria's inclusion on the State Department's State Sponsors of Terrorism list. Syria has close economic relations with Russia and the Islamic Republic of Iran.

The war in Syria is not a domestic conflict. This is a war imposed on Syria by Israel, the U.S., and other Western capitalist powers. The primary promoter of Wahhabi extremism around the world has been the Kingdom of Saudi Arabia, a U.S. client state. Turkey and Jordan, U.S.-aligned countries bordering Syria, keep their borders open so that weapons, supplies and money can continue to flow into the hands of Daesh and other anti-government terrorists.

At least 470,000 people are dead, and millions of others have been forced to become refugees, but Western leaders and their allies do not end their campaign. The insane chorus of "Assad Must Go" has transformed a small, domestic episode of unrest into a full-scale humanitarian crisis. The war has nothing to do with the calls for democratic reform and the peaceful protests of 2011.

As Daesh now threatens the entire world, the consequences of the Wall Street regime change operation, promoted with "human rights" propaganda, are becoming far more extreme. The Syrian government rallies a coalition of Christians, Communists, Islamic Revolutionaries, and other forces who are fighting to maintain stability and defeat Takfiri terrorism. (The term "Takfiri" refers to groups of Sunni Muslims who refer to other Muslims as apostates and seek to establish a caliphate by means of violence.)

The only real peace plan for Syria is for the U.S., France, Britain, Saudi Arabia, Turkey, Jordan, and other powers to end their neoliberal crusade. The internationally recognized and recently re-elected Syrian government could easily defeat the insurgents if foreign meddling ceased.

As U.S. media bemoans the humanitarian crisis, somehow blaming on the Syrian government and its president, and the U.S. directly sends its military forces into the country, the people of the world should ask Western leaders and their allies: Why are you prolonging this war? Why can't you just leave Syria alone? Why do you continue funding and enabling the terrorists? Isn't five years of civil war enough? Is overthrowing the Syrian government really worth so much suffering and death?

Originally Published in Mint Press News

Syria, Western Capitalism & The Psychology of Mass Shootings

On June 12th, 2016, the Syrian revolution visited the Pulse nightclub in Orlando, Florida. A fanatical extremist, armed with a US-made weapon, visited a public place. Innocent people, just trying to relax on a Saturday evening and enjoy their lives, were killed. Spouting loyalty to Saudi Arabia's distortion of the Islamic faith, commonly called Wahabbism, a crazed fanatic slaughtered 49 innocent men and women. If this event had taken place in Damascus, US media would not have called Omar Mateen a mass murderer. Rather, Mateen would be a "revolutionary" and "freedom fighter." Meanwhile, the police who tried to stop the rampage would be described as "agents of a dictatorship." Reports of the massacre would be dismissed as "Assad Propaganda," and those who pointed out Mateen's vicious actions would be dismissed as "conspiracy theorists" or "tankies" who are "brainwashed."

In the name of toppling Bashar Assad, tens of thousands of Omar Mateens from across the region have been transported into Syria. Saudi Arabia, Jordan, Qatar, and Turkey continue to ship US-made weapons into Syria in order to strengthen the crusade of foreign terrorists. US-allies are openly funding the Al-Nusra Front, previously known as Al-Queda in Syria, in hopes of bringing down the Baath Arab Socialist Party.

While commentators in the Wall Street-controlled US political establishment disagree about their analyses of the shooting, none of them will admit to the direct link to US foreign policy.

The absolute hypocrisy of both wings of the US political

establishment can be demonstrated in response to the country's mass shootings. When Dylan Roof, a young Ku Klux Klan enthusiast shot a number of African-American Christians at their church, the political right-wing downplayed the obvious political nature of the mass murder. Republican analysts attempted to change the conversation to issues like mental health, and ignored the fact that the shooter was spewing Neo-Nazi ideology.

In response to the recent shooting in Orlando, it is the political left that is downplaying the ideological motivation of the shooter. Despite the fact that the shooter's father was a Taliban-aligned figure in Afghan politics, and the shooter swore allegiance to ISIS, the political left wants to make the conversation around Omar Mateen about mental health and gun control. The media seems to fixate on the idea that Mateen was a self-hating homosexual, motivated purely by some kind of identity crisis, while the right-wing responds with standard Islamophobia and anti-immigrant bigotry.

There is certainly no question that both Omar Mateen and Dylan Roof were mentally ill. Sane individuals don't go on shooting sprees, and randomly open fire on unarmed people. Mateen and Roof may have both acted alone, and not be part of some wider conspiracy to commit their mass shootings, but both of them were armed with ideologies, in addition to their legally purchased firearms. The ideologies of both Wahabbism and Ku Klux Klanism have been actively promoted by Wall Street and London in order to strengthen western capitalism's control of the planet.

Ku Klux Klanism, the Weapon of Wall Street & London

The US Civil War was really the second American Revolution. The southern plantation system was defeated. Abraham Lincoln built a beautiful coalition that included labor unions, small farmers, northern industrial capitalists, and black revolutionaries like Harriet Tubman and Frederick Douglas.

In the aftermath of the Civil War the former slave owners in Tennessee drafted a former Confederate General, Nathan Bedford Forrest, to build the Ku Klux Klan. The KKK was a violent terrorist organization that actively sought to prevent African-Americans from voting, and to squash the talk of land redistribution and social reform that was beginning to take place during the Reconstruction period.

The primary business partner of the southern plantation owners, both before and after the Civil War was the British empire. The emerging British textile industry depended on cheap cotton from the US South. Wall Street began as a financial district by insuring slave ships, and New York City was a stronghold of pro-Confederate sentiments during the war.

As President, former Union Army General Ulysses S. Grant used federal troops to crush the Ku Klux Klan. However, after his administration, troops were pulled out of the South and the plantation owners were able to establish the Jim Crow system. The slave owners maintained their power with impoverished black and white workers laboring as tenant farmers on their plantations. British capitalists continued to receive its cheap cotton, and Wall Street blossomed as a global financial empire.

Decades later in 1915, Hollywood produced the first full-length film ever made. *The Birth of a Nation* retold the story of the US Civil War, and glorified the Ku Klux Klan as heroes. Shortly afterward, the KKK was revived in a mass hate rally in Stone Mountain, Georgia.

In the lead-up to WWI, the Ku Klux Klan mobilized the US population into a fit of national chauvinism and anti-black hate. Throughout the 1920s and '30s the Ku Klux Klan was utilized to violently attack labor activists and other progressives.

In the 1950s and '60s, the Ku Klux Klan slaughtered civil rights activists. In 1979, KKK members killed five activists from the Communist Workers Party in broad daylight at the famous "Greensboro Massacre." Despite their actions being recorded on film by a local TV crew, the Klansmen were acquitted in court. It was later revealed that among the Klansmen in Greensboro was an undercover agent of the Bureau of Alcohol, Firearms, and Tobacco, as well as a few FBI informers.

During the 1970s, the main spokesman for the Ku Klux Klan in the US media was David Duke. Duke eventually moved on to become a Republican and was elected to the US House of Representatives. Duke admits that he spent nine months with his father in Laos. While teaching English, Duke flew missions with "Air America," the CIA's air and cargo line that distributed anti-Communist propaganda across southeast Asia.

According to Duke's writings, the Bolshevik revolution was a conspiracy by Jews to harm the white race. Much like many figures within the Poroshenko government in Ukraine, Duke believes that the Nazis were justified in invading the Soviet Union and killing 27 million people. It should be no surprise that after seizing power after the Euro-maiden riots, the ultra-Nationalists unfurled the US Confederate Flag and the Ku Klux Klan's Celtic cross symbol in Kiev's city hall.

The variation of white supremacist ideology, correctly called Ku Klux Klanism, that Dylan Roof embraced before slaughtering people in South Carolina is an ideology that has been actively supported by the US government and the financial elite. The Klan was formed to serve the Wall Street- and London-aligned plantation owners. The KKK was revived in 1915 with a Hollywood movie and, in its more recent incarnations, has openly cooperated with government officials to assassinate dissident activists.

Unlike other far-right and white supremacist ideologies throughout the world, the Ku Klux Klan never called for any kind of "National Socialism" or "Corporatism." The KKK always preached the need for free market capitalism, and opposed any attempt at establishing a planned economy or restrict the activities of the financial elite. Aside from demagogic statements about Wall Street being "controlled by the Jews," the Ku Klux Klan has never embraced any kind of economic populism, and generally champions austerity, perpetuating the myth that only African-Americans benefit from social welfare programs.

Though Dylan Roof was certainly an unstable, psychologically disturbed individual, he latched onto an ideology that has been actively promoted and enabled by Western capitalism. If Ku Klux Klanism had not been repeatedly embraced and utilized by the wealthiest and most powerful people in the United States, it would have been forgotten long ago. The same can be said for the teachings of Muhammad Ibn Al-Wahhab.

Wall Street and Wahabbism

The Wahabbi interpretation of the Islamic religion began in the 1700s with Muhammad Ibn Al-Wahhab, a fanatic who believed in establishing a repressive, autocratic government through violent means. Wahhab's extreme interpretation of Sunni Islam would be meaningless if he were not able to work with Muhammad bin Saud, who used the teachings of Wahhab to organize his kingdom. Muhammad bin Saud's descendents, the successive Kings of the House of Saud have embraced "Wahabbism" as a justification for their dynasty.

The British empire saw Wahabbism and the House of Saud as being very useful in enabling them to control the oil resources of the Middle East region. While it is debatable whether or not the British empire actually worked directly with Muhammad Ibn Al-Wahhab, there is no debate about the fact that they actively promoted his teachings. The British funded, trained, and armed the House of Saud in order fight the Ottoman Empire, and to secure control of the Middle East region for themselves.

After the Second World War, the United States established a close relationship with the Saudi monarchy. All four major US oil companies—Exxon-Mobil, British Petroleum, Royal Dutch Shell, and Chevron—actively do business with Saudi Arabia. Saudi Arabia purchases billions of dollars worth of weapons from the United States every year.

The Wahabbi ideology remained almost exclusively on the Arabian Peninsula until the 1970s. After the OPEC boycott, when the Saudi regime began to make a much larger margin of profits, Wahabbism began to spread itself across the world with Saudi money.

In the 1980s, Wahabbism became a key aspect of US foreign policy in Afghanistan. Osama bin Laden, the billionaire heir of a wealthy Saudi construction firm traveled across the Muslim world promoting Wahabbism. Bin Laden recruited thousands of young men to fight against the People's Democratic Party and the Soviet Union in Afghanistan.

In Afghanistan, a Wahabbi army called the "Mujiahadeen" was built. The group poured acid on the faces of women who did not wear burkhas, and lynched teachers who taught women how to read. The United States actively supplied the Mujihadeen with weapons, and the US media portrayed the Mujihadeen as "freedom fighters" and "revolutionaries." The Columbia School of Journalism revealed that CBS news was airing fake battle footage in order to portray the Mujihadeen as romantic revolutionaries.

Among the Afghans who aligned with the Mujihadeen in Afghanistan during the 1980s was Siddique Mateen, the father of Omar Mateen. Siddique Mateen was able to get a visa and become a resident of the United States. From the United States he broadcast political messages into Afghanistan urging hostility toward Pakistan. Siddique Mateen was also a supporter of the Taliban government, often speaking positively of it in his broadcasts.

Omar Mateen embraced the Wahabbi ideology his father had aligned himself with during the Afghan Civil War. He visited the Wahabbi homeland of Saudi Arabia on two occasions. He came to admire the Wahabbi terrorist organization known as ISIS, which currently operates in Syria.

ISIS emerged as a faction among the forces fighting against the Syrian government in 2014, and was supported by the United States and its allies in the Middle East. Israel has provided ISIS fighters with medical care in the occupied Golan Heights. A number of ISIS fighters were trained by the United States in Jordan. Most of ISIS' weapons were manufactured in the United States, and ISIS fighters generally drive Toyota trucks, which the US supplied to supposedly "moderate" rebels in Syria.

Turkey allows its borders to remain open so supplies can flow into the hands of ISIS, and continues to conduct airstrikes against the Kurdish Nationalists who are fighting ISIS.

Fifty one US diplomats recently signed a "dissent channel" cable, urging the United States to act as ISIS air force, and smash their primary battlefield enemy, the Syrian government.

The hateful ideology that Omar Mateen embraced did not arise from nowhere. This is a brand of fanaticism and hate that was actively funded and promoted in order to serve US foreign policy objectives.

Where Do Psychopaths Come From?'

Even the question of mental health cannot be separated from US society and the financial elite that runs it.

In the United States, many myths surrounding mass

shooters and their beliefs have emerged. After the 1999 Columbine Massacre, many believed that the incident was a response to bullying. The media promoted the myth that the two shooters were taking revenge after years of abuse from their peers. This was false.

The media now admits, two and half decades later, that students did not recall Eric Harris and Dyland Klebold being bullied, but rather the opposite. At least one of the Columbine killers was a known bully himself, who enjoyed mistreating his fellow students.

Mass shooters are psychopaths. They admire cruelty, and see the world as a heartless place where might makes right. Often psychopaths are victims of extreme child abuse, who come to subconsciously admire and glorify their abusers. The archetypical mass shooter tends to find life to be dull and pointless, and hopes to carry out some horrific act of cruelty and brutality in order prove their worth, before committing suicide.

Among mass shooters who are white men, a keen interest in Ku Klux Klanism is a common trait. The Ku Klux Klan's history is particularly appealing to psychopaths, as the Klan was known for lynching. The Klan's trademark activity was to take unarmed African-American men and extra-legally execute them in a carnival-like atmosphere. Klansmen and their supporters often posed for pictures with the dangling corpses of black men, and kept their body parts as souvenirs.

Psychopaths tend to be aroused and impressed by such activities, and admire those whose moral compass is so weak that they can so blatantly prey on the weak, and harm those who cannot protect themselves or fight back.

Much like the Ku Klux Klan, the videos produced by ISIS are very appealing to psychopaths. ISIS does not film itself engaging in fair fights. Rather, much like the Ku Klux Klan, ISIS celebrates and promotes acts of sadism and cruelty against defenseless people.

It has been widely noted that before turning to ISIS, Omar Mateen attempted to join the New York City Police Department. Omar Mateen most likely admired the NYPD because of its reputation for brutality and cruelty. Mateen failed the entrance exam, and was not permitted to join the police force that intentionally killed Ramarley Graham, Sean Bell, Amadou Diallo and many other unarmed African-American men.

Like ISIS, which celebrated Mateen's killings, the NYPD routinely packs the court rooms in support of officers who kill innocent people, and then applaud when their "brothers in blue" are acquitted. When asked about innocent people who are shot for running, or holding their wallets in the air, representatives of the police routinely blame the unarmed victims for the entire incident, and think that the officers who gun down innocent people acted heroically.

Psychopathy is particularly prevalent in the United States, to the extent that works of literature promoting this mental illness are widely circulating. Ayn Rand, the novelist and philosopher, actively encouraged people to work toward slaying all of their altruism and compassion, and to replace it with "rational self-interest."

After immigrating to the United States from the Soviet Union in the 1920s, the young Ayn Rand admired the famed

Chicagoan murderer, William Hickman. Her diaries spoke of the man who strangled his wife as if he were some kind of hero.

Ayn Rand's novel "The Fountainhead" contains a scene in which the protagonist breaks into a woman's home and forcibly rapes her. Rand's prose describes the event as glorious and justified.

Rand's psychopathy, like that of Klansmen and Wahabbis, has been widely promoted by the financial elite of the United States. Ayn Rand's protege Alan Greenspan was at one time the most powerful figure in the US economy as the chairman of the Federal Reserve. He also served as a leader of the Council on Foreign Relations, the primary think tank of the CIA.

Rand's writings promoting psychopathy are widely promoted on US television and in US universities. Paul Ryan, the Chairman of the Republican National Committee, calls himself a follower of Ayn Rand.

There's no question that Omar Mateen and Dylan Roof were mentally ill, but they embraced a mental illness that is being actively promoted throughout US society.

The Politics of Mass Murder

The US right-wing described Dylan Roof as mentally ill, and ignored his open preaching of fascist hate. The US political left ignores Mateen's family ties and professed belief in Wahabbism, and insists that Mateen was only a mentally ill, self-hating homosexual.

In the aftermath of the ISIS attacks in Paris, the US political establishment revealed similarly partisan and confused responses. The US right-wing attempted to blame all of Islam for what ISIS had done, and the US Congress even passed visa regulations restricting visa for those have travelled to the Islamic Republic of Iran. The law was particularly insulting, as Iran's Revolutionary Guards continue to risk their lives each day on the battlefields, fighting against ISIS.

The US political left responded with confused pacifist statements and calls to oppose Islamophobia. One organization held a protest saying "Police Brutality is Terrorism Too!" No one, on the left or on the right, dared point out that US foreign policy is actively enabling and supporting Wahabbism, and specifically the ISIS organization operating in Iraq and Syria.

Currently, the US Congress is debating a new law which would prevent individuals on the terrorism watch list from purchasing firearms. Neither Dylan Roof nor Omar Mateen were on the terrorism watch list when they purchased their weapons. Mateen had temporarily been on the list, but was removed in 2014.

The US Supreme Court considers the right to purchase firearms to be a constitutional right. The US Constitution clearly states that a constitutional right cannot be removed without due process. Individuals can be placed on the "terrorism watch list" for a variety of reasons including, countries they travel to and political statements they make, among other things.

While different forces seek to politicize the killing, it should be obvious that from every angle, the phenomena of the "mass shooters" is uniquely American. The ideological and psychological drive behind it is deeply rooted in the destructive nature of modern capitalism and US foreign policy.

These underlying roots must be addressed if there is any hope of ending the horrific phenomena

Originally published in New Eastern Outlook

Napoleon Has Left The White House

The November 20th White House Statement, given on
behalf of US President Donald Trump, contained a level
of crass honesty previously unheard of in US politics. The
statement admitted Saudi involvement in the murder of
journalist, Jamal Khoshoggi, but justified continued US-Saudi
relations in the following terms:

"After my heavily negotiated trip to Saudi Arabia last
year, the Kingdom agreed to spend and invest $450 billion in
the United States. This is a record amount of money. It will
create hundreds of thousands of jobs, tremendous economic
development, and much additional wealth for the United
States. Of the $450 billion, $110 billion will be spent on
the purchase of military equipment from Boeing, Lockheed
Martin, Raytheon and many other great U.S. defense
contractors. If we foolishly cancel these contracts, Russia
and China would be the enormous beneficiaries – and very
happy to acquire all of this newfound business. It would be a
wonderful gift to them directly from the United States!"

Unlike almost all of Trump's predecessors, US policy was
not being defended in the name of democracy or human
rights, or even fighting terrorism. What Noam Chomsky
and Michael Parenti spent their careers trying to prove is
now being stated openly: US foreign policy is about money.
It's about oil profits and weapons contracts, not lofty ideals
about freedom and security. One is almost reminded of the
Saturday Night Live character, Nathan Thurm. Thurm was the
caricature of a crooked, corporate lawyer. When confronted
with the misdeeds of his clients, the Thurm character would
nervously inhale from a cigarette and say phrases like "Of
course, do you think I don't know that?" and "What's your
point?"

246

While some of the Pentagon brass and some elderly conservatives may appreciate Trump's frankness and "telling it like it is," one can be sure that many within the intelligence community are fuming with rage. Trump's crass honesty is undoing years and years of work, mainly the work of managing the image of the United States and building relationships with potential proxy fighters. However, this "soft-power" strategy of maneuvering and manipulating Muslim extremists had ultimately climaxed during the term of Trump's predecessor, Barack Obama.

Barack Obama: A 21st Century Napoleon

Napoleon Bonaparte was not a Muslim, and most likely, not a genuine Christian either. Bonaparte rose to power in the aftermath of the French Revolution, when atheism was in fashion within the circles of power. Napoleon arranged for the Pope to coronate him as Emperor, but then dramatically took the crown from the Pope and placed it on his own head. Napoleon was excommunicated by Pope Pius VII, but eventually reconciled with the Church shortly before his death in 1821.

However, when Napoleon waged his Middle Eastern campaign, he worked very hard to convince the Arab people that he was a devout Muslim. The following statement was issued on July 2nd, 1798 when he marched into Alexandria: "People of Egypt! You will be told by our enemies that I am come to destroy your religion. Believe them not. Tell them I am come to restore your rights, punish your usurpers, and revive the true worship of Mohammed. Tell them that I venerate, more than do the Mamelukes, God, his prophet, and the Koran."

Napoleon's words were false. He apparently joked
about them with his officers saying: "A change of religion,
inexcusable for the sake of private interests, becomes
comprehensible when immense political results are
involved.... Do you think the Empire of the East and perhaps
the subjugation of the whole of Asia was not worth a turban
and some loose trousers?" In the hopes of conquering the
Arab people, Napoleon pretended to share their religious
beliefs and understand their woes.

Flash forward to 2009, when another western leader was
in Egypt, he presenting himself as a friend of Arabs and
Muslims. Barack Obama proclaimed: "I've come here to
Cairo to seek a new beginning between the United States and
Muslims around the world, one based on mutual interest and
mutual respect and one based upon the truth that America
and Islam are not exclusive and need not be in competition.
Instead, they overlap and share common principles, principles
of justice and progress, tolerance and the dignity of all human
beings."

The Muslim world had far more cause than simply polite
words to believe him. After all, Obama's middle name is
Hussein. He had attended a Muslim elementary school in
Indonesia as a child. He had met face to face with Palestinian
intellectual, Edward Said. His biological father had been a
Muslim, and his mother had remarried to a Muslim General
in the Indonesian military. Obama's critics constantly accused
of him of being a "secret Muslim." While such allegations
may have harmed him at home, they made the 44th President
of the United States immensely popular in the Arab world.

For decades, the United States had already been working
with religious extremists to counter their rivals. In the 1980s,

the USA had worked with a young Osama Bin Laden to build an army of Mujihadeen to wage civil war and eventually topple the People's Democratic Republic of Afghanistan.

The Muslim Brotherhood and the Arab Spring

The wave of revolts that swept the Middle East in 2011 was not entirely spontaneous. Social media was key in making it happen. Certain videos got promoted, and calls for protest went viral. Jared Andrew Cohen, a google executive and member of the Council on Foreign Relations, was is very open about how closely he was working with the US State Department during these events. Al-Jazeera, a TV network owned by the Qatari monarchy, was very key in promoting the uprisings, as was the religious/political organization aligned with Qatar and Turkey, the Muslim Brotherhood.

The Muslim Brotherhood is a religious and political entity created in 1928 in Egypt. The Muslim brotherhood rejects Arab nationalism and Marxism, and favors a free market economy based on Islamic values. Currently, the Muslim brotherhood tends to recruit small business owners and professionals, mobilizing them to provide charity and services to low income people. Then these desperately poor people are used by the Brotherhood as foot soldiers against rival political factions.

The Central Intelligence Agency of the United States began actively funding, training and working with the Muslim Brotherhood in efforts to counter the Arab Socialist President, Gamal Abdul Nasser during the 1950s. In the following decades, the Muslim Brotherhood was key in US covert operations to combat the Baathist Arab Socialist Party in Syria and Iraq, as well as efforts against the Islamic Socialist government of Libya. With the help of the CIA, a Muslim brotherhood uprising against the Syrian Arab Republic was staged in 1982, resulting in thousands of deaths. Turkish President, Recep Tayyip Erdoğan was elected in an alliance with the Muslim Brotherhood and the Qatari monarchy continues to fund the Brotherhood's activities around the world.

During the 2011 Arab Spring the Muslim Brotherhood, the Kingdom of Saudi Arabia and the US State Department, all marched in lockstep, with Facebook, Twitter, and Al-Jazeera broadcasts providing support in the form of propaganda. The poor people of the Middle East, many of whom were quite desperate in the aftermath of the financial crisis, were mobilized to topple "dictators."

Tunisia's dictator, Zine El Abidine Ben Ali was toppled in the first uprising, sparked by a viral video of a frustrated street vendor lighting himself on fire. When the dust settled after the revolution, the Muslim Brotherhood won the elections and became the ruling party of Tunisia. In Egypt, the dictator Hosni Mubarak was toppled and replaced by a Muslim Brotherhood leader, Mohammed Morsi, who was eventually removed by the military in 2013. In Libya, the Muslim Brotherhood was key in mobilizing armed brigades and foreign fighters against Colonel Moammar Gaddafi's Islamic Socialist government. In Syria, the Muslim Brotherhood has been key in waging the ongoing civil war against the Syrian Arab Republic and the Baath Socialist Party.

A New Approach To The World

In 2018, the Napoleonic alliance of Saudi Wahabbi extremists and Muslim Brotherhood activists working to conduct regime change for the United States, is crumbling. Qatar and Saudi Arabia are at loggerheads. Turkey, despite being a member of NATO, is becoming far friendlier to Russia, and facing more condemnation from Washington.

Meanwhile, the Trump presidency seems to be actively working to sever the intelligence community's relationship with the Muslim Brotherhood. Trump has floated the idea of putting the Muslim Brotherhood on the list of designated Foreign Terrorist Organizations. The 'Travel Ban' enacted by the Trump White House prevented the CIA from rewarding allies in the seven listed countries with visas to live in the United States.

Trump boasts about selling weapons for Pentagon contractors. Trump talks of the Saudi relationship being economically important. Trump seems to court the Netanyahu wing of Israeli politics, and emphasize opposition to Iran. Trump also makes statements like 'Islam hates us' which do not increase US popularity among the global Muslim community.

Its pretty clear that Napoleon has left the White House. The USA is no longer trying to win friends and influence people in the Middle East region. Rather, the current strategy seems to be a kind of crass self-interest presented under the slogan "America First," along with a kind of reverence for weaponry, summed up in the slogan "Peace Through Strength."

The Pentagon may appreciate the Trump administration's shift away from Obama-era consolation and soft power manipulation, but it is likely that many in the intelligence community are furious. In essence, the work of decades, winning the trust of Muslims and Arabs, building relationships with potential proxy forces, is all being undone by a leader who very much fits the stereotype of an "ugly American." The fact that hostility to the current president seems to be flowing from the highest seats of American power should not be shocking to anyone.

Originally published in New Eastern Outlook

POMPEO REVEALS TRUMP-ERA CONFUSION ON IRAN

The foreign policy strategies of the previous two US administrations were very straight forward. George W. Bush favored "spreading democracy" through regime change. Barack Obama had come to office amid frustration with these hawkish neoconservative policies, and instead favored soft-power and manufactured revolutions coordinated with NATO allies.

But what is the foreign policy of the Trump administration? No straight forward answer can be given, even after a sloppy attempt to define the "Trump Doctrine" regarding Iran in an essay from Secretary of State Mike Pompeo. In the publication Foreign Affairs, printed by the Council on Foreign Relations, Pompeo attempted to explain the actions and objectives of the United States in regards to the Islamic Republic. The article was confused, inaccurate, and much like the Trump administration itself, seemed to be trying to please many different people at the same time.

Hypocrites or Fanatics? – They Cannot Be Both

In attempting to explain the "Iranian Threat," Pompeo proclaims: "And today, no regime has more of an outlaw character than that of Iran. That has been the case since 1979, when a relatively small cadre of Islamic revolutionaries seized power…" Those who are familiar with the history of the Islamic Republic know very well that the outpourings of people who brought down the brutal, US backed Pahlavi regime and created the Islamic Republic, were anything but small. The millions of people who took to the streets, some of them actually wearing burial shrouds as they marched because they expected to be gunned down, were quite massive. The crowds that greeted Imam Khomeni at the airport when he returned from exile were equally large.

For almost four decades the Islamic Republic has effectively withstood a lengthy war with Iraq, as well as continued efforts by Sunni, Arab, and Kurdish separatists, among other hostile elements, to break it apart. The Islamic Republic draws its support from local Basij organizations, which enforce the goals of the revolution on a local level. Iran is organized, block by block, neighborhood by neighborhood, city by city, and region by region. To characterize the mass movement that gives strength to the Islamic Republic as a "small cadre" is either intentionally deceptive propaganda, or simply ignorance.

Following his initial mischaracterizations, Pompeo's attempts to demonize Iranian leaders becomes contradictory. He writes "Two years ago Iranians rightfully erupted in anger when leaked pay stubs showed massive amounts of money inexplicably flowing into the bank accounts of senior government officials. For years, clerics and officials have wrapped themselves in the cloak of religion while robbing the Iranian people blind."

Indeed, the issue of corruption and misuse of resources is a big one in Iran. However, the people who raise this issue the most, and have done the most to combat it, are the individuals that Pompeo probably cares for the least. It is the "hardliners" and "principalists" who constantly seek to reassert the religious anti-imperialist and anti-capitalist goals of the revolution, who express the greatest frustration with the market liberalization, the gap between rich and poor, and what they perceive as a revision of the Islamic Republic's revolutionary ideology. Pompeo seems to agree that the most conservative clerics are correct in their criticism of the Rouhani government and the reformist movement.

But yet, while Pompeo accuses Iran's leaders of being phonies who simply mouth an ideology they don't believe in, he seems to believe that they are simultaneously a group of fanatics hell bent on destroying the world. He writes earlier in the piece that Iran created the Quds force, an "elite special forces unit, and tasked it with exporting revolution abroad." He writes "regime officials have subordinated all other domestic and international responsibilities... to fulfilling the revolution."

He accuses Iran of aiding the Palestinians, the Iraqi Shia community that faces attacks from Saudi backed Sunni extremists, the Syrian Arab Republic that faces an onslaught of terrorism, as well as the people of Yemen in the face of Saudi Arabia's criminal bombardment. Not all of these accusations are accepted by independent observers, but if they are indeed true, they are hardly the act of cynical phonies and hucksters. So, is the Iranian government made up deceptive con-men who do not believe in the radical principals they espouse? Or is it made up of bloodthirsty fanatics, constantly taking great risks and sacrificing the country's wealth and resources in order to fulfill their revolutionary agenda?

Pompeo argues that somehow the Iranian leaders are both of these things. This should reveal to any careful reader how disingenuous his statements actually are.

Escalate Confrontations, But No War?

Pompeo's statements seem just as contradictory when he describes the leadership of his own country. He writes

"Trump does not want another long term U.S. military engagement in the middle east or any other region… Pundits may gin up the fear over the idea that this administration will get the United States into a war…"

Yet, he goes on to describe how "President Trump has made clear the pressure will only increase if Iran does not live up to standards…" He goes on to say "This widespread agreement about the Iranian threat leaves no room for countries to remain ambivalent about whether to join the global effort to change Iran's behavior, an effort that is big and getting bigger."

Yes, the USA will threaten Iran and continue to impose sanctions, i.e. economic warfare, on Iran. The Trump administration has already pulled out of the Nuclear Deal and is working hard to punish allies who have tried to have cordial relations with Iran. However, the USA doesn't want a new war and in fact wants to get along better with the country?

Pompeo argues that Trump doesn't want a war, but will continue to push Iran around with threats and economic warfare. The obvious contradiction of such words shouldn't be lost on anyone. Threats are meaningless if there is no intention of ever carrying them out.

Furthermore, isolating any country from the world economy is hardly a way to win them to be friendly. Does Trump really believe that sanctions that make it harder for cancer stricken Iranians to get treatment is going to somehow result in improving relations? Does Pompeo believe that Trump's threats with Iran do not contain the danger of escalating into a large conflagration that could endanger millions of lives? If

Pompeo believes Trump's threats against Iran are completely idle, why would he announce this to the world, publicly? How would revealing that Trump's threats are not genuine help the United States gain leverage in negotiations?

America Faces Iran in Utter Confusion

Pompeo's article contains a large number of comparisons of the Islamic Republic of Iran to the Soviet Union. The article also quotes and makes reference to US President Ronald Reagan on several occasions. The reason for this is that Reagan has practically been canonized by the right-wing of US mainstream media. Pompeo's narrative presents Iran as the new USSR and Trump as the new Ronald Reagan, an analogy that is so obviously inaccurate it is almost laughable. Despite the inaccuracy, it is an analogy that the will cause well trained FOX news viewers and the Rush Limbaugh 'ditto-head' audience to weep.

The article feeds into a fantasy which many of those who were attracted to the "Make America Great Again" slogan would love to be drawn in by. With Reagan-esque bombast against Iran, Trump is bringing back the "good ol' days" when the USA was "number one" in the world, and the "evil empire" of the Soviet Union was in decline. Rather than stating actual intentions of policy, Pompeo words are intended to win the hearts and minds, and probably the votes of elderly rustbelt residents.

Other contradictory points in the article serve a similar propaganda purpose, pleasing specific constituencies that hate the Islamic Republic. Calling Iran a group of hateful fanatics fits the message of Netanyahu, the Likud Party, and its staunch ally and Trump-backer Sheldon Adelson.

Iran's crazed fanaticism and supposed "threat" is routinely presented as a justification for Israel's behavior. While many Israelis, including top Generals, opposed Netanyahu's 2015 speech to the US Congress opposing the Nuclear Deal, the Likud Party is fixated on building up the Israeli military under the pretext of "the Iranian threat." Statements about Iran "spreading chaos" will win the Trump team more donations from Adelson and more support for the Likud Party faction of pro-Israeli lobbyists.

Meanwhile, Iran's supposed wasting of resources abroad is a favored talking point of Pahlavists in southern California and wealthy Persians within Iran's borders who dislike the Islamic Revolution. Racism and the belief that Persians are Hitler's "Master Race" of Aryans was a central tenant of the Shah's ideology. Pahlavists consider themselves to be white and detest the fact that the Iranian government has worked to improve the living conditions of Arabs and Kurds as well as others it deems to be inferior, both within its own borders, as well as abroad. Pompeo hopes to appear to be championing the quiet bitterness found in the wealthy districts of Northern Tehran, as well as Sunset Park, among those who feel the 1979 revolution deprived of them of their rightful positions of wealth and power. He hopes that more Persian nationalists can be duped into risking their lives for his regime change agenda, which in reality aims to beat down and destroy, not simply the Islamic Republic, but the entire Iranian nation.

It is not hard to understand that Iran's foreign policy is hardly needless charity or mere fanaticism. If the Syrian Arab Republic were to be toppled and made into a hotbed of sectarian fanaticism, Iran would be in even greater danger. Iran helps Shia in Iraq for the same reason, knowing that the presence of violent, fanatical Wahhabis on its border is a security concern, as are the Sunni separatists operating on the Afghan border. Furthermore, no matter how supremacist and bitter a Pahlavist may be, it is hard to imagine that any self-respecting nationalist would want to see their homeland go the way of Afghanistan, Libya, and Iraq. US "regime change" is not "nation building" but generally results in the destruction of nations.

Pompeo's contradictory characterization of Iran's leaders as phonies who do not actually believe in or act out the ideals of the 1979 revolution, feeds into the narrative of the crazed terrorist cult known as Mujahadeen E-Khalq. Unlike the Pahlavists and Israelis who hate the 1979 Islamic Revolution, the Mujahadeen E-Khalq (MEK) believes it did not go far enough. The MEK cult believes that its founder Massoud Rajavi is a prophet sent to earth to lead some kind of apocalyptic Islamo-Marxist revolution. The MEK cult of torturing, suicide bombing, fanatics began its campaign of terrorism against the Islamic Republic after it was removed from several leadership positions in 1980. After a long period of collaboration with Saddam Hussein, the MEK now works with Israel and the United States in efforts to destabilize Iran. Pompeo's attempted dog-whistling of the MEK's rhetoric against Iranian leaders is blatantly obvious.

Pompeo's murky attempted explanation of the Trump administration's policy toward Iran is display of contradictory virtue signaling. The piece reflects how deeply confused and divided the US ruling elite truly is. Even among those loyal to Trump, there is no clear agreement on what should be done regarding Iran, or even what the perceived flaws of the Iranian government, or of the Nuclear Deal, actually are.

Some may point to the article as a "brilliant" way of being

"unpredictable" at a future negotiating table by giving so many mixed messages. However, those within the United States can see that this is hardly a brilliant maneuver to confuse an opponent. In reality, the American deep state and the American ruling elite are being pulled in many different directions, unsure of how to proceed, as the waters of a domestic and international crisis rise around them.

The persona of Trump, long known for his arrogance and refusal to admit errors amid a history of blunders and contradictions, seems to fit the overall situation perfectly. Despite pounding the podium, the leaders of the United States have no idea what to do regarding Iran, but pressure for them to do something is rising, and coming from many different sources, with many different goals.

Originally published at New Eastern Outlook

PART FOUR:
THE ALTERNATIVE

Historic Speech: Xi Jinping Upholds Progress

Belief in historical progress was once abundant in the western world. In fact, some of the uglier crimes of western colonialism were justified in the name of progress. Colonizers and imperialists often claimed to be more advanced than those they repressed and brutalized, and justified their mistreatment of others in the name of somehow "civilizing" and "advancing" their victims. However, in recent years, this very western concept has been largely eroded.

Harvard Psychologist Steven Pinker tried to put forward a western, capitalist conception of historical progress in his article "The Enlightenment is Working" published by the *Wall Street Journal* on February 13th, 2018. Observing the condition of American discourse, he began his article saying: "For all their disagreements, the left and the right concur on one thing: The world is getting worse. Whether the decline is visible in inequality, racism and pollution, or in terrorism, crime and moral decay, both sides see profound failings in modernity and a deepening crisis in the West. They look back to various golden ages when America was great, blue-collar workers thrived in unionized jobs, and people found meaning in religion, family, community and nature." Pinker's article went on to give a defensive attempt to assert the concept of progress in an atmosphere where it is notably absent, and say that such progress is indeed coming from western countries.

Those who still have faith in the future most certainly breathed a sigh of relief when Chinese President Xi Jinping, whose ideological breakthroughs have been added to the Communist Party's constitution, took the floor at the China International Import Expo in Shanghai for his widely viewed keynote address.

Belief in historical progress is a central tenant of Marxism and the ideology of the Chinese Communist Party. Marx drew much of his philosophical outlook from Hegel, and his concept of the dialectic. Hegel argued that history was advancing through contradictions, in which a thesis clashed with an antithesis, ultimately resulting in a synthesis. While Hegel understood historical progress primarily in the sense of a battle of ideas, Marx developed historical and dialectical materialism, arguing the struggle to advance productive forces and raise the conditions of human existence drove civilization forward.

President Xi Jinping's remarks included this particularly glowing passage:

"People with vision in the world would agree that economic globalization, as an irreversible trend of history, has greatly boosted global growth. This is an overarching trend, something that is independent of people's will. What we mankind can do is to understand, adapt to, and apply the law of history instead of trying to prevent it from happening. The wheel of history, indeed, will keep rolling forward no matter what."

However, the speech reached its climax when he spoke about China's role in the global economy and human history, proclaiming:

"China is the world's second largest economy. We have a market of more than 1.3 billion consumers who live on the land of over 9.6 million square kilometers. To use a metaphor, the Chinese economy is not a pond, but an ocean. The ocean may have its calm days, but big winds and storms are only to be expected. Without them, the ocean wouldn't be what it is. Big winds and storms may upset a pond, but never an ocean. Having experienced numerous winds and storms, the ocean will still be there! It is the same for China. After going through 5,000 years of trials and tribulations, China is still here! Looking ahead, China will always be here to stay!"

"I am convinced that as long as we have strategic confidence, deepen reform and opening-up across the board, intensify supply-side structural reforms and make greater efforts to solve outstanding problems, then the Chinese economy will surely make a quicker transition to high-quality development, the Chinese people will surely overcome all challenges coming our way, and China will surely embrace a brighter future of development."

The audience of both international guests and important Chinese leaders responded to these statements with dramatic applause. Xi's his words presented the long term aspirations of the Chinese nation, and presented sentiments that many across the planet are longing for.

In his widely studied essay "On The Role of the Individual in History" Yuri Plekhanov, the father of Russian Marxism and mentor of Vladimir Lenin, wrote: "A great man is great not because his personal qualities give individual features to great historical events, but because he possesses qualities which make him most capable of serving the great social needs of his time, needs which arose as a result of general and particular causes.

Xi Jinping's boldness in upholding and continuing the Chinese Communist Party's vision for the rejuvenation of a great country, and his ability to offer hope, not just to his own people, but to the entire world, certainly points to the status of a "great man" by Plekhanov's definition.

There is no question that in age with so much pessimism, isolationism, fear and retreat from the global economy, Xi Jinping's speech served as a breath of fresh air and ray of hope and inspiration to many, many people.

Originally published in New Eastern Outlook

CHINA HAS REAL GROWTH, NOT DEBT-BASED ILLUSIONS

As Americans become ever more nervous about pending problems in their economy, projecting these fears onto China is quite irresponsible and completely unjustified.

The consistent rate of long-term economic growth in China over several decades is quite different than Trump's superficial boasts about stock market numbers.

The nervous reaction that followed the dramatic Oct. 10 drop on the New York Stock Exchange are fully justified. The increase in spending due to the Trump administration's initial wave of tax cuts, and the de-regulation drive is coming to an end. The problems involving an American public with declining ability to spend in a low-wage economy and amid crumbling infrastructure continues to assert itself.

Many economists are critical of the fact that any continued American ability to spend is dependent on debt. Real incomes are not increasing; neither are personal savings and real wealth. The country is getting poorer, despite the lending spigot occasionally being cranked open wider.

Amid the fears about the health of the U.S. economy, claims that China is in a similar situation are popping up throughout the American financial press. Stories highlight the debt of various local governments, as well as the recent sell-off of some of the U.S. debt owned by China. They go on to claim that China could soon be facing the same difficulties currently being experienced by America.

However, actual data disproves such assertions. Unlike the United States, which has been witnessing a steady overall decline in spending power among the population, the opposite trend has been taking place in China. There's abundant proof, all of it quite visible.

According to CNN, every day, a new Chinese millionaire is created. The number of Chinese billionaires is rapidly rising. The rising number of new cash-rich Chinese tourists is greatly boosting the global hospitality and travel industry.

This is real economic growth. The wages of industrial workers, the profits of business owners, and the overall prosperity of society, are all rising. Government spending on infrastructure, poverty alleviation, technology, and programs working toward medium and long-term development goals has certainly been a factor driving this growth.

However, spending and debt have not been the only factors. Chinese society is becoming increasingly prosperous overall.

On Oct. 19, the National Bureau of Statistics presented the real facts about the economic situation. One of its top statisticians, Mao Shengyong, reported: "The Chinese economy has, on the whole, remained stable in the first three quarters with deepened transformation and upgraded development." For the first three quarters of 2018, China's GDP increased by roughly 6.7 percent.

Such a rate of growth is almost unheard of in recent American history. For example, the GDP growth rate in 2017 was a mere 2.7 percent. The closest the United States has come to China's GDP growth rate in recent history was in 1999, with a rate of 4.7 percent.

It should be clear to observers that the ability of the

Chinese government to control the centers of economic power has given the country a special ability to keep growing. The model of "Socialism with Chinese Characteristics" engineered by Deng Xiaoping utilizes foreign investment and the market, but allows the State to maintain control and protect society from capitalist chaos.

While Americans grow nervous about their declining standard of living amid record levels of government, household and student debt, they shouldn't seek to try and project their own difficulties onto China. China's economic growth is society-wide and based on overall gains for the entire population. It is not a debt-based illusion.

Originally published at China.org.cn

WILL CHINA SAVE US FROM HOLLYWOOD?

As right-wing conservatives in the United States have pointed out for decades, Hollywood is a very political place. However, a new and growing source of political influence may be changing how the global entertainment industry, US film studios included, portrays events on the silver screen. China, led by the 90-million members of its Communist Party, could gradually be pushing back the blatant pro-western, neoliberal tone that has been so prevalent in modern cinema.

Hollywood Has Always Been Political

Attempts to say that the products of the film studios located in southern California are "art for art's sake" and have no political agenda are highly disingenuous. Hollywood's politics have often been very blatant, so blatant that the US government has stepped in either to utilize or control them.

The first full length movie ever produced was D.W. Griffiths *The Birth of a Nation*, released in 1915. The film contained lengthy quotations from the writings of the sitting President, Woodrow Wilson, and was screened at the White House. The film was a blatant work of political propaganda, designed to strengthen the Democratic Party. The film retold the history of the American Civil War, portraying Lincoln as a cruel tyrant and the Ku Klux Klan as heroes. The film lauded the defeat of attempts at creating social equality in the post war period, and the establishment of Jim Crow. The title is derived from the belief that the unity of southern and northern whites against African-Americans constituted The Birth of a Nation.

The film was shown across the USA, and in Boston and Philadelphia, the audiences were so inflamed with hate, that they left the theaters to go attack African-Americans. Not only did the film inspire race riots, but shortly after its release, the previously illegal Ku Klux Klan was revived as a mass white supremacist movement.

In the late 1930s, Hollywood swung to the left. As President Franklin Delano Roosevelt faced a wave opposition from big business, bankers, and industrialists; the artists, actors, and film directors of Hollywood saw him as their friend and ally. Movies like *Mr. Smith Goes to Washington* portrayed capitalists as selfish villains ruining the lives of the common people. Meanwhile, films like Humphrey Bogart's *The Black Legion* portrayed far-right politics as a destructive scam. Charlie Chaplin ended his anti-fascist comedy film, *The Great Dictator* with a four minute anti-capitalist speech saying "Soldiers, don't give yourself to brutes! … Machine men, with machine minds and machine hearts!… Let us fight for a new world…Let us do away with national barriers, let us do away with greed… In the name of democracy, let us all unite!"

When the Second World War broke out, Hollywood films crossed into blatantly pro-Communist territory. The 1942 film *The North Star* portrayed Ukrainian guerrillas fighting off Nazi invaders while singing the praises of socialism in the USSR. The film *Mission to Moscow* portrayed the Moscow Trials of 1937 in a positive light, presenting Stalin as heroically exposing a domestic conspiracy of Japanese Imperialists and German Nazis, in league with Russian Trotskyites.

After the war, in the late 1940s and early 50s, Hollywood

faced a huge crackdown on its hard left elements. The House Un-American Activities Committee investigated people working in entertainment who held pro-Soviet and anti-capitalist sentiments. Ten screenwriters who had associated with the Communist Party famously went to prison for refusing to testify against their co-workers. Charlie Chaplin fled the country. Pete Seeger was banned from performing his folk music on national television for over a decade.

Since the 1950s, Hollywood has largely strayed from anti-capitalist or Marxist themes, though it has never been a bastion of social conservatism. Almost since its inception Hollywood has been pushing back the standards of "decency" by including explicit sex, drug use, homosexuality, sacrilege, and other things that both offend people in middle America, and also sell lots of tickets. Hollywood encompasses both ends of the American political spectrum. American cinema generally worships the right-wing capitalist ideal of wealth and profits, while promoting a more liberal cultural hedonism that opposes tradition and community obligation.

A few of the Oscar winning films of recent years have been quite political. The 2012 Academy Award Winning Film *Argo* portrayed the Iran's 1979 Islamic Revolution as cruel mob of fanatics, persecuting the well intentioned Americans. The 2008 "Best Picture" winner was a film called *Slumdog Millionaire,* which portrayed the people of India as uncultured primitive barbarians, whose only hope for salvation was the investment of western corporations. In one scene, an American tourist actually hands the young protagonist some cash saying "This is what the real America is all about."

A "Red Dawn" at the Box Office

When preparing to release the 2012 film *Red Dawn*, the Hollywood producers at MGM realized they had a problem. The action movie portrayed the United States being taken over by an army of Chinese invaders who commit horrific atrocities. Such a film would undoubtedly be quite offensive to Chinese audiences. At the last minute, the film was digitally edited, so that invaders were no longer Chinese, but rather soldiers from the Democratic People's Republic of Korea.

Why did MGM change the film at the last minute? The Chinese box office is very important. In 2018, it is predicted that movie ticket sales in China will surpass those of the United States for the first time. Furthermore, with theaters rapidly opening across China's countryside, giving its population of more than a billion people access to the big screen, it is predicted that the already high cinema revenue will double by 2023.

Recent articles in the US press have highlighted the huge amount of influence that the Chinese market, and by default, the Chinese Communist Party has on global entertainment. The AMC Movie Theater chain is owned by the China based Dalian Wanda Group. Dalian Wanda Group, like many supposedly private corporations in China, does not function according to the laws of the market. Just like Huawei, the largest telecommunications manufacturer in the world, or the various "groups" that make up the Chinese steel industry, Dalian Wanda Group is completely subservient to the government.

The CEO of Dalian Wanda Group is Wang Jianlin, the richest man in China. Wang Jianlin may be very wealthy, but he is also a member of the Communist Party. Wang's father was a hero in the Chinese revolution who marched alongside Mao on the legendary long march. Wang spent 16 years in the military before going into business, and his market activities, which have attracted lots of foreign investment, have always been completely in accordance with the State Development Plans. The *Wall Street Journal* quoted a former executive of AMC Theaters, Gerry Lopez, complaining about how the directives of Wang, a loyal Chinese Communist Party member, had priority over everything else: "He's total control. Every decision period, gets made by one guy."

The products of China's blossoming domestic film industry are certainly different than those put out by American studios. Chinese films, especially in recent years, tend to promote a sense of duty to the homeland. A large percentage of Chinese films and TV programs promote heroes from the country's history such as Zhou Enlai or Lei Feng.

An NPR article on Chinese influence on global media gives the impression that Chinese media is almost totalitarian. It complains how about how Chinese government officials insist that films not contain "offensive" content, and that their overall message be consistent with the Communist Party's goals for society.

While this certainly sounds upsetting to adherents of western liberalism, it is more consistent with society's view of artists throughout most of human history. In most civilizations that have existed over the past 4,000 years, artists were considered to be public servants, who had a duty to improve people with their art. Throughout the vibrant history of human civilization, painters, writers, and performers were not expected dumb down their art, and make it appeal to the most crass and primitive instincts within people in order to maximize revenue for production companies. Rather than lowering their standards to broaden their appeal, artists were expected to educate, inform, persuade, and challenge their audiences. Art served the purpose of making all of society better, not simply making profits.

Chinese cinema is a business, but it fits its business into the overall goals of the Communist Party for a prosperous society. In 2014, China's President Xi Jinping condemned artists who "are salacious, indulge in kitsch, are of low taste and have gradually turned their work into cash cows, or into ecstasy pills for sensual stimulation." The Chinese government urges film and TV producers to make art that promotes "socialist core values, as well as patriotism and Chinese fine traditions." Chinese companies are forbidden from working with films that "harm national dignity and the interest of China, cause social instability, or hurt the national feeling."

According to the *Wall Street Journal*, American producers are already limiting the amount of films that contain certain themes like "homosexuality and the undead" because Chinese audiences disfavor them. Furthermore, Hollywood is working hard to include more Chinese actors in supporting roles to appease the desire of Chinese audiences.

Qingdao: "Popularity Should Not Necessitate Vulgarity"

Woodrow Wilson, the American President who worked with D.W. Griffith to create the racist propaganda film *The*

273

Birth of a Nation in 1915, was widely hated, far beyond American shores. In 1919, the he was burned in effigy across the Chinese mainland, and hated most especially in the streets of a city called Qingdao.

Qingdao is part of the Chinese mainland that was forcibly seized by the German empire in 1897. The Germans used Qingdao to host a naval base. While building it, the Germans deported thousands of Chinese people from their homes in order to erect railroads and munitions factories. After Germany was defeated in the First World War, US President Woodrow Wilson, refused to allow Qingdao to be returned to China at the Paris Peace Conference.

In response, Chinese students revolted across the country, burning Wilson in effigy and boycotting American and Japanese products. The May Fourth Movement, a huge explosion of anti-imperialism in response to Wilson's humiliation of the Chinese people, is often considered to be the opening battle of the Chinese revolution.

Among the young street fighters who forced a boycott on foreign goods and denounced the Versailles treaty was an organization called the "New People's Study Society" led by a young man named Mao Zedong. Eventually the New People's Study Society abandoned the Anarchist teachings of Peter Kropotkin and helped to form the Chinese Communist Party. Qingdao was finally returned to China in 1922, after decades of foreign occupation. It was seized by the Red Army in 1949, just weeks before the People's Republic of China was declared in Beijing.

While Qingdao has played a huge role in the armed battles between western capitalism and China's drive for independence, today it is at the center of a cultural and intellectual battle.

Today, Qingdao is the home of the "Oriental Movie Metropolis." Already there are 30 sound stages that have been constructed. The world's largest studio pavilion, set to be over 10,000 square meters, is currently being constructed there. The area will also be home to a research center on IMAX theater technology, and a museum on the history of cinematography. The site is set to become fully operational in 2018.

China's planned economy, which has already overtaken the rest of the world in telecommunications and steel manufacturing, now moves ahead in the cultural arena. The many thousands of Chinese people involved in film production are guided in their work by the recent words of President Xi Jinping.

In discussing the role of art, he said: "Popularity should not necessitate vulgarity and hope should not entail covetousness... Pure sensual entertainment does not equate to spiritual elation.... The true value of a masterpiece lies in its intellectual depth, artistic exquisiteness and skillful production."

Originally Published in New Eastern Outlook

THE "GREAT SATAN" & THE SILK ROAD

In February of 2015, China heralded the opening of
its month leading the Security Council with a cultural
performance at the United Nations Headquarters. The
performance, done in the form of traditional Chinese ballet
was called *The Dream of the Maritime Silk Road.*

The theatrical performance told of events that took place
hundreds of years ago, as Asian silk was first exported across
the planet. The performance specifically highlighted the
relationship between China and the ancient society of Persia,
located in what is now called the Islamic Republic of Iran.

The theme of the performance was not merely an obscure
historical reference, and its selection for performance at the
United Nations was no accident. The respective histories of
China and Iran in the last century have many similarities. In
the current period, though the two countries have distinctly
different ideologies and perspectives, they are increasing
becoming bound together in economics. Both of them are
facing increasing hostility from the United States.

US Backed Terrorism Against Popular Revolutions

Following the Second World War, even though the
Communist Party played a key role in defeating the Japanese
invaders, a US backed dictator named Chiang Ki-Shek barred
it from participating in the elections. Members of the heroic
"Eighth Route Army" were being rounded up and arrested.

In response to this, Mao Zedong rallied the people of China
to take up arms once again, this time targeting the domestic
tyrants in the Nationalist Party. From 1945 to 1949, the

Chinese Communist Party and its allies battled against the US aligned Nationalists. In 1949, the Chinese Communist Party was victorious, and the "People's Republic of China" came into existence. Mao Zedong proclaimed "the Chinese people have stood up!" Land was redistributed, education and employment was provided to the population, and industry was developed. Western capitalism was thrown out, and China began on an independent course.

Since that time, China has been subjected to an endless campaign of terrorism and subversion. In the 1950s, Tibetan separatists, trained in Colorado, were airdropped into the country to wage an ugly campaign of violence. The US backed Nationalists set up shop on China's island of Taiwan, and used it as a base for terrorism and subversion against the mainland. Currently, the CIA has a cozy relationship with the Falun Gong, a crazed religious extremist group that kidnaps children among other atrocities. The CIA and western NGOs have funded "Occupy Central" protests in Hong Kong, and other schemes to destabilize Chinese society. US media has recently been filled with a wave of allegations about "cyber warfare" from China. The current Chinese President, Xi Jinping, is described as a dictator in the US press, and statements condemning him are becoming very frequent.

The Islamic Republic of Iran, was also born in a popular revolution against a US backed dictator. The Shah of Iran was a brutal repressive tyrant, trained by the US government and the CIA, to repress and torture the Iranian people. In 1979, a massive uprising of the Iranian people brought the Shah of Iran down. A new government based on religious principles called the "Islamic Republic" was established.

The Islamic Republic utilized the country's vast oil

resources to develop the economy. Strong government control over industry and economic activity resulted almost full employment in Iran, in addition to the wiping out of illiteracy and the vast expansion of healthcare and education.

In response to the Iranian revolution, the US supported Iraqi President Saddam Hussein in attacking Iran. Over one million people died in an eight year war, in which the US provided chemical weapons, funding, and military support to the Iraqi aggressors.

The Islamic Republic of Iran continues to be the victim of US backed terrorism. The Mujahadeen-E Khalq Organization, a violent terrorist group, is currently coddled by the US, even as it has assassinated Iranian scientists and professors. The organization has a record of slaughtering innocent people, and sided with Saddam Hussein during the Iraq-Iran War. US intelligence forces also have a cozy relationship with Jindallah, another terrorist group that facilitates drug smuggling and bombings along the Iran-Afghanistan border.

Thousands of Iranians and Chinese people have died as a result of US attacks. Though Iran is currently negotiating with the United States, and China has vast US investments, the blatant hostility has not ceased. US media demonizes both China and Iran, and the Pentagon and the CIA openly long to smash both societies with "regime change."

"Neither East Nor West"

As the cold war neared its end in 1991, both China and the Islamic Republic of Iran were officially neutral. The People's Republic of China originated as a Soviet aligned country, but in 1961 this relationship was abruptly terminated. By the

1970s, Chinese leaders spoke of "Soviet Social Imperialism" and often aligned with the United States in global conflicts.

Imam Khomeni, the founder of the Islamic Republic of Iran was highly critical of capitalism and the power of money. In his speeches he often invoked the "battle of poverty against wealth." He referred to the United States as Sheitan-E Bozorg (The Great Satan).

However, Imam Khomeni was also highly critical of the Soviet Union. The Iranian revolution was not part of the current of Soviet aligned forces in the Persian Gulf Region. Instead of preaching secular Marxism, Khomeni raised the slogans of "Neither East nor West" and "Not Capitalism but Islam."

Iran's economic model has never been like the soviet style command economy, or the Arab nationalist model of central planning. Iranian revolutionaries have always maintained that markets and capitalism are absolutely necessary to develop the country, but they must be controlled. They argue that an Islamic Revolutionary government, based in committees and neighborhood organizations, must keep control of the capitalists who are naturally deceptive and greedy.

In the late 1970s, China transitioned to a very similar economic model. Deng Xiaoping argued "Poverty is anti-Communist, but to get rich is glorious." China currently has a vast capitalist market, that is tightly regulated and controlled by the Communist Party. The Chinese Communist Party has millions of members throughout the country. The Communist Party functions in a highly disciplined manner, watching over the capitalists and society as a whole, to ensure that the goals of the revolution remain intact.

Both China and Iran have military structures which are partisan and based on revolutionary anti-imperialist principles. Iran's Revolutionary Guard Corps are not accountable to the President or any elected official, but only the Supreme Leader. The Revolutionary Guards are highly ideological, with each of its members well trained in the teachings of Imam Khomeni and the principles of the Islamic Revolution.

In China, the People's Liberation Army is not under the dominion of the government, but under the direct control of the Communist Party. People's Liberation Army soldiers are given highly political training and education. Recently, Chinese President Xi Jinping has been showing Chinese soldiers films about the events leading up to the collapse of the Soviet Union, and the criminal record of US military aggression.

Wall Street Aggression and Internal Disruption

The Islamic Republic of Iran faces crippling economic sanctions from the United States. These sanctions are based on the false allegation that Iran seeks to develop nuclear weapons. The sanctions target the peaceful nuclear energy program, and every effort is being made to push Iran out of the international economy. These sanctions are economic warfare, making it impossible for Iran to purchase necessary things like airplane engine parts, medical equipment, and other vital products.

Meanwhile, China is facing a growing level of hostility from the United States. US airplanes are violating China's airspace, and the US military presence in the pacific is greatly expanding.

Internally, both Iran and China face similar difficulties. In an ironic twist of reality, the anti-capitalist revolutions have both in a huge expansion of domestic capitalism.

Prior to the 1979 revolution, Iran was highly impoverished. Wall Street corporations made huge profits from Iran's oil, but most Iranians lived in extreme poverty, with a very limited domestic economy. The 1979 revolution in Iran has allowed many Iranians to open businesses and become wealthy. In comparison to its neighbors, Iran has a very vast economy, and there are many wealthy Iranian business owners. The northern section of Iran's capital city of Tehran is filled with wealthy young people, who drive Mercedes and BMWs. These young wealthy Iranians eat hamburgers, wear American style clothes, and idealize everything about the United States.

Though they do not display it in public, it is no secret that these wealthy Iranians have absolute contempt for the Islamic revolution. During the "Green Movement" of 2008, many of them were in the streets, violently attacking government officials, disrupting society, directed by the CIA and cheered by US media.

China faces hostility a from a similar domestic grouping. The revolution launched by the Chinese Communist Party has allowed China's economy to become a booming world center. Compared to its asian neighbors, China has a much larger number of business owners, and a very large population of wealthy, US worshipping youth. Many young Chinese people study at US universities, and openly espouse contempt for Mao Zedong, the Communist Party, and the Chinese revolution itself.

The United States, the CIA, and its apparatus of NGOs and Non-Profits, is doing all it can to cultivate a close relationship with these sectors of Chinese and Iranian society. US media, showing a filtered, glamorized image of US society plays an invaluable propaganda role.

If the US had kept its grip on China and Iran, this huge number of domestic capitalists would never have come into existence. However, this strata of newly rich people, especially its youth, are unsatisfied with their already vast level of prosperity. They have been sucked into the delusion that somehow US intervention and "regime change" will lead to even greater riches.

The reality of US intervention in Iraq, Afghanistan, Libya, Eastern Europe, and so many other places points to a far less desirable result. However, this reality is not highlighted in western media.

Friendship and Revolutionary Revival

In response to increasing hostility from the United States, Iran and China are becoming much closer. In the region of Hormuz in Southern Iran, an entire city has practically sprung up in the last three years alone. Economic activity in Bandar Abbas, the port where 90% of Iran's maritime trade activity takes place, is rapidly expanding. The city's skyline is dotted with Chinese language signs.

Chinese leaders announced on June 5th that they would be expanding investment in Iran's energy sector. China is already the top purchaser of Iranian oil.

As the countries grow closer, leaders of both China and Iran are urging a revival and reinforcement of their anti-imperialist principles.

The Supreme Leader of Iran, Ayatollah Ali Seyed Khamenei, gave a lengthy address on June 4th, at a ceremony commemorating the 26th anniversary of the death of Imam Khomeni, who lead the country's 1979 revolution. In front of a crowd of Iranians who had bussed in from all across the country, he re-emphasized that Iran's founder was a champion of the poor, oppressed, and downtrodden. He emphasized that Khomeni had opposed people living "aristocratic" lifestyles.

Khamenei warned that some figures were distorting the ideas of the Islamic Republic's founder. He emphasized that while Imam Khomeni was not a "like the leaders of the French Revolution and Marxist Revolutions", he also made clear that Khomeni saw the United States as "The Great Satan." Khamenei emphasized that Iran has always "stood with the oppressed," and opposed "international bullying" from the United States. As the crowd thunderously applauded and chanted against US imperialism, Khamenei's speech made references to police brutality in the United States, and emphasized Iran's solidarity with Palestine.

Meanwhile in China, Xi Jinping is waging a "Mass Line Campaign" against corruption by government officials. Leaders who take bribes are facing harsh penalties. Symbolic one day prison sentences are being handed down by Chinese courts as a warning to officials who are moving in a corrupt direction, or living extravagant lives.

Xi Jinping recently reached out to China's religious community, and said that religion should be incorporated into Chinese society. In the same speech, however, Xi urged

Chinese religious leaders not to become collaborators with the United States, as many have done in the past.

Driven Together By History

The growing relations between China and Iran are not faultless. Many Iranians distrust China, and speak of corruption and malpractice they have observed by Chinese capitalists. Iran's supreme leader has emphasized that Iran's "resistance economy" must involve a large amount of domestic production and self-reliance. Despite the growth of foreign trade, Iran must not become dependent.

In addition, while Chinese leaders are growing more friendly to Iran, there is still a level of mutual distrust. China, despite continuing to invest in Iran, has a very close relationship with the US, and has not boldly opposed the sanctions. Chinese leaders are often accused of having a condescending attitude of superiority in their relations with Iran, as well as in their growing relations with African and South American countries.

China and Iran are two very different countries, with two very different ideologies and histories. However, they are being driven together by the forces of history. Both of them want development, and are struggling to improve the living standards of their peoples. Both of them have rejected Wall Street and London, and seek to develop independently. Both countries refuse to be colonies, subjugated by foreign powers. Both of them have governments based in popular organizations of the population and supported by independent, politicized armed groupings.

While neither of these countries are "socialist" in the

sense of the Soviet Union, it would be incorrect to describe their governments or economic models as being fully capitalist. Both of these societies are strong opponents of neo-liberalism, western economic domination, and free market insanity. As a result, they have both become victims of extreme attacks and subversion.

The relationship between Iran and China is greatly expanding, because Wall Street cannot tolerate such things. The only response of the Pentagon to self-reliance and independence is sanctions, subversion, attack, and war. The outmoded global set-up, where western bankers enrich themselves at the expense of the planet, is in severe decline.

However, the imperialist global set-up is not exiting the global stage peacefully. The recent bloodbaths in Syria, Yemen, and Ukraine are clear demonstrations of this. The vicious billionaires of Wall Street, armed with nuclear weapons, intend to go down fighting, as history marches past them, and more countries assert their freedom.

As a result of Wall Street's attacks, countries across the world who want economic independence are pulling together and learning from each other. Despite the intentions from Iranian and Chinese leaders, in reality it is the increasing aggression and desperation of Wall Street that is constructing the "New Silk Road."

Originally published in New Eastern Outlook

Cuba's Support for Revolutions & Self-Defense Has Not Changed

President Barack Obama's visit to Cuba was roundly condemned by his right-wing opponents. The fact that the visit coincided with the Brussels bombing was not omitted from conservative diatribes. The conservative press voiced further outrage when it was revealed that Secretary of State John Kerry had met with representatives of the Revolutionary Armed Forces of Colombia, or FARC, who were in Cuba for negotiations with the Colombian government.

The right-wing press seethed with anger that Obama, who is supposedly fighting a "war against terrorism," would visit Cuba, which was only officially removed from the State Department's State Sponsors of Terrorism list last May, several years after the State Department confirmed that the Cuban government "no longer actively supports armed struggle in Latin America and other parts of the world."

Desiree DeLoach is an organizer for the Venceremos Brigade, a group that, in an act of civil disobedience, routinely violates the ban on Americans traveling to Cuba. When asked about Cuba's former designation as a state sponsor of terrorism, she told MintPress News that "its hypocrisy is abhorrent."

DeLoach described how, in her analysis, the United States has actually waged a campaign of terrorism against Cuba. "There have been over 600 assassination attempts against Fidel Castro's life, bombings of hotels and many other acts of terrorism carried out or backed by the United States," she said, further noting the example of the refusal to extradite Luis Posada Carriles, a man who confessed to having bombed a Cuban airplane and remains safe and free in Miami.

Looking beyond the hypocrisy, the relationship between the Cuban government and armed groups throughout Latin America — the basis for its former official designation as a state sponsor of terrorism — has evolved based on changing circumstances. However, Cuba's ideological principles remain consistent.

The reason for Cuba's apparent shift in favor of peaceful methods of social activism points toward an unacknowledged and concealed reality about revolutionary left-wing politics.

'Making violent revolution inevitable'

In 1982, Cuba was officially designated as a state sponsor of terrorism. According to a CIA report, Cuba was included on the list because:

"Havana openly advocates armed revolution as the only means for leftist forces to gain power in Latin America, and the Cubans have played an important role in facilitating the movement of men and weapons into the region. Havana provides direct support in the form of training, arms, safe havens, and advice to a wide variety of guerrilla groups. Many of these groups engage in terrorist operations."

Indeed, Cuba was supporting armed groups throughout Latin America in 1982. The CIA document lists, among others, the 19th of April Movement in Colombia; the Sandinista National Liberation Front in Nicaragua; and the Farabundo Marti National Liberation Front in El Salvador — all as receiving support from the Cuban government in their armed campaigns. The report also quotes Cuban officials saying "acts by legitimate national liberation movements cannot be defined as terrorism."

When asking why Nicaraguans, Salvadorans, and Colombians were engaged in armed revolutionary violence — and why the Cubans supported them — rather than quoting Cuban officials, the CIA report should really quote President John F. Kennedy, who famously said: "Those who make peaceful revolution impossible will make violent revolution inevitable."

Those who accuse Cuba of "supporting terrorism" forget that the M-19 revolutionaries in Colombia, the FMLN in El Salvador, and the Sandinistas in Nicaragua all took up arms not against democratic states but against brutal, repressive, human rights-violating autocracies. In Colombia, paramilitaries armed and trained by the U.S. kidnapped, assassinated, and tortured almost all peaceful opposition. Many thousands of labor activists, socialist organizers, and religious leaders were killed.

The M-19 took up arms alongside FARC and other Colombian groups in the context of extreme political repression, violations of human rights, and routine slaughter of innocent civilians. Explaining the situation in Colombia, Fidel Castro said:

"The Colombian Communist Party never contemplated the idea of conquering power through the armed struggle. The guerrilla was a resistance front and not the basic instrument to conquer revolutionary power, as it had been the case in Cuba."

The Sandinistas in Nicaragua, which Cuba is also accused

of supporting, took power in an armed revolution in 1979 against a military dictatorship led by Anastasio Somoza. In 1972, when Nicaragua was struck by an earthquake that killed 10,000 people, the regime's military shocked the world as it forcibly stole food and money from the quake's victims. In his 2012 book "Latin American Dictators of the 20th Century," Javier A. Galván wrote: "The military engaged in an indiscriminate operation of torture, rape, savage beatings, unjustified incarceration, and the assassination of thousands of poor peasants. The soldiers confiscated their land and kept it for themselves. In the meantime, the urban areas were simultaneously suffering under strict martial law and further censorship of all communications media."

It was in a fight against this heavily corrupt and human rights-violating regime that the Cuban-aligned Sandinista revolutionaries seized power in 1979.

The guerilla fighters in El Salvador, who also received Cuban support, took up arms in 1979 after a repressive military junta deposed the elected government in a coup d'état. The United Nations Truth Commission on El Salvador described the situation this way:

"[V]iolence became systematic and terror and distrust reigned among the civilian population. The fragmentation of any opposition or dissident movement by means of arbitrary arrests, murders and selective and indiscriminate disappearances of leaders became common practice."

Nearly all the armed groups Cuba was accused of supporting in 1982 took up arms not out of bloodlust, but only when other means of struggle were made fruitless and impossible by extreme political repression. Cuba is accused

289

of supporting Guatemalan indigenous people who armed themselves against what human rights observers have since described as genocide. Cuba is alleged to have supported armed groups who battled against the brutal military dictatorship of Augusto Pinochet in Chile, where dissidents were frequently "disappeared" and their mangled corpses eventually dumped on the street.

The regimes opposed by Cuba's Latin American allies were staffed by people trained in the School of the Americas (now known as the Western Hemisphere Institute for Security Cooperation, or WHINSEC) in Georgia. At this CIA facility, paramilitaries and counterinsurgency specialists from all across the American hemisphere were trained in the art of torture, kidnapping, and other methods designed to terrify civilian populations into subservience and obedience. In the context of such brutal repression and autocracies throughout South America, the Cuban government worked with the Soviet Union to provide arms, weapons and military training to resistance forces.

Support for the violent insurgencies of Colombia, Chile, Nicaragua, El Salvador, Guatemala, and elsewhere is certainly consistent with the Cuban government's ideological heritage. The Marxist-Leninist ideology most certainly permits its adherents to take up arms in the context of extreme political repression and a mass movement for social justice. As de facto leader of the Communist International, Josef Stalin explained the context and theory of armed revolutionary violence to British novelist H.G. Wells in 1934, saying: "Communists do not in the least idealize the methods of violence. But they, the communists, do not want to be taken by surprise, they cannot count on the old world voluntarily departing from the stage, they see that the old system is violently defending itself, and that is why the communists say to the working class: Answer violence with violence; do all you can to prevent the old dying order from crushing you, do not permit it to put manacles on your hands, on the hands with which you will overthrow the old system."

In current times, Cuba's allies are largely not taking up arms. The Sandinistas of Nicaragua and the FMLN of El Salvador are in power, but this power was not won by means of armed insurrection. The Sandinistas and the FMLN took power in peaceful, democratic, internationally-observed elections. Cuba's allies in the Venezuelan United Socialist Party, or PSUV, the Movement Toward Socialism, or MAS, in Bolivia, and other anti-imperialist, socialist-oriented governments in Latin America, have taken power by legal, electoral means.

Genuine communists favor peaceful methods

But how can this be possible? Isn't the Cuban Communist Party still a Marxist-Leninist Party? Do they not still uphold the same ideological beliefs and principles as they upheld in 1982? Do they not advocate "dictatorship of the proletariat" and the "smashing of the bourgeois state," among other communist ideas?

The Cuban government maintains its Marxist-Leninist political line, but the circumstances have changed. The Latin America of the 21st century is not the same as the Latin America of the 1970s and 80s. The tactical principles of Marxism-Leninism are widely misrepresented. In reality, they do not fetishize or celebrate the use of violence.

Communist Party leader William Z. Foster — not a

moderate, but considered to be a "hardliner" and "Stalinist" by historians of American communism — accurately articulated the Marxist-Leninist position on violence in 1948. He wrote:

"The working class and other toiling elements are always and instinctively champions of peace and democracy...This fact is so because the toilers are the ones who always have to suffer the most from tyranny and from war's destruction. They pick up the sword against those who oppress, exploit, or would butcher them only when they have no other alternative, only when the road of peace is closed to them."

Even in the context of the brutal czarist autocracy, Lenin and the Bolsheviks condemned "adventurism." Marxist-Leninists throughout the world have always opposed revolutionary strategies based on isolated acts of violence. Describing political assassinations and bombings as ineffective, Vladimir Lenin wrote: "We know from the past and see in the present that only new forms of the mass movement or the awakening of new sections of the masses to independent struggle really rouses a spirit of struggle and courage in all. Single combat however, inasmuch as it remains single combat... has the immediate effect of simply creating a short-lived sensation, while indirectly it even leads to apathy and passive waiting for the next bout."

The world situation, not Cuba, has changed

In the context of the 21st century, progressive activists in Latin America are not compelled to take up arms. In most Latin American countries they are free to organize demonstrations and labor unions, as well as to participate in elections.

In this new context, Cuba worked to resolve— not to expand or exacerbate — one of the longest-lasting armed conflicts on the continent. In 1993, the Communist Party of Colombia and FARC terminated their relationship with each other. At that time, Cuba ended its alliance with FARC. Fidel Castro criticized the FARC leader, Manuel Marulanda, by saying: "He conceived a long and extended struggle; I disagreed with this point of view. But I never had the chance to talk with him. … I have expressed, very clearly, our position in favor of peace in Colombia; but we are neither in favor of foreign military intervention nor of the policy of force that the United States intends to impose at all costs on that long-suffering and industrious people. … I have honestly and strongly criticized the objectively cruel methods of kidnapping and retaining prisoners under the conditions of the jungle."

After 1993, Cuba was now neutral in the conflict between the Colombian government and the FARC rebels, and eventually negotiated an end to the conflict.

Those who misunderstand the methods and tactics of genuine revolutionaries portray Cuba as a country of bloodthirsty revolutionaries who spread violence throughout the continent. Cuba has supported progressive forces who, like the Cubans did in 1959, took up arms in self-defense against brutal and repressive autocracies. However, like all sensible forces advocating social justice, they would prefer a peaceful transition to a better world.

The Cuban government and its allies throughout the region have demonstrated to the world that they are not violent psychopaths. Rather, they are individuals who are dedicated to social justice, and will make great sacrifices in order to achieve that. Violent methods may be used in some contexts, but only if necessary.

The reestablishment of diplomatic relations with the U.S. certainly opens a new chapter in U.S.-Cuba relations. As tensions rise in Venezuela, Brazil, and other countries throughout the region, many hope that the possibility of peaceful, democratic struggle can remain open, and that the use of brutal military dictatorships to halt social progress will remain in the history books.

Originally Published in Mint Press News

US Led Economic War, Not Socialism, Is Tearing Apart Venezuela

The political and economic crisis facing Venezuela is being endlessly pointed to as proof of the superiority of the free market.

Images and portrayals of Venezuelans rioting in the streets over high food costs, empty grocery stores, medicine shortages, and overflowing garbage bins are the headlines, and the reporting points to socialism as the cause.

The *Chicago Tribune* published a Commentary piece titled: "A socialist revolution can ruin almost any country." A headline on Reason's *Hit and Run* blog proclaims: "Venezuelan socialism still a complete disaster." The Week's U.S. edition says: "Authoritarian socialism caused Venezuela's collapse."

Indeed, corporate-owned, mainstream media advises Americans to look at the inflation and food lines in Venezuela, and then repeat to themselves clichés they heard in elementary school about how "Communism just doesn't work."

In reality, millions of Venezuelans have seen their living conditions vastly improved through the Bolivarian process. The problems plaguing the Venezuelan economy are not due to some inherent fault in socialism, but to artificially low oil prices and sabotage by forces hostile to the revolution.

Starting in 2014, the Kingdom of Saudi Arabia flooded the market with cheap oil. This is not a mere business decision, but a calculated move coordinated with U.S. and Israeli foreign policy goals. Despite not just losing money, but even falling deep into debt, the Saudi monarchy continues to expand its oil production apparatus. The result has been driving the price of oil down from $110 per barrel, to $28 in the early months of this year. The goal is to weaken these opponents of Wall Street, London, and Tel Aviv, whose economies are centered around oil and natural gas exports.

And Venezuela is one of those countries. Saudi efforts to drive down oil prices have drastically reduced Venezuela's state budget and led to enormous consequences for the Venezuelan economy.

At the same time, private food processing and importing corporations have launched a coordinated campaign of sabotage. This, coupled with the weakening of a vitally important state sector of the economy, has resulted in inflation and food shortages. The artificially low oil prices have left the Venezuelan state cash-starved, prompting a crisis in the funding of the social programs that were key to strengthening the United Socialist Party.

Corruption is a big problem in Venezuela and many third-world countries. This was true prior to the Bolivarian process, as well as after Hugo Chavez launched his massive economic reforms. In situations of extreme poverty, people learn to take care of each other. People who work in government are almost expected to use their position to take care of their friends and family. Corruption is a big problem under any system, but it is much easier to tolerate in conditions of greater abundance. The problem has been magnified in Venezuela due to the drop in state revenue caused by the low oil prices and sabotage from food importers.

The Bolivarian experience in Venezuela

Americans have been trained by decades of Cold War propaganda to look for any confirmation that "socialism means poverty." A quick, simplistic portrait of the problems currently facing Venezuela, coupled with the fact that President Nicolas Maduro describes himself as a Marxist, can certainly give them such a confirmation. However, the actual, undisputed history of socialist construction around the world, including recent decades in Venezuela, tells a completely different story.

Hugo Chavez was elected president of Venezuela in 1999. His election was viewed as a referendum on the extreme free market policies enacted in Venezuela during the 1990s. In December, when I walked through the neighborhoods of central Caracas, Venezuelans spoke of these times with horror.

Venezuelans told of how the privatizations mandated by the International Monetary Fund made life in Venezuela almost unlivable during the 1990s. Garbage wouldn't be collected. Electricity would go off for weeks. Haido Ortega, a member of a local governing body in Venezuela, said: "Under previous governments we had to burn tires and go on strike just to get electricity, have the streets fixed, or get any investment."

Chavez took office on a platform advocating a path between capitalism and socialism. He restructured the government-owned oil company so that the profits would go into the Venezuelan state, not the pockets of Wall Street corporations. With the proceeds of Venezuela's oil exports, Chavez funded a huge apparatus of social programs.

After defeating an attempted coup against him in 2002, Chavez announced the goal of bringing Venezuela toward "21st Century Socialism." Chavez quoted Marx and Lenin in his many TV addresses to the country, and mobilized the country around the goal of creating a prosperous, non-capitalist society.

In 1998, Venezuela had only 12 public universities, today it has 32. Cuban doctors were brought to Venezuela to provide free health care in community clinics. The government provides cooking and heating gas to low-income neighborhoods, and it's launched a literacy campaign for uneducated adults.

During the George W. Bush administration, oil prices were the highest they had ever been. The destruction of Iraq, sanctions on Iran and Russia, strikes and turmoil in Nigeria — these events created a shortage on the international markets, driving prices up.

Big oil revenues enabled Chavez and the United Socialist Party to bring millions of Venezuelans out of poverty. Between 1995 and 2009, poverty and unemployment in Venezuela were both cut in half.

After the death of Chavez, Nicolas Maduro has continued the Bolivarian program. "Housing Missions" have been built across the country, providing low-income families in Venezuela with places to live. The Venezuelan government reports that over 1 million modern apartment buildings had been constructed by the end of 2015.

The problems currently facing Venezuela started in 2014. The already growing abundance of oil due to hydraulic fracturing, or fracking, was compounded by Saudi Arabia flooding the markets with cheap oil. The result: massive price drops. Despite facing a domestic fiscal crisis, Saudi Arabia continues to expand its oil production apparatus.

The price of oil remains low, as negotiations among OPEC states are taking place in the hopes that prices can be driven back up. While American media insists the low oil prices are just the natural cycle of the market at work, it's rather convenient for U.S. foreign policy. Russia, Venezuela, Ecuador, and the Islamic Republic of Iran all have economies centered around state-owned oil companies and oil exports, and each of these countries has suffered the sting of low oil prices.

The leftist president of Brazil, Dilma Rousseff, has already been deposed due to scandal surrounding Petrobras, the state-owned oil company which is experiencing economic problems due to the falling price of oil. Although much of Brazil's oil is for domestic consumption, it has been revealed that those who deposed her coordinated with the CIA and other forces in Washington and Wall Street, utilizing the economic fallout of low oil prices to bring down the Brazilian president.

The son of President Ronald Reagan has argued that Obama is intentionally driving down oil prices not just to weaken the Venezuelan economy, but also to tamper the influence of Russia and Iran. Writing for *Townhall* in 2014, Michael Reagan bragged that his father did the same thing to hurt the Soviet Union during the 1980s:

> *"Since selling oil was the source of the Kremlin's wealth, my father got the Saudis to flood the market with cheap oil.*

Lower oil prices devalued the ruble, causing the USSR to go bankrupt, which led to perestroika and Mikhail Gorbachev and the collapse of the Soviet Empire."

The history of socialist construction

Prior to the 1917 revolution, Russia was a primitive, agrarian country. By 1936, after the completion of the Five-Year Plan, it was a world industrial power, surpassing every other country on the globe in terms of steel and tractor production. The barren Soviet countryside was lit up with electricity. The children of illiterate peasants across the Soviet Union grew up to be the scientists and engineers who first conquered outer space. The planned economy of the Soviet Union drastically improved the living standards of millions of people, bringing them running water, modern housing, guaranteed employment, and free education.

There is no contradiction between central planning and economic growth. In 1949, China had no steel industry. Today, more than half of all the world's steel is produced in China's government-controlled steel industry.

Cuba has wiped out illiteracy, and Cubans enjoy one of the highest life expectancies in Latin America.

When the Marxist-Leninist governments of Eastern Europe collapsed in the early 1990s, economists like Jeffrey Sachs of Columbia University, who can be counted among capitalism's "true believers," predicted rapid economic growth. Since the 1990s, conditions in what George W. Bush called the "New Europe" have become far worse than under socialism. The life expectancy has decreased and infant mortality has risen.

Human and drug traffickers have set up shop. In endless polls, the people of Eastern Europe repeatedly say life was better before the defeat of Communism.

Russia's recovery from the disaster of the 1990s has come about with the reorientation of the economy to one centered around public control of its oil and natural gas resources — much like Venezuela. The Putin government has also waged a crackdown on the small number of "oligarchs" who became wealthy after the demise of the Soviet Union. Once strong state to control the economy was re-established, Russia's gross domestic product increased by 70 percent during the first eight years of Putin's administration. From 2000 to 2008, poverty was cut in half, and incomes doubled.

Neoliberal capitalism has failed

It is only because these facts are simply off-limits in the American media and its discussions of socialism and capitalism that the distorted narrative about Venezuela's current hardships are believed.

American media has perpetuated a cold-war induced false narrative on the nature of socialism.

When discussing the merits of capitalism and socialism, American media usually restricts the conversation to pointing out that socialist countries in the third world have lower living standards than the United States, a country widely identified with capitalism. Without any context or fair comparison, this alone is supposed to prove the inherent superiority of U.S.-style capitalism.

If the kind of neoliberal "free trade" advocated by U.S.

corporations was the solution to global poverty, Mexico, a country long ago penetrated with the North American Free Trade Agreement, would be a shining example of development, not a mess of drug cartels and poverty. The same can be said for oil-rich countries like Nigeria, where exports are massive but the population remains in dire conditions.

The governments of Bangladesh, Honduras, Guatemala, Indonesia, and the Philippines have done everything they can to deregulate the market and accommodate Western "investment." Despite the promises of neoliberal theoreticians, their populations have not seen their lives substantially improve.

If one compares the more market-oriented economy of the U.S., not to countries in the global south attempting to develop with a planned economy, but to other Western countries with more social-democratic governments, the inferiority of the "free market" can also be revealed.

The U.S. is rated 43 in the world in terms of life expectancy, according to the CIA World Factbook. People live longer in Germany, Britain, Spain, France, Sweden, Australia, Italy, Iceland — basically, almost every other Western country. Statistics on the rate of infant mortality say approximately the same thing. National health care services along with greater job security and economic protections render much healthier populations.

Even as the social-democratic welfare states of Europe drift closer to the U.S. economic model with "austerity cuts," the U.S. still lags behind them in terms of basic societal health. Western European countries with powerful unions, strong socialist and labor parties, and less punitive criminal justice systems tend to have healthier societies.

The American perception that socialism or government intervention automatically create poverty, while a *laissez faire* approach unleashes limitless prosperity, is simply incorrect. Despite the current hardships, this reality is reflected in the last two decades of Venezuela's history.

A punishment vote, not a vote for capitalism

The artificially low oil prices have left the Venezuelan state cash-starved, prompting a crisis in the funding of the social programs that were key to strengthening the United Socialist Party.

It is odd that the mainstream press blames "socialism" for the food problems in Venezuela, when the food distributors remain in the hands of private corporations. As Venezuelan political analyst Jesus Silva told me recently: "Most food in Venezuela is imported by private companies, they ask for dollars subsidized by the government oil sales to do that; they rarely produce anything or invest their own money."

According to Silva, the economic sanctions imposed on Venezuela by the U.S., in addition to the oil crisis, have made it more difficult for the Venezuelan government to pay the private food importing companies in U.S. dollars. In response, the food companies are "running general sabotage."

"Venezuela's economy depends on oil sales. Now that oil prices are dropping down, the challenge is to get other sources of economic income," he explained. "Meanwhile, the opposition is garnering electoral support due to the current economic crisis."

303

When the United Socialist Party and its aligned Patriotic Pole lost control of Parliament in December, many predicted the imminent collapse of the Bolivarian government. However, months have passed and this clearly has not taken place.

While a clear majority cast a *voto castigo* ("punishment vote") in December, punishing the government for mismanaging the crisis, the Maduro administration has a solid core of socialist activists who remain loyal to the Bolivarian project. Across Venezuela, communes have been established. Leftist activists live together and work in cooperatives. Many of them are armed and organized in "Bolivarian Militias" to defend the revolution.

Even some of the loudest critics of the Venezuelan government admit that it has greatly improved the situation in the country, despite the current hardships.

In December, I spoke to Glen Martinez, a radio host in Caracas who voted for the opposition. He dismissed the notion that free market capitalism would ever return to Venezuela. As he explained, most of the people who voted against the United Socialist Party — himself included — are frustrated with the way the current crisis is being handled, but do not want a return to the neoliberal economic model of the 1999s.

He said the economic reforms established during the Chavez administration would never be reversed. "We are not the same people we were before 1999," Martinez insisted.

The United Socialist Party is currently engaging in a massive re-orientation, hoping to sharpen its response to economic sabotage and strengthen the socialist direction of the revolution. There is also talk of massive reform in the way the government operates, in order to prevent the extreme examples of corruption and mismanagement that are causing frustration among the population.

The climate is being intensified by a number of recent political assassinations. Tensions continue to exist on Venezuela's border with the U.S.-aligned government of Colombia. The solid base of socialist activists is not going to let revolution be overturned, and tensions continue to rise. The Maduro and the United Socialist Party's main task is to hold Venezuela together, and not let the country escalate into a state of civil war.

Originally published in Mint Press News

VIET NAM'S ECONOMIC MIRACLE HAUNTS
US-KOREA TALKS

.

While free market countries across the developing world remain deeply impoverished, China and Viet Nam have both seen impressive increases in living standards during the past several decades. Public voices in the western world give all credit for this to "liberalization," but a recognition of other key factors seems to underlie US sluggishness in Korean Nuclear talks.

Economic discourse in the United States seems to take place almost exclusively in neoliberal terms. It is assumed that free competition and market solutions always render the best results, and state central planning has proved to be nothing but a total failure. Even among the emerging democratic socialist current in the United States, there have been no calls for state control of production. Supporters of Bernie Sanders and Alexandria Ocasio-Cortez simply call for a bigger welfare state and heavier taxes on the rich. Their respective platforms do not contain a single call for the nationalization of any industry or resource. Any advocate of the Marxist definition of socialism is simply told "Look at Venezuela" or "Look at the Soviet Union" for `proof` that free markets are the only solution for creating growth.

However, an article published in September of 2018 from the World Economic Forum gushes with praise for the economic successes of Viet Nam. The article asks: "A mere 30 years ago, the country was one of the poorest in the world. How did this southeast Asian nation grow to become a middle-income country?"

The analysis of the text gives most credit to liberalization and market reforms, but also admits some other key factors: "Viet Nam has invested heavily in human and physical capital, predominantly through public investments... Viet Nam invested a lot in its human capital and infrastructure. Facing a rapidly growing population – it stands at 95 million today, half of whom are under 35, and up from 60 million in 1986 – Vietnam made large public investments in primary education. This was necessary, as a growing population also means a growing need for jobs. But Vietnam also invested heavily in infrastructure, ensuring cheap mass access to the internet. The Fourth Industrial Revolution is knocking on Southeast Asia's door, and having a sound IT infrastructure in place is essential preparation. Those investments paid off."

As much as the article tries to give credit to free markets, the fact remains that Vietnam is a socialist country. The country is led by the Communist Party, and despite the huge market sector, the state ultimately controls and plans the economy. Like China, Vietnam has 5 five-year plans, and the private corporations exist at the behest of the government.

Viet Nam is not like Bangladesh, Malaysia, Indonesia, Haiti, Guatemala, Honduras, or Nigeria. In these countries, the western corporations have been given almost completely free reign. Instead, Viet Nam has followed China's strategy of utilizing foreign investment and a market sector to strengthen socialism. As a result, Vietnam enjoys a GDP growth rate of roughly 6-7%, rivaling China's.

NEOLIBERALISM HAS FAILED, MARKET SOCIALISM WORKS

Viet Nam's recent successes fit in with an overall pattern during the post-Cold War years. During the 1980s, the Soviet economic model of almost total state control suffered from stagnation. The Communist Bloc was effectively cut out of the computer revolution and, within the state-run apparatus, many intellectuals, engineers, technicians, and innovative people felt stifled. The revolutionary enthusiasm that had enabled Stalin to mobilize the Soviet people during the 1930s and the patriotic zeal that allowed miracles in post-war construction across Eastern Europe, had worn off. Underlying the Marxist-Leninist rhetoric of Warsaw Pact governments was a kind of cynicism and frustration that was widespread among the population.

The toppling of socialism in Poland, Czechoslovakia, East Germany, Romania, Albania, and eventually the Soviet Union was a political defeat, not an economic one. Despite stagnation, the countries maintained a decent living standard and functional economy. The much-heralded "collapse of communism" was ultimately a seizure of power by pro-western forces within the respective governments, spurned by the alienation and frustration of the intellectual strata. George Soros and western intelligence agencies effectively manipulated these factors for their own geopolitical ends.

In eastern Europe, capitalism, not socialism, brought about an economic collapse. As free market policies swept the region, the results were utterly catastrophic. Governments sold off state enterprises and let Wall Street and London set up shop. The result was mass unemployment; mass starvation accompanied a drastic rise in crimes such as the drug trade and human trafficking. However, amid the failure, the World Bank and the International Monetary Fund thundered that "free markets" and neoliberalism were the only way forward. Milton Friedman and Jeffrey Sachs became the respected voices, and their policies of deregulation and economic plunder expanded far beyond the former Eastern Bloc. In

South and Central America, and in Africa, the promises of free market capitalism creating prosperity and abundance never materialized.

Russia's recovery for these years of disaster came about as a result of a sudden break with neoliberal economics. Russia was able to restore its economic power by nationalizing oil and gas. Gazprom and Rosneft, two national champions, became the basis of the state apparatus reasserting its control over the Russian market under the Putin administration. The process was slow and complex and involved many long negotiations. Many of the newly rich Russian oligarchs fled the country, seeing that playtime was over, and the state would no longer allow them to enrich themselves at the country's expense.

While countries across the developing world became impoverished under neoliberal policy, China continued to see extensive growth. Why? Because in China, the market was controlled. The private sector that expanded in China during the 1980s and 90s was closely controlled by the party, and forced to operate in accordance with its central plans and vision.

The Fears About Korea

The World Economic Forum article praises Viet Nam's achievements, speculating that it could continue to see growth:

"Both domestic and international retailers are eyeing rapid expansion in the country, as more and more people gain the purchasing power to consume goods and services. It may mean that one day, instead of the hustle and bustle of small

*shops and scooters, Viet Nam will be characterized by large
malls and cars. But for now, Viet Nam is growing, at its own
pace, and in its own way."*

And while such conversations are hidden from public
discourse, as the Korea talks seem to stall, and strange attacks
against the North Korean embassy in Spain have taken place,
a debate is happening behind the scenes. The more strategic
voices within the US government do not agree with Jim
Roger's view that North Korea is a huge economic boom
waiting to happen.

There is a real fear on the part of the more long-term
thinking circles within the American power structure, because
the facts speak for themselves:

In the 1980s, free market advocates predicted that
the "reform and opening up" would lead to the Chinese
Communist Party's downfall. In fact, the opposite has
happened. The Chinese Communist Party and its "Socialism
with Chinese Characteristics" are stronger and more popular
than ever.

The "socialist-oriented market economy" has not led
to the toppling of the Communist Party of Vietnam or the
restoration of capitalism, either. It has led to the opposite.
The Communist Party is stronger and more popular than ever
because it has delivered effective results; reducing poverty
and improving living standards.

The Workers' Party of Korea has studied these trends and
would like to maneuver toward carrying out similar reforms.
Western leaders, who greatly fear socialism and anti-
imperialism, see this as a real danger.

The fact is that while the Soviet model of the 1980s needed to be updated, this form of socialism was not collapsing economically. The post-Cold War years have demonstrated that neoliberalism has failed to deliver growth and prosperity, and socialism, specifically a market-oriented version, works quite well. As much as their ideology states otherwise, western leaders know this on some level, and fear what it could mean for the future of geopolitics.

Originally published in New Eastern Outlook

Brzezisnki & Kissinger in Southeast Asia

The Socialist Republic of Vietnam is set to host a US aircraft carrier from the pacific fleet. The USS Carl Vinson will be docked in Vietnam, and this will send a clear message of hostility from Vietnam to the People's Republic of China.

The South China Sea has been a point of contention in recent years, as China works to secure the route of oil tankers and other importing vessels destined for Shanghai and other Chinese ports. The USA seeks to maintain its ability to stop China's oil supply at any time with a heavy military presence in the pacific. China has escalated its military presence in the South China Sea, looking to make sure that no matter what happens in international relations, the huge apparatus of production on the Chinese mainland cannot be shut down by a US blockade. A Chinese corporation is currently working to construct a canal through Nicaragua, so that imports to China crossing into the Pacific can never be compromised.

While Donald Trump cancelled the Trans Pacific Partnership, and promised a divergence away from the Obama-era strategies, he has continued courting Vietnam as an ally against China.

In the early months of his administration, the Trump White House promoted dissidents and religious activists who sought to overthrow the Communist Party of Vietnam. Trump seemed to be reassuring the anti-Communist Vietnamese exile community that he would not continue Obama's overtures toward Hanoi. However, Trump has not reinstated the arms embargo against Vietnam which was lifted in 2016, and the docking of the USS Carl Vinson will be the largest US military presence in the Southeast Asian country since the "Fall of Saigon" in 1975.

Dividing Countries, Manipulating Leftists

The strategy of playing China and Vietnam against each other did not begin with Barack Obama, but goes as far back as the Nixon administration. In the aftermath of the Sino-Soviet split, China attempted to present itself as a bastion of third world anti-colonial revolution. China escalated its support for the Vietnamese National Liberation Front, accusing the Soviet leadership of being "revisionists" and "betrayers of people's war."

But as China's Cultural Revolution escalated, and the Gang of Four of ascended following the fall of Lin Biao, China's tensions with the Soviet Union took on a different character. China began to speak of the Soviet Union as "Social-Imperialists" and "the main danger" to the world. The "Theory of Three Worlds" laid the ideological basis for Mao Zedong to welcome Richard Nixon to Beijing, and establish diplomatic relations with Washington. Henry Kissinger, advisor to Richard Nixon, is widely credited with the strategy of recruiting China as an ally against the Soviet Union in the Cold War.

The withdrawal of the USA from Vietnam after Nixon's "secret plan" of mass bombing failed, was viewed as a humiliating defeat for the United States. The Pentagon strategy of "peace through strength" fell out of favor in Washington, and those who advocated covert action and the funding of proxies had the upper hand in foreign policy strategy.

President Jimmy Carter called himself a student of CIA strategist Zbiegnew Brzezinski. The Carter administration talked a language of detente and non-interventionism to the world, while the USA escalated its covert operations in Latin America and Central and Southeast Asia under the surface.

While Kissinger's strategy for normalization of relations between the USA and China on the basis of opposing the Soviet Union laid the basis for the divisions, the Kampuchea War, in which thousands of Vietnamese, Cambodian, and Chinese people lost their lives, came about by utilizing the strategies of Brzezinski.

USA covertly supported Pol Pot wing of the Communist movement in Cambodia, which slaughtered the Marxist-Leninists and put forward a bizarre ideology of "Agrarian Socialism." Pol Pot was nominally a Communist, but he opposed industrial development. Pol Pot's regime persecuted intellectuals, evacuated the urban centers, and abolished all currency, arguing that Cambodia could remain "pure" in its communist ideals by remaining a deeply impoverished, agricultural military state. The world communist movement widely condemned Pol Pot as ultra-left and semi-anarchist. His government of "Democratic Kampuchea" rejected the notion of historical progress and development, which is central to Marxism. Not surprisingly, it also condemned Vietnam for its alliance with the Soviet Union, echoing the position that the USSR was a bastion of "Soviet Social Imperialism."

This was the same strategy that Brzezinski had implemented in Eastern Europe. In Czechoslovakia, Hungary, and many other parts of the Eastern Bloc, Brzezinski had mastered the art of manipulating youth and intellectuals. Most of the young people who received covert support from US intelligence as they destabilized Marxist-Leninist governments did not advocate capitalism, but articulated some brand of middle class leftism. The Prague Spring of 1968, the Hungarian Revolt of the 1956, and many other anti-communist uprisings fomented by the CIA involved young people who believed they were "anarchists," "Trotskyists," "syndicalists" or "democratic socialists." These young people, often from intellectual strata, with grievances against their government were effectively manipulated to serve the west. The ultra-leftist rhetoric served as a cover, as Washington manipulated them as pawns against the Soviet Union and its allied Marxist-Leninist states.

Pol Pot was a wealthy Cambodian intellectual who had studied in France. He considered Soviet society to be overly rigid and authoritarian, and wanted to implement a more utopian and anti-industrial leftist vision in his home country. Whether he was aware of it or not, much like the idealists in European color revolutions, the US Central Intelligence Agency aided him in implementing his ultra-leftist, anti-communist potpourri. The Khmer Rouge served as a counter gang of sorts, preaching Communist sounding rhetoric as they rallied people in Cambodia to fight against Vietnam and the Soviet Union.

Disagreements in Hanoi

While the US backed government in south Vietnam collapsed in 1975, Vietnam was unable to begin the process of peaceful socialist construction until 1980. War with China and Pol Pot's "Democratic Kampuchea," covertly supported by the United States, kept the country in a state of war for another half decade. Since peace was established in 1980, the Vietnamese Communist Party has made huge achievements in raising the life expectancy and increasing the standard of living for the population. The official position of the Vietnamese Communist Party is that they have not fully achieved the construction of modern socialism like China, Cuba, and other countries, but that they are diligently working toward that end, utilizing foreign investment in the process.

While Washington's strategy in the late 1970s was to support China and Pol Pot against Vietnam, which was a soviet aligned country at the time, in the present time, when China has ascended to the role of a global superpower, the strategy has flipped. Now US leaders court Hanoi, hoping to maneuver it toward becoming a satellite against Beijing. The hope is that Vietnam can become a mechanism in the operation of preventing China from securing the South China Sea, and maintaining the potential US "oil veto" over Chinese industry.

While there is a long history of war and hatred between the people of China and Vietnam that goes back centuries, the people of Vietnam and the people of China are now both led by Marxist-Leninist Parties. Both countries have overturned capitalism, are constructing state controlled planned economies, utilizing market mechanisms.

While Vietnam continues to respond in-kind to Washington's overtures, there are clear disagreements about this within the Communist Party. The fall of Nguyen Tan Dung, the most anti-Chinese voice within the party, seems to indicate that anti-Chinese sentiment is not universal. The Vietnamese Communist Party seems to be clashing internally when it comes to many issues, including economic policy, as well as foreign relations.

While Vietnam's path forward is unclear, Washington's strategy is very clear. The hope is that Vietnam and China, despite being led by ideologically similar parties, and having the same goal of eliminating poverty and raising the standard of living with socialist planned economies, can be turned against each other. "Divide and Conquer," the catch phrase of conquerers in ancient Rome, remains applicable in 2018, as Wall Street and London seek to keep their grip on the world.

Originally published in New Eastern Outlook

11 MILLION REASONS FOR WALL STREET AND LONDON TO HATE RUSSIA

Why does the US media have an anti-Russian fixation? It's not what the American people want to hear. 71% of the Ronald Reagan-loving, military-obsessed Republican Party approve of Trump meeting with Putin. On the other side, top liberal CNN commentator and former President Obama's adviser, Van Jones has admitted in a video recording that the "Russiagate" story is a "big nothing burger" which Democrats are not interested in. The Russia-fixated, Hillary Clinton-DNC liberal establishment now faces an upsurge of opposition from Democratic Socialists like Alexandria Ocasio-Cortez and Bernie Sanders, who emphasize the need for populist economics reforms.

Conservatives don't want to hear it. Liberals don't want to hear it. Hating Russia is just not a bandwagon the U.S. public is ready to jump on. Yet, if one turns on American television, in the aftermath of the summit in Helsinki, the rhetoric and accusations against the government of the Russian Federation are almost endless.

Like Trump, Obama was also unable to resolve the tensions now being described as the "New Cold War." Let's not forget that Obama was elected saying he would "talk to Putin". In the early years of Obama's first term, he said he intended to "reset" relations with the Eurasian superpower, and was attacked for it by the Tea Party. The American people favor better relations with Russia, and politicians win votes for promising it, yet the dangerous trajectory continues. Why?

A New Day in the Energy Markets

One answer can be found in the field of economics. On July 18th, crude oil production in the United States reached 11 million barrels per day. This is the highest it has ever been. The drilling and fracking rigs are pulling more oil out of the ground and shale than ever before in U.S. history.

The longtime liberal aspiration for "Energy Independence" has been achieved. The U.S. is no longer dependent on overseas oil. A new OPEC boycott wouldn't be anything like the catastrophe of 1973. The longtime oil export ban has been lifted, and crude pulled from US shale and soil is now being shipped off to China and other countries.

Meanwhile, the spell of low oil prices that began in 2014 is long over. Oil prices are climbing high, having reached over $80 per barrel in May, and remaining around $70 since then. With high prices, oil companies are raking in profits.

But, amid the energy boom, another entity is also getting stronger. The world's largest publicly traded oil company is not Chevron, BP, Exxon-Mobil, or Shell. The largest publicly traded petroleum corporation is called Rosneft. It is a government owned super corporation in Russia.

Rosneft, alongside Gazprom, are the two "National Champions" that Vladimir Putin wrote about as a university student. In 1997, as a graduate student, Vladimir Putin published his dissertation *Strategic Planning of the Reproduction of the Resource Base*. In it, he laid out how Russia, which was reeling in poverty and massive internal turmoil after the fall of the Soviet Union, could restore its strength. Putin argued that two gigantic government

319

corporations could harness Russia's natural resources and make the country once again economically powerful.

Russia: A Competitor with Wall Street Monopolists

Putin's academic work has manifested itself in reality. As President, Putin proceeded to utilize government power and reorient the economy around two super-corporations. As oil prices shot through the roof during the invasion of Iraq and its aftermath, Russia's government raked in new revenue. The oil and gas money rebooted industrial production. Poverty was drastically reduced, and wages multiplied. The massive crisis of the 1990s was resolved by economic planning. Russia is now an energy giant, selling on the global market in competition with Wall Street and London.

As record amounts of crude oil is churned out of the United States, the Trump White House talks of "Energy Dominance." The USA is also the top producer of natural gas, which is also due to the invention and widespread use of hydraulic fracking.

All of this oil and gas is worthless to the western oil monopolists, unless they can sell it. Every barrel of oil and every ounce of natural gas sold by Russia is a barrel of oil or an ounce of gas not purchased from the Wall Street and London oil banking elite. Russia is a competitor on the global energy markets, selling two of the most vital products in the world economy.

Trump recently lashed out at the Germans for their natural gas deal with Russia. The German public finds the idea of importing natural gas from the United States, on the other side of the planet, to be absurd compared to pumping it in from nearby Russia. The Wall Street energy giant and fracking cowboys naturally disagree, furious that somebody else has captured the German market.

As China's oil and gas consumption rapidly expands, their neighbor to the north is supplying the fuel they need. American oil companies have just recently gotten in on the Chinese market, while Russia has been selling to the government in Beijing for decades.

Relations between the U.S. and Russia were very good when Boris Yeltsin was running the country. Naomi Klein's 2007 book The Shock Doctrine describes the Yeltsin years in detail. From 1991 to 1998, 80% of Russian farms went bankrupt. Russia was forced to start importing food from U.S. agriculture companies. 70,000 factories closed down. 1 in 4 people were living in conditions of extreme poverty, with unemployment often between 20% and 30%.

In the 1990s, as Russians were dying, being sold into sexual slavery, committing suicide and dying of heroin at massive rates, the US government and the Russian government were fast friends. The Clinton administration saw its relationship with Boris Yeltsin, and his relationship with the International Monetary Fund and the World Bank, to be a great achievement.

In the 1990s, Russia was a dependent, impoverished "sphere of influence" for American corporations. Russians were poor, and not producing very much. They were a captive market for Wall Street and London monopolies, having been economically demolished after losing The Cold War. In addition, British hedge fund managers and stock traders tied with HSBC Bank, among them Bill Browder, proceeded to loot the country's natural resources.

But that disaster is long over with. Vladimir Putin leads a Russia that is "back in business." The new Russia is selling oil and gas across the planet. The Russian government has now overseen a mass revival of agriculture, with farms springing up across the country, even in the sparsely populated Far East regions. Russia produces a large amount of the world's titanium, and sits at the center of the Eurasian Economic Union, a bloc dedicated to overseeing similar revivals in other nations.

Now, as 11 million barrels of crude are pulled from American soil and shale each day, and the USA remains the top producer of natural gas, Russia is a barrier to global dominance on the energy markets.

The forces that seek to maintain a global monopoly are not concerned with "election meddling", "collusion", "human rights", "nationalism", or any of the other endless canards flickering across U.S. television. What they can't stand is a solid competitor.

Originally Published in New Eastern Outlook

SMARTPHONE WARS

The arrest of Chinese telecommunications CFO Meng Wanzhou has sent shockwaves through the global markets. The context of the smartphone industry and the new challenges facing big western monopolies from Russia and China is vital background information for anyone who wants to understand these recent, dramatic events.

One of the favorite talking points of defenders of free markets is "capitalism made your iphone." According to the meme, those who believe in socialism or Marxism are presented as total hypocrites if they own a smartphone as only the profit system's rewarding of entrepreneurship could ever produce such a technological creation.

However, a little investigation reveals that the entire premise of the meme is false. The first cellphone was created by Leonid Ivanovich Kupriyanovich, a Moscow-based engineer in 1955 who conducted his research in state-run facilities. Furthermore, the screens of most smartphones are illuminated by Light Emitting Diodes (LED), the first of which was invented in 1927 by Oleg Vladimirovich Losev. Losev was also a Russian who conducted his research in state sponsored facilities.

The computer revolution itself can largely be attributed to the work of Alan Turing and his decoding machine created during the Second World War. This research was done in the context of heavy military control over industry, when Britain was aligned with the Soviet Union against Nazi Germany, hardly a free market situation.

Cell-phones are simply not the product of some objectivist fantasy about a misunderstood "great man" tinkering in his

323

garage unabated and untaxed. Cell phones, LED lights, and the Computer Revolution itself came about as a result of central planning and the overall mobilization of society by the state to reach technological and production goals.

Today, the largest cell phone manufacturer on earth is Huawei Technologies based in the Chinese tech hub of Shenzhen. This huge manufacturer of smartphones that are purchased and celebrated all over the world, is closely tied to the Chinese government and military.

The Chief Financial Officer of Huawei was recently arrested in Canada at the request of US officials. Meng now faces extradition to the United States. Charges have not formally been named, but it is widely speculated that it is related to accusations that Huawei has violated US sanctions against the Islamic Republic of Iran.

Independent Telecom on the Rise

It is perhaps a strange coincidence that just as Huawei's CFO has been arrested, Yandex, the Russian internet corporation has announced that it is producing a smartphone of its own. On December 5th, the world became aware that soon a "Yandex Phone" produced by the government subsidized tech entity will be available for purchase. Yandex has also recently gotten in on the ride hailing and other high tech endeavors.

Even the deeply impoverished nation of Angola, led by the Socialist MPLA, was able to create its own independent cell phone company. Isabel Dos Santos utilized revenue from the state controlled oil corporation, and assistance from the People's Republic of China, to create and expand a corporation called Unitel. Santos pushed for the creation other independent telecommunications apparatus in southern Africa and in Portuguese speaking countries.

Prior to the arrest of Meng Wanzhou, the US FBI urged Americans not to buy Chinese smartphones. The reason given was the corporation's ties to the Chinese government, and fears that information could be compromised.

However, it is widely known thanks to the revelations of Edward Snowden, that the National Security Agency of the United States has a close relationship with many American cellular and tech companies. Google, Facebook, Apple, and other high tech companies have routinely cooperated with federal officials, and the individuals whose information is being subpoenaed or requested from the tech giants is often never informed that their privacy has been violated.

In the context of a rising challenge to the western smartphone monopolies by independent manufacturers around the world, one must find it suspicious that Federal Officials in the USA have suddenly become concerned about the privacy of American citizens, and alleged sanctions violations by China's telecommunications giant.

One must wonder if underneath the hysteria, there is a desperate attempt to preserve a western semi-monopoly on the smartphone market that is quickly slipping away.

Originally published in New Eastern Outlook

WHY DOES CHINA LOVE ELECTRIC CARS?

The numbers speak for themselves. 746,000 New Energy passenger cars were sold in China between January and October. By the end of 2018, all buses and taxis in the vital tech hub city of Shenzen will be electric. The central borough of the city of Dalian is expected to reach this benchmark by 2020. Chinese manufacturers created 358,000 non-fossil fuel buses from 2014 to 2017.

The *Wall Street Journal* quotes Sandra Retzer of the German Agency for International Cooperation as saying that when it comes to electric cars: "China is the only one in the race; it's all Chinese manufacturers."

The push for New Energy Vehicles is at the center of the "Made in China 2025" technology project heralded by Xi Jinping and the Communist Party. From 2009 to 2017 the Chinese government spent $48 billion to subsidize electric cars.

Meanwhile, the White House is singing a different song. Lawrence Kudlow of the White House National Economic Council announced on December 3rd that subsidies to US automakers to create electric cars are on the chopping block. He announced "We want to end, we will end those subsidies and others of the Obama administration…" This announcement comes in the aftermath of an agreement between Trump and Xi Jinping to end China's 40% tariff on US made cars.

So, why is it that China is pushing electric cars like mad, while US leaders seem reluctant? So far the only moves by the US government have been weak subsidies to automakers, and even these small moves are on the verge of being rolled back.

The Fossil Fuel Economy: An Economic Prison for Humanity

As a small clique of western financiers emerged to dominate the global economy, oil was essential. John D. Rockefeller's Standard Oil, the descendent of which is the supermajor known as Exxon-Mobil, rides high over the world. Oil was discovered on the Arabian Peninsula in 1938, and soon the British were working to empower the House of Saud with weapons and other support.

The Russian Empire granted access to the oil fields of Azerbaijan to the Rothschild banking dynasty and various Swiss and British oil corporations. Following the Russian Revolution of 1917, British troops were deployed to Azerbaijan to fight the Bolshevik Red Army in a vein attempt retake the oil that had been seized by the new Soviet government.

Wall Street and London have cornered the global oil market. Saudi Arabia, United Arab Emirates, Kuwait, and other despotic vassal states secure their access and control in the Middle East. Nigeria's impoverished, corrupt state apparatus enables unlimited access for BP, Shell, Exxon-Mobil and Chevron. Hydraulic Fracking has made the USA an oil exporting, rather than importing country.

The Russian Revolution of 1917 opened the door for countries to challenge this economic setup. In 1920, the Bolsheviks convened the "Conference of the Peoples of the East" in Baku. Eventually the Soviet Union became aligned with the Patriotic Officers and the Baathist movement in the oil rich Middle East, as well as various socialists and nationalists throughout Africa and Latin America.

As a result of the process that began during the Cold War Russia, Venezuela, Iran and a few other countries have seized control of their oil resources. They now sell oil in competition with the Wall Street, London monopolists and have used the proceeds to build independent economies. These countries battle constant acts of subversion and sabotage, intended to secure the monopoly of western bankers and push them off the market. The independent, oil exporting socialist governments of Iraq and Libya were directly toppled by US-led intervention leading to humanitarian catastrophe, a refugee crisis and a rise in terrorism.

During the administration of George W. Bush, oil prices skyrocketed to above $110 per barrel, some of the highest in history. Then, under the Obama administration in 2014, oil prices dropped to catastrophically low levels, below $27 at one point. These dramatic shifts caused huge problems for people all over the world. In an economy centered on petroleum, developing countries were left at the mercy of the selfish manipulations of western bankers as carried out by their puppets governments and hired vassals.

The Chinese Dream of National Rejuvenation

As the oil banking global financial system emerged, the five thousand year old civilization of China faced unprecedented humiliation. The British waged two Opium Wars, forcing the country to import narcotics and not erect protective tariffs. The Germans, the British, and other western powers lined up with Japan and ravaged China economically, holding back development.

However, the Chinese people fought back. Dr. Sun Yat Sen's Nationalist Movement gave birth to the Chinese Republic, and after Chiang Kai Chek betrayed the ideals of his predecessor, the Chinese Communist Party stepped up to lead the battle to create a new country.

In the battle against western economic domination and domestic backwardness, the Chinese Communist Party received significant support from the Soviet Union, just as the Chinese Nationalist KMT had during the 1920s. In the 1930s the Soviet Union became a world superpower, becoming the top producer of steel, wiping out illiteracy, and bringing running water and electricity to the entire country. It also began extracting and refining its vast oil resources.

When the Chinese Communist Party took power in 1949, it was closely aligned with the Soviet Union. The first steel mills and a number of power plants in China were constructed with Soviet assistance. The first 11 years of the People's Republic of China involved a deep level of friendship and cooperation with Russia.

After 1961, China no longer received Soviet support but continued to work toward industrializing. China began constructing the massive China Pakistan Friendship Highway in 1966. This is the most elevated roadway in the world and it has laid the basis for the China Pakistan Economic Corridor (CPEC) rapidly emerging in 2018.

One of China's weaknesses is that it has very little domestic oil resources. As the Chinese Communist Party has taken the country down the road of modernization and industrialization, dependence on foreign oil and natural gas has increased.

China imports oil from many different countries, but the oil market remains a sphere dominated by Wall Street and London bankers, enabling them to rule over developing countries. Because much of China's oil is imported by sea, it has become vitally important for China to maintain security in the South China Sea. Tensions between the US military and the Chinese military in this maritime region have increased during recent years.

China has also pushed to build an alternative to the US controlled Panama Canal. China is currently working with the socialist government of Nicaragua on a $40 billion project to construct an alternative route for trade vessels.

Learning From The Fall of Rome

The fossil fuel economy is essential to Wall Street and London's domination of the world economy. For this reason, they see technological progress as dangerous. Meanwhile, many countries around the world, including countries like Iran and Russia that are very dependent on fossil fuels themselves, have joined with China's efforts to push for a way out of the oil based global order.

Kaivan Karimi, a high-ranking executive at Blackberry, recently spoke up about how China isn't only leading the world in New Energy Vehicles, but also in the exciting potential for driverless ones. Karimi is quoted as saying: "When autonomous driving takes off, I believe China will be the leader, just by the fact that you will have the infrastructure in place, which means you will be producing and actually putting cars on the road versus everybody else, who will still be trying because the infrastructure is not in place."

Many attribute the fall of the Roman Empire to its refusal to embrace technological progress. Rather than developing new farming techniques and methods of producing tools and goods, the Romans oversaw the gradual decline of their agricultural output. As their own ability to produce decreased, the Romans simply made up the difference by conquering other people and plundering their crops and resources.

The Roman Empire fell because it stopped trying to advance productive forces. It entered an arrangement with the world, where its rule depended on holding back social progress and beating down other nations and peoples.

China, on the other hand, has rapidly transformed itself and restored its position as a global superpower with the opposite approach. The Chinese Communist Party is guided by Marxism and historical materialism and sees human progress as essential. Furthermore, in 1978 China launched its reform and opening up, and openly repudiated the ultra-leftist clique known as the Gang of Four, who distorted Marxism and worshipped poverty.

History is marching forward, and China intends to march forward with it. The question remains, however, will the United States continue to try and hold back an outmoded economic setup? While Wall Street and London bankers are certainly making super-profits, the people of America, like the ancient Romans, are seeing their standard of living and productive capacity decreased. Will they be able to force their government to change its priorities? Only time will tell.

Originally published in New Eastern Outlook

PART FIVE:
THE BROKEN POLITICAL COMPASS

CHAOS FROM ABOVE & THE CRISIS OF GEOPOLITICS

The traditional aesthetics of left and right are lost in
the unfolding confusion of the 21st century. Wall Street
bankers, the most powerful entities on the London Stock
Exchange, the Silicon Valley elites, speaking to us through
CNN, Facebook, Twitter, and every high tech mechanism for
molding opinion, are screaming "revolution!"

The Arab Spring seemed to be the opening explosion, and
the fallout from that geopolitical disaster continues. Libya
went from being the African country with the highest life
expectancy and most prosperous economy to its present
condition as a failed state, with refugees fleeing and terrorists
setting up shop. Syria has faced over half a decade of civil
war, as western-backed "revolutionaries" who beheaded
children and bombed churches unleashed hellish conditions
in the hopes of toppling a government led by Baathist Arab
Socialists. Western media now cheers for mobs of enraged
students and armed extremists who work to topple the
governments of Nicaragua and Venezuela, decrying the
popular, elected Bolivarian leaders as "dictators."

Powerful voices from the western world are screaming almost in unison: "revolt!" But revolt against what? For what purpose? What is the goal of this highly romantic, but ideologically vague CNN-led revolution? No answer has been provided. It is as if the ghost of Leon Trotsky has shed his socialist aspirations, kept only his fixation on barricades and firing squads, and taken the helm of western geopolitics.

The nightmare playing out before our eyes is very much the consequences of Wall Street and London's new "revolutionary" impulse. Refugees are pouring into western countries. Acts of terrorist violence are becoming far less infrequent. Among CNN's beloved "revolutionaries" in Syria and Libya, an entity called "Islamic State" has emerged, utilizing all the media savvy that Hollywood and Silicon Valley has perfected to sell destruction. In reaction, among the less powerful sectors of the European and American elite, a "new right" of "anti-globalists" and "isolationists" now calls for a retreat from these horrors of the "global community."

During the Cold War, the leaders of NATO countries accused the Soviet Union of "spreading chaos." They invoked memories of the Communist International, and presented the Soviet Union as attempting to conquer the world under the guise of a proletarian revolution. Yet, today, the calls for revolution come from Washington, London, Paris, and Berlin. Those who oppose this call, and champion stability and security are deemed to be "fascists."

The Economic Roots of a Civilization Crisis

Like most things, the roots of these bizarre political manifestations in our time can be found in economics. At

333

the time of the Arab Spring in 2011, the primary issue was mass unemployment; millions of rural jobless people were piling into the urban centers of the Middle East, sleeping in graveyards and rioting for food. But joblessness and underemployment wasn't unique to the region. Jobless young Americans occupied Zuccotti Park in lower Manhattan, after observing jobless Greeks and Spaniards occupying their universities and town squares months before.

The computer revolution has forced the human race to remember the prophecies of Karl Marx. While Marx's call for a glorious international worker's revolution may have been disappointed his more scientific predictions about the fundamental workings of the profit-centered economy are ringing truer than ever.

Marx's close collaborator, Frederich Engels explained his comrade's basic, non-moralist critique of capitalism this way:

"We have seen that the ever-increasing perfectibility of modern machinery is, by the anarchy of social production, turned into a compulsory law that forces the individual industrial capitalist always to improve his machinery, always to increase its productive force....

"The extension of the markets cannot keep pace with the extension of production. The collision becomes inevitable, and as this cannot produce any real solution so long as it does not break in pieces the capitalist mode of production, the collisions become periodic..."

"Commerce is at a stand-still, the markets are glutted, products accumulate, as multitudinous as they are unsaleable, hard cash disappears, credit vanishes, factories

are closed, the mass of the workers are in want of the means
of subsistence, because they have produced too much of the
means of subsistence; bankruptcy follows upon bankruptcy,
execution upon execution. The stagnation lasts for years;
productive forces and products are wasted and destroyed
wholesale, until the accumulated mass of commodities finally
filter off, more or less depreciated in value, until production
and exchange gradually begin to move again."

Little by little, the pace quickens. It becomes a trot. The
industrial trot breaks into a canter, the canter in turn grows
into the headlong gallop of a perfect steeplechase of industry,
commercial credit, and speculation, which finally, after
breakneck leaps, ends where it began — in the ditch of a
crisis."

This is the crisis of the 21st century. As 3-D printers
churn out products that once required hundreds of industrial
workers to produce, as fast food workers sweat on hamburger
assembly lines with the 'short order cook' as a distant
memory, as fracking wells and deep sea drills extract more
oil and gas than ever before, as online retailers close down
shopping centers, as a vast, globalized high tech apparatus
of production rolls onward, seemingly without workers, the
overall standard of living is dropping.

The millions who are left "outcast and starving" cannot
even begin to purchase the huge amount of goods being so
efficiently produced without them. The 2008-2009 financial
crises were rooted in attempts to solve an unsolvable problem
with credit deregulation. The spending power of the global
working class is dropping, while the efficiency of production
has risen higher than ever before.

The strength of western governments during the Cold War came from the "aristocracy of labor" i.e. the working class people of America, Britain, France, Norway, and Sweden, who enjoyed a comfortable lifestyle, high wages, and thus were patriotic and loyal to the "free world" against Marxist opposition.

The construction workers who beat up anti-war activists in the Hard Hat riots of 1970, the "Archie Bunker" base of American militarism, signified a strata of comfortable conservatives that was essential in maintaining order. But this strata is now fading away into nothing, The reality of a low wage, service sector economy and a rising police state is replacing the "white picket fence" American dream of the post-war industrial days.

The Eurasian Alternative

However, elsewhere, a different political and economic model is thriving. If one looks at Iran, Russia, China, Venezuela, Nicaragua and Syria, it is hard to find ideological consistency. These governments are Secular, Atheist, Catholic, Orthodox, and Islamic. They are nationalists, theocrats, Baathists, Communists, and social-democrats.

Yet, in all of these countries the state has taken control of the centers of economic power. Russia re-emerged from the nightmare of the 1990s with an economy centered around Rosneft and Gazprom, two gigantic state-controlled corporations. They were "National Champions" controlled by state central planners, functioning to serve the nation. In Iran, the largest economic entity is the Islamic Revolutionary Guard Corps, controlling major industries and vital resources. China's market reforms have allowed a large, private sector to prosper, but at the end of the day, the party's control over the state-controlled banks and industries dictates production. Bolivarianism, Baathism, and other anti-capitalist theories from the formerly colonized world may be a deviation from the Marxism of Soviet textbooks, but all of the 21st century anti-imperialists are quite clear about who should control the means of production, and why the rule of profits keeps the world chronically poor.

As western capitalism drowns in the high-tech- market-spawned chaos, the societies where the state is strong enough to mobilize the population and control the economy continue to march forward, slowly but surely. The Belt and Road from China, Moscow's Eurasian Economic Union, and other alternative economic structures have made it possible for nations to flourish without the IMF and World Bank.

Neoliberalism has reduced governments to the role of helpless bystanders amid economic catastrophe, but the concept of Statecraft which built civilization, is alive and well across Eurasia. In sections of the globe not gripped by dropping wages alongside endless ipods, or homelessness amidst skyrocketing rent, the government is not keepings its hands off. In the rising alternative, the mantra is not "the government is best which govern least." Rather, the government is deemed best when it delivers the goods, and advances the interest of the population directed by it.

As farms sprout up across Russia's Far East, and the state controlled steel industry of China grinds forward, despite Trump's tariffs, it is clear that the crisis of overproduction does not menace societies in which the economy is not "free to choose." When the state has the power to direct economic activity and manage production, the irrational horrors of starvation amidst plenty can be abetted.

The forces that dominate the crashing and burning global economy are not motivated by ideology. They seek to make profits, and the key to maintaining profits is monopoly. They seek a planet that can function as a captive market, buying and selling only from them.

Holding Back Technological Progress

Oil is central to maintaining this monopolistic power. The Wahabbi Saudi Monarchy and its Arab state vassals, Africa's Niger Delta displaying poverty drenched in black gold, the fracking colonies of North Dakota, and the Gulf of Mexico's deep sea oil rigs, all function as tentacles of the western financial centers. Chase Bank (Exxon-Mobil), HSBC Bank (British Petroleum), all see independent oil and gas producing states like Russia, Venezuela, and Iran as annoying competitors. If they suffered the same fate as Libya and Iraq, profit margins would only expand.

The real danger to the monopolist global order of Wall Street and London oil bankers comes from new technology. China's "New Energy Vehicle" laws made the mineral markets explode with demand. Fusion energy, artificial intelligence, supercomputers, hyperloop trains, all the hope for humanity made possible by the computer revolution, spell the end of those who have cornered the oil market and the economy of the dying old world.

Meanwhile, Silicon Valley attempts to control the information explosion it launched, realizing that sooner or later social media and cybernetics will no longer be under their dominion. Tightening their grip only expedites the process of the new world utilizing new technology against the old world that created it.

So, what is their only hope? Chaos. Revolution. Regime change. Deconstruction. Destruction. Disobedience. Dysfunction. Maintaining underdevelopment.

The only hope for staying on top of the mountain is to reduce the valley to chaos. In our bizarre post-modern civilization crisis, the emperors of a falling Rome are themselves dispatching the barbarians. The forces who once screamed "containment" and "law and order" hoping to hold off the Marxist menace, now unfurl an ideologically cleansed banner of revolution in the hopes of tearing down any possible alternative or rival.

Like the feudal-preservationists who rallied around Robert Malthus, they talk of "reducing the population" to hold off the inevitable. Meanwhile, Hollywood movies churns out repeated psychological rehearsals for the apocalypse.

The only hope for the dying order is that history can be stopped by a wave of chaos and destruction. But history marches forward, regardless, and civilization has not surrendered.

Originally Published at United World International

IMMIGRATION, 'PEASANT CULTURES," & THE NEW RIGHT-WING NATIONALISTS

Global media is abuzz with talk of the "New Nationalism" that is sweeping the western world. US media talks specifically of the "Alt Right." So, why is it that figures like Marine Le Pen, Donald Trump, Steve Bannon and Nigel Farrage on the rise? In a desperate attempt to explain it, some analysts have gone as far as to say that the new political shift is due to some sort of Russian conspiracy. The reason for the revival of right-wing populism and authoritarianism is in fact rooted in a deeper reality currently plaguing western politics.

Two well-known American pundits, Cenk Uygur and Ann Coulter, recently sat down for a debate at a conference called *Politicon* in Los Angeles. The exchange got heated as the two barbed back and forth about a variety of political issues.

Ann Coulter, the right-wing analyst who is also the daughter of the anti-Communist witch-hunter Jack Coulter, did her best to focus the conversation on the issue of immigration, which is part of her recent political makeover. Coulter's career began during the late years of Clinton, and escalated under the Bush administration. The books that defined her career, with titles like *Slander, Treason* and *How to Talk to a Liberal* were neoconservative defenses of aggressive US foreign policy and free market capitalism. In the picture her earlier works painted of the United States, those who faced economic hardship were a bunch of lazy whiners who needed to go out and get a job, while US foreign policy was a benevolent form of international charity in which the Pentagon selflessly liberated people being oppressed by dictators and terrorists.

Coulter has had to re-invent herself in recent years. The base of the Republican Party, the suburban and rural white American working class, are no longer economically prosperous. They are increasingly isolationist in their views and do not approve of continued US meddling around the globe. With her nose to the ground, Coulter has shifted from the neocon narrative, in which America is perfect and dissidents are traitors, and has slowly evolved into a nationalist and right-wing populist along the lines of Britain's Nigel Farrage.

The New Right & The Global Crisis

During the debate, Coulter went on a tirade against immigrants from both the Middle East and Latin America. She said "It's simply a fact: we are bringing in peasant cultures." She cited the fact that many Middle Eastern countries have primitive, medieval style legal systems. She cited the fact that many of the immigrant children from Central America had never seen a flushing toilet before.

The response of Cenk Uygur and his liberal audience was to boo and accuse Coulter of being "racist" and "bigoted." Aside from holding her feet to the fire regarding her statements about nuclear weapons, Uygurs response was not very persuasive, especially to those within Coulter's right-wing fan base. Those who admire Ann Coulter and voted for Donald Trump are impressed with the boldness of those who are "not politically correct" and break taboos of politeness and cultural sensitivity.

The facts that Coulter cited were in many ways accurate. Saudi Arabia, Qatar, Bahrain, Jordan, UAE and Oman do indeed have primitive legal systems. Many impoverished people in Central and South America do not have access to running to water. Criminal gangs plague Latin America, and terrorist and extremist groups like Al-Queda, ISIS or the Muslim Brotherhood have a lot of influence in the Middle East. All of this is true, though Coulter points it out in a rather crass and insensitive way.

The reality is that millions of people throughout the world, not only in Latin America and the Middle East, but also in Southeast Asia, the islands of the pacific, and many other places, simply cannot live in their homelands any longer, and are fleeing in big numbers. The occurrence is widely recognized as a global crisis of mass migration.

The liberals of Cenk Uygur's ilk, and even some of the hard left "socialists" and "communists" celebrate mass migration like it is somehow a good thing. They talk about "the American dream" of "coming to a new land." They shout slogans like "no one is illegal" and "we are all immigrants" with a big smile on their faces. While the political left rightly opposes bigotry and any further repression of immigrant workers, in the process, they ignore a very real humanitarian catastrophe which is shaking the planet. Corpses are discovered on a daily basis on the US border with Mexico. Many migrants have died attempting to cross the Mediterranean to Europe.

It should be no surprise that many working class people in the United States and Europe, who directly observe this inflow of impoverished workers, see a rise in violence, and are increasingly afraid of being killed in terrorist attacks, are rallying behind right-wingers like Trump, Farrage, and Coulter, who at least acknowledge that the problem exists, and claim to offer solutions to it.

Wall Street Oil Bankers & Primitive Regimes

The reason that anti-immigration politicians and activists are often called "racist" is because much of their rhetoric insinuates that those from foreign lands who travel to the west are inherently criminal, dirty, violent or somehow inferior to the westerners. This belief that some peoples are just naturally inferior to others is the textbook definition of racism. Though this kind of blatant racism was widely promoted and accepted by western capitalist powers at one time, it has now become largely unacceptable in public discourse, mainly as a result of the political upheavals which took place the 1960s and 70s.

If one can reject notions of racial supremacy, certain facts must still be addressed surrounding the issue of immigration and cultural diversity.

"Peasant Cultures," the derogatory and disrespectful phrase used by Ann Coulter is not completely off the mark when describing the legal systems of certain parts of the Middle East. Saudi Arabia is certainly a "peasant culture," or more accurately a "Bedouin culture." The ruling elite still live in tents, and Saudi women are not legally permitted to drive cars. People are routinely beheaded and crucified for crimes like "sorcery" or "insulting the King." More than 30% of the population are foreign born "guest workers," who exist essentially as slaves. The setup of Saudi society is indeed barbarism, and many within Saudi Arabia, especially Shia Muslim oil workers who endure the horrors of this backward system on a daily basis, are the first to point this out.

Those who would attempt to dismiss the horrific, repressive nature of Saudi society as merely "a different culture" or a "different way of life" are completely disingenuous and should not be taken seriously. However, Saudi Arabia is not the natural outgrowth of Arab civilization. The borders of the Arab world were drawn in the Sykes-Picot Agreement, a secret treaty among western powers. The House of Saud was selected and propped up by the British empire for geo-strategic reasons.

In the 1940s, the Saudi Royal Family became fast friends of America's financial elite. The Wall Street monopolists of Exxon-Mobil, many major politicians of both the Democratic and Republican Parties, are deeply tied to the Saudi regime. Saudi Arabia sells oil to American oil giants, and purchases a huge number of weapons from Pentagon contractors. Ronald Reagan's administration made clear in 1981 that it would send troops to protect the regime "if there should be anything that resembled an internal revolution in Saudi Arabia."

Like Saudi Arabia, the primitive regimes that repress women, torture, behead, and have absolutist monarchs across the Middle East region, are close allies of the United States government and the financial western monopolists. They sell oil to western corporations, and purchase weapons from US military contractors. Almost all of these regimes, be it Kuwait, Bahrain, or United Arab Emirates; nearly all of these primitive, barbaric monarchies are deeply involved in NATO backed efforts to topple the Syrian government. They also echo in Israeli officials fiery denunciations of the Islamic Republic of Iran as being somehow a threat to world peace.

Targeting the Modernizers, Halting Development

While the most savage and backward autocracies have been propped up by the USA, what regimes are targeted by the Pentagon and NATO? Iraq was led by the Baath Arab

344

Socialist Party. Saddam Hussein was a secular leader, who vastly improved the conditions of women in his country, and also modernized and industrialized Iraq. The US invaded Iraq, destroyed the country's infrastructure, and hung Saddam Hussein. What was once a stable, independent economy that was gradually becoming more modern and civilized, has been reduced to chaos.

The Syrian Arab Republic, currently in the crosshairs of the Pentagon and US funded "regime change" operations, is yet another independent, nationalist government. The Syrian Baathist government has worked with Russia and China to industrialize the country and bring in infrastructure, while at the same time modernizing the society. In Syria, Christians, Alawites, Druze, and Sunnis have lived together in peace for decades. Women in Syria have full constitutional equality. Many Syrian industrial workers are organized into unions that exercise collective bargaining power. Syria, unlike its Wall Street friendly Arab neighbors, is not a "peasant culture" but an impoverished country in a strategic region, led by independent patriotic forces that are desperately trying to modernize and develop.

After the Islamic Revolution of 1979, the leader of the revolution, Ayatollah Khomeni called forth a "construction Jihad." Iranians were mobilized to build highways, airports, and other infrastructure. Unlike all the Emirates, Kingdoms, and US backed oil autocracies, Iran has contested elections in which "hardliners" and "moderates" compete for elected office. In Iran, the majority of those attending public universities are women. University education and healthcare is free to all citizens, and the society is tightly organized with the Basij organizations volunteering and enforcing the revolution on a local level.

US media fixates on portraying Bashar Assad as a dictator. They claim Syria's elections are illegitimate, and that the ruling Baath Arab Socialist Party is corrupt. However, the King of Saudi Arabia makes no pretense of being democratically elected. Neither does the King of Jordan, the King of Bahrain, or those who rule Kuwait, the United Arab Emirates, and other US aligned regimes in the region. Syria does not conduct public floggings or beheading. Syria allows religious diversity.

Criticism of Iran and Syria can most certainly be made, but compared to the autocratic oil monarchies who are aligned with Wall Street and the Pentagon, they are very advanced in terms of human rights, the rule of law, and basic societal health. The Islamic REPUBLIC of Iran and the Syrian Arab REPUBLIC exist as "Republics" in a region full of Kingdoms, Emirates and Sultans who openly behead, torture, and deny basic human rights to their people. Yet it is these independent regimes, republics, with elections and leaders who pursue modernization that are targeted by the western capitalist powers and their allies, who simultaneously prop up and align with the most barbaric "peasant cultures."

Furthermore, while liberals insist on being "politically correct" and just shout "Islamophobe" at anyone who dares say it, in addition to political backwardness, another issue that plagues the Middle East region is terrorism and violent extremism. But why is terrorism so prevalent in the Middle East?

The ideology embraced by ISIS, Al-Queda, Al-Nusra, and almost every other murderous terrorist organization in the Arab world is an extremist distortion of Sunni Islam called "Wahabbism." Wahabbism is the state ideology, not of Iran or Syria, but of Saudi Arabia. Osama Bin Laden, said to be the mastermind behind the 9/11 attacks, comes from one of the most wealthy families in Saudi Arabia. The multi-billionaire Bin Laden family has a state enforced monopoly on construction within the Kingdom, and is extremely well connected. The previously redacted 28 pages of the 9/11 commission report, reveal all kinds of links between the government of Saudi Arabia, and Wahabbi terrorism.

Bahrain, Kuwait, the United Arab Emirates and the Hashemite Kingdom of Jordan are deeply involved in cooperating with Wahabbi terrorists and fanatics, some of whom are linked to Al-Queda, in an effort to topple the Syrian government. The majority of the hijackers who carried the 9/11 attacks were openly identified as being Saudi citizens.

Who Supports The Terrorists & Drug Dealers?

Barbaric, murderous terrorist groups certainly exist in the Arab world. However, these groups are linked to US backed regimes, and have been utilized by western countries to attack the independent states which are desperately trying to modernize. Starting in 1979, the USA spent over a decade funding Wahabbi terrorist groups as they fought to topple the secular People's Democratic Party in Afghanistan. The United States currently cooperates with such organizations in its efforts to topple the Syrian government.

The political left mostly refuses to acknowledge the Wahabbi terrorism is a real problem in the Middle East. It screams about "Islamophobia" and holds parades to "welcome the refugees." It cheers for the "Syrian Revolution" led by Wahabbi terrorists. When the right-wing makes bigoted, ignorant statements about the Arab peoples, or those who practice the Islamic faith, the left's only response is a kind of semantic scolding. They scold the right for breaking taboos and saying certain things, but do not dig into the reality of the region or its history. This shrill tone and lack of any real depth or analysis allows the crass right-wing to create a racist caricature of all Muslims, Persians, and Arabs. The right-wing looks like it is being "bold" by acknowledging what the left refuses to permit any discussion of.The same can be said for Latin America. Guatemala, Honduras, and Mexico are a mess of poverty and criminal violence. Central American countries hold the world's top murder rates. South of the US border, drug cartels and other criminal organizations engage in crimes that are horrifying to any rational person. These thugs and murderers operate near the US border, on both sides, and do horrendous things. Their activities have intensified in recent years, and the areas of the United States near the southern border have not been immune to their violence.

Pointing out this reality is not "racist" as the cowardly, non-ideological left screams at all who point it out. The victims of these monstrous criminals are primarily other people of Central American and Latino backgrounds, and they are the first to denounce these crimes, and point out the crisis. A wave of vigilante anti-drug groups have formed across Mexico to fight the drug cartels.But what is the roots of the drug related violence and chaos in this region? The infamous "School of the Americas" in the US State of Georgia trained many murderous thugs in the art of torture, assassination, and war crimes. Many of the "contras" funded by the United States in Nicaragua, and paramilitary groups propped in Colombia, were directly involved in the drug trade during the 1980s.Even today, the majority of the weapons used by the drug cartels in Mexico originate in the United States. Drug cartels in Mexico have, not only the kind of hunting rifles and hand guns that can be legally purchased in the USA, but also military grade assault rifles and other equipment that was somehow acquired from the US military. The United States trains the Mexican police forces and supplies them with weapons, when they have a reputation for being completely corrupt and bought off by the drug cartels in many areas. Guatemala has endured decades of violence. The roots of this chaos goes back to when the United States supported violent paramilitaries who slaughtered the indigenous peoples throughout the 1970s and 80s.

Honduras elected a socialist President, Manuel Zelaya who wanted to stabilize the country and sought independent economic development. The United States supported the military in toppling him in 2009 with a brutal military coup d'etat. Hillary Clinton discussed her support for the Honduran coup in her book *Hard Choices*. Since the independent socialist President Manuel Zelaya was overthrown, Honduras has been a mess of crime and poverty, and though the recent statistics are quibbled about, it is often listed as "murder capital of the world." The new western right would like to present peoples of Latin-American decent as inherently criminal and inferior. The political left simply screams "racist" at anyone who dares point out the reality of poverty and criminal violence in the region. What is ignored is that the real problem of gang and drug violence in Central and South America is a result of international bankers trying to hold back development and secure a monopoly for themselves. While Mexico, Guatemala, and Honduras are a mess of violence, Nicaragua is a bastion of stability in Central America. The Sandinista government, which is routinely decried as a "dictatorship" in American media, has drastically reduced poverty, provided housing and education to the population. Just like in the Middle East, it is the independent, nationalist governments, like Nicaragua, Venezuela, Bolivia, and Ecuador that are targets of US intervention and destabilization. Like Wahabbi terrorism in the Middle East, the drug related violence and instability in Central and South America is something that has been imposed on Latin America.

The funding of paramilitaries and drug linked criminal organizations was part of US efforts in the 1980s to topple various Marxist governments in the region. While independent nationalist governments like the Sandinistas have tried to develop, build infrastructure, and modernize their countries, it is the west that has unleashed drugs and violence in an effort to hold back development.

Impoverishing, Not Developing The World

Why is it that children from so many countries around the world have never seen a flushing toilet? Is it because they are inherently "dirty" or inferior peoples as Coulter would have us believe? No. It is because Wall Street monopolists and bankers have held back development.

Nigeria is the top oil exporting country on the African continent. The oil rich Niger Delta Region is home to some of the most impoverished peoples on the planet. Photographs show the horrendous and primitive conditions lived in by these people. The ground the beaches they play on are often stained black with oil. Western corporations like British Petroleum and Royal Dutch Shell have made countless billions from the Niger Delta, but the people there live in extreme poverty.

Nigeria, the top oil exporting country in Africa is now facing a massive crisis of malnutrition according to the world food program.

Libya was once the top oil producing country on the African continent. The Islamic Socialist government of Moammar Gaddafi created Africa's most efficient water system. Free University education was provided, and Libyans had a lifestyle that the envy of almost everyone else on the continent. Women in Libya held important roles in local levels of the government. It was the USA and NATO that toppled this independent nationalist government. Now, Libyans are fleeing their home country as refugees. The formerly prosperous country has been completely wrecked. Poverty has been forcibly imposed on the people of what was once the most prosperous African country.

What is worse, is that the same kind of controlled economic demolition imposed on Libya, Central America, and the Middle East is now taking place, to a much milder degree, within the borders of the United States.

The new low wage economic order is devastating places like Michigan, Pennsylvania, Ohio, and Wisconsin, states that were key in securing Trump's victory. These places no longer have good paying industrial jobs, but instead have short term service sector employment. The rates of opiate overdoses, suicide, mental illness, crime and other societal ills spawned by a sudden drop in the standard of living are rising. In the last 8 years, the number of Americans applying for nutritional assistance has increased by 32%.

Silicon Valley, New York City, and some gentrified urban areas of the USA are seeing a new level of stability, but for the rustbelt it's a very different story. Millions of people in the economically devastated areas voted for Donald Trump because he acknowledged these problems, while Clinton spoke of Obama's presidency as being successful and promised more of the same.

Trump spoke about the suffering of millions of Americans. He blamed "international bankers" for wrecking the lives of America's working people. Trump even went as far as to acknowledge the negative results of US foreign policy in Iraq and Syria, where terrorism has been strengthened. Trump dared to condemn Saudi Arabia. His rhetoric embraced the rising isolationist sentiments, which have increased on both the left and the right.

The New Nationalists Fill A Void

Trump's right-wing nationalism filled a void among an entire strata of American society which is disgusted by the current conditions wrought by American capitalism. Due to the fact that the organized political left makes no solid appeal to the rustbelt working class, they are rallying behind Trump, who appeals to them as a savior. The crowds of protesters outside of Trump's rallies offered no explanation for why millions of refugees and immigrants are pouring into the western countries, or how the crisis could be stopped. Many of the left-wing activists who protested Trump have openly supported the "regime change" operations in Libya and Syria which have unleashed terrorism and a wave of refugees into Europe. The only message the left has offered the Trump supporters is a nasty rebuke of "racist!"

The surprise victory of Donald Trump was not because millions of Americans were impressed with his program or proposed solutions. Trump's proposals were rather fluid and inconsistent. Other than his plan for a big wall between the USA and Mexico, and to "bring back the jobs" he statements were often quite vague. Some of Trump's economic agenda seemed populist and social-democratic, other parts of it seemed free market and neoliberal. Trump did emphasize support for policing agencies, and seemed to play into a disgust at "Black Lives Matter" protests among white Americans who sympathize with the police.

The rise of Trump, as well as the rise of various right-wing populist currents across western Europe is not the result of a Russian conspiracy. It is also not indicative of a pending mass genocide or the creation of a new Third Reich, as certain alarmist voices claim. The situation is this: Nations, countries, and communities all over the world are being impoverished and thrown into chaos by global capitalism. Working people's lives are being destroyed in both the first and third worlds.

Stability is one of the most basic human needs. People need to feel in touch with the world around them. The lives of people in the western world once involved a higher level of stability and security than any other peoples in the world, but this has been swept away. The day to day insecurity and fears associated with short term, low wage employment, as well as the increased presence and over site of government surveillance and policing agencies is drastically changing the lifestyle of people in western countries.

Multiculturalism is causing an increasing amount of ideological insecurity and confusion, with many becoming increasing unsure of what is right and wrong, and looking desperately for purpose in their lives. This is all compounded by the fear of terrorism and crime, which is visibly increasing.

The political left allows no real discussion of these issues, and sticks to abstract slogans against "racism." To millions of people in the west, the left has become synonymous with the political establishment, which holds no answer to the crisis. To millions, "socialism" is no longer a call for a new political system in which society controls and plans the economy, but instead has become a euphemism for expanding social welfare programs. Many confused Americans will say things like "the USA is half socialist already."

The left has exists in a kind of "movementist" vacuum where slogans and protest chants take the place of substantive analysis or proposals. The left does not explain that mass migration, drug gangs and Wahabbi terrorism is caused by the international financial order. The left does not offer radical proposals about how improve the lives of working people in the western countries. The left does not expose the criminal nature of US foreign policy, and often cheers on State Department "revolutions" across the planet. While the far-right embraces a bombastic and radical sounding tone filled with anger and demanding change, leftist political rallies often sound like a kind of group therapy involving "safe spaces" and "self-care."

As a result the newly remolded right-wing, which offers a watered down version of 20th century right-wing nationalism and populism, is providing a worldview and program for moving forward. The far-right is stepping up to the plate, giving voice to peoples anger, as bigoted as it may be, and offering its own solutions, as flawed as they are. In western political discourse, the far-right wing is almost the only radical sounding alternative to the status quo that delivers a coherent message, and acknowledges the problems that are radicalizing and politicizing people.

The new nationalist right-wing is in ascendancy for one reason: disaffected people who want solutions will only turn to those who actually claim to offer them.

Originally Published in New Eastern Outlook

WALL STREET PRIMITIVISM

Wall Street, London, and the Bretton Woods institutions like the World Bank, and the International Monetary Fund claim to support development and the eradication of poverty around the world. They also claim to support scientific progress and raising the global standard of living. However, often they seem to make friends and allies with very different goals. As Nicaragua proceeds with a huge construction project that has dynamic global implications, one can see a certain international pattern repeating itself, with quite dangerous implications.

"Native Activists" Fighting To Preserve US Maritime Dominance

Control of the Panama Canal by the United States has been vital in asserting control over the world economy. The US military has intervened militarily in Panama on many occasions to secure its control of this vital global shipping and transportation hub.

While the USA currently allows vessels to pass through, this could easily change in the case of a military confrontation. With so much of the world's industrial shipping passing through this vital point, control of the canal gives the USA a level of unchecked power in the global economy. At any point they could "veto" a country's economy by stopping ships.

However, a construction project currently in the works in Nicaragua could change that. The Chinese government and corporations based in China are cooperating with the socialist government of Nicaragua to construct a new canal, parallel to the Panama Canal. This canal will not be under US dominion, but under the dominion of the Sandinista government and the People's Republic of China.

The announcement of the project was followed by all kinds of reports in western media claiming it would be an ecological disaster and contribute to global warming. Now, as the project proceeds, voices of the establishment are crying crocodile tears for the indigenous people who will be forced to move by the project. The Guardian has run stories bemoaning their plight. Amnesty International is warning Nicaragua not to interfere with their protests.

The USA is in the process of putting sanctions on Nicaragua, for their support of Venezuela. A bill currently in the US congress called the NICA Act aims to cripple the socialist government.

While it is ignored in US press reports, the Sandinista government has done a great deal to improve the lives of its population, a large percentage of which is indigenous. Poverty in Nicaragua has been reduced by 30%. The United Nations World Happiness Index reports the great increase of happiness in any country in 2016, as having taken place in Nicaragua.

The socialist government is asserting public control over major industries, guaranteeing jobs, housing, and education to the population, and moving toward a centrally planned economy. The Sandinistas are cultivating a layer of patriotic small business owners, who cooperate with the state to develop the economy with foreign investment. Their methods are similar to those employed by Deng Xiaoping when opening up China during the 1980s.

Though the Sandinistas are widely popular, the forces who oppose the canal project have found a number of indigenous leaders to align with. 76% of people in Nicaragua have some indigenous ancestry. The overwhelming majority of the country is ethnically "mestizo" meaning it has a mixture of European and native ancestry.

However, the forces being rallied to oppose the project are not from the overwhelming majority of the population which has indigenous ancestry, but rather to a specific group of just over 4% of the population, which is described as "unmixed indigenous inhabitants." These are individuals who have cut themselves off from Nicaraguan society at large, and much like the Amish or Mennonites in the USA, maintain a lifestyle without technology, immersed in religious tradition. While the majority of Nicaraguans are Christians, these forces are Shamanists and practitioners of polytheistic faiths. They reject all "european" concepts and lump Marxism, dialectical materialism, and Christianity into the same basket.

The relationship between this isolated minority in Nicaragua and the US Central Intelligence Agency is not a new development. During the 1980s contra war, the CIA supplied weapons and military training to the indigenous Mosquito peoples to fight the Sandinistas. In addition to the weapons and funding they received from the USA, a number of Anti-Communist US Native American activists such as Russell Means joined with them. Many of these indigenous, anti-technology, and anti-science fanatics stood against what they called the "Racist European Marxism" of the Sandinista government, which was made up largely of dark skinned people with indigenous blood. While they claimed to oppose both "capitalism and communism" as European concepts, they quietly and sometimes not-so-quietly, worked with the

Pentagon and the CIA.

Just as they took up guns in the 1980s in alliance with Washington, they now get promoted by pro-US Non-Governmental Organizations and Non-Profits, who conveniently see maintaining US maritime dominance as the latest, trendy, ecological, liberal cause, done to rescue some "mystical people" with "beautiful ancient traditions" being crushed by "racist" "dogmatic" Marxists.

"Traditionalist" CIA-Allies in China

Western utilization and manipulation of primitivist, conservative, and reactionary social forces in order to stop economic development is not restricted to Latin America. The political allies of the United States on the Chinese mainland, who work against the People's Republic, often while spouting rhetoric about "human rights" are a rather interesting bunch.

The Chinese government has just cracked down on an extremist cult known as "Eastern Lightning." The group is also known as the "Church of the Almighty God" and worships a woman who they claim is the second coming of Jesus Christ. They are reported to torture, mutilate, and even execute members who attempt to leave. Members of the group famously murdered a man in a Mcdonalds restaurant for refusing to allow his daughter to give her phone number to them.

While some would dismiss this simply as an obscure religious cult, it is important to note that the lead minister of the Church, along with the woman who claims to be Jesus Christ, both currently live in the USA. In 2001, they sought "political exile" in the United States, and while thousands of people die attempting to cross the US border, the US government happily grants visas to anti-China activists, order to help them escape "persecution" from the US government.

Another friend of the USA in China is the Falun Gong, a strange buddhist sect. The group calls for the public execution of homosexuals and opposes inter-racial marriage. Li Hongzi, the group's founder, lives in Queens, New York. His organization has been presented with awards by the Heritage Foundation.

Much like Eastern Lightning, the Falun Gong preaches that the Chinese Communist Party's leadership, in particular its policies advancing the position of women, are harmful to society. The Falun Gong argues that the Chinese Communist Party's rule represents a "Dharma Ending Period" and that its efforts to include women in government positions is one of its most grievous crimes. The group is also known for separating young people from their families, and threatening ex-members.

Following this pattern, the USA has worked endlessly to promote the deposed feudal theocratic monarchy of Tibet. The Dalia Lama, who ruled Tibet with an iron fist and executed and tortured all who questioned him, is presented as a harmless self-help, spiritual guru in US media.

While he is presented as a man of peace, it is widely known that his brother was given military training in Colorado, and air dropped into the Tibet Autonomous Region in the 1950s. With guns and weapons from the USA, the Tibetan separatists waged a violent proxy war in the mountains for years. This is all boasted about in the right-wing, anti-China book *The CIA's Secret War in Tibet.*

All these bizarre religious groups aligned with the USA in China seem to glorify feudal, pre-Communist China. They all oppose the Chinese Communist Party for its modernization. While they speak different languages, and glorify different traditions, they probably would agree a lot with the Nicaraguan, US-backed "indigenous activists" who oppose the socialism of the Sandinistas. Meanwhile, it is a similar crowd of western liberals who admire them, and would accuse any who criticized them of "racism" and "whitesplaining."

Not only does Washington have a history of aligning with primitivist and feudalist forces, so do European fascists. Julius Evola, the Italian far-right ideologue who spoke of a "revolt against the modern world" had a particular admiration for feudalism and primitive societies around the world. In his book *Man Among Ruins* he speaks of "the demonic nature of the economy" in western countries, which people are always trying to advance, create, and become more prosperous. He admires pre-capitalist civilization for its poverty and "stability" amid starvation.

As members of the European far-right, the Nazis also admired primitivism and poverty. Heinrich Harrier, the author of the beloved *Seven Years in Tibet*, practically a holy book for advocates of Tibetan seperatism, was actually an SS officer. The Nazis believed Germans to be descended from Tibetans, and sent scientists to measure ancient skulls in order to somehow prove this. The Nazis had similar admiration for the caste system in ancient India, and adopted the swastika as their symbol for that reason.

361

CIA Loves Islamic Extremists

It was the British empire that first discovered the political value of Wahabbism. The Saudi monarchy owes its origins to a cleric named Muhammad ibn ʿAbd al-Wahhab. His interpretation of Islam in 1700s enabled the Saudi royal family to establish its brutal, repressive theocratic monarchy. The British cooperated with the Saudi royal family, which conveniently allowed them access to oil in exchange for propping up the barbaric regime. In 1945, the USA joined with the British is coddling the Saudi autocracy.

Today, Saudi Arabia is one of the only countries in the world where housing in bedouin tents, not modern buildings is widespread. The lack of infrastructural development accompanies a government that outlaws women from driving cars, conducts public floggings and beheadings, and punishes crimes with mutilation. Every person and everything in Saudi Arabia is the property of the King. Citizens are routinely executed for "insulting the King" or "sorcery" among other crimes. Sometimes bodies are crucified and left on public display after execution.

A large percentage of the Saudi population are guest workers who live as slaves with no human rights. Even among the Saudi born population, the Shia oil workers face brutal discrimination and exploitation on the job, with their religious freedom often denied.

While the western economic institutions and governments all claim to support "poverty alleviation" and "development" in the third world, they embrace the Saudi Monarchy in all its horror and backwardness. Meanwhile, the targets of the USA and NATO in the Middle East, are not the primitive oil autocracies, but rather, regimes that work toward modernization.

The Iranian revolution of 1979 deposed western capitalism, and established a government under the slogan of "not capitalism, but Islam." After the revolution, even in the context of a massive war with Iraq, Imam Khomeni launched a "construction Jihad." In this effort inspired by Stalin's Five Year Plans and the rapid industrialization of socialist countries, Iranians were mobilized to build highways, schools, hospitals, power plants, and so much else in order to bring the country out of poverty. Despite sanctions and attacks from the west, Iran has utilized oil revenue and central planning to construct a highly modern country, with a comparatively prosperous population. The Islamic Republic of Iran that emerged from the 1979 revolution, and has made huge strides toward modernization, is now the target of western leaders.

The Syrian Arab Republic, born in the Baath Socialist revolution, is also targeted by the west. This is a government that has multiple parties in office, and has worked with Russia and China to construct huge power plants and highways. Syrian industrial workers are organized into labor unions, and have legal protections on the job. The Communist Party and the Communist Party (Baghdash) are permitted to participate in the government process. Religious freedom is guaranteed with Sunnis, Shia, Alawi, Christians, Druze, and other religious groups all freely practicing their faith. The achievements of Syria's state controlled healthcare system are widely praised by international bodies, with many doctors and medical professionals trained the state run Universities.

Fitting with this pattern, western leaders are now arming

and training Wahabbis, a force representing primitivism and barbarism of the Saudi variety, in the hopes of toppling the Syrian government. It is worth noting that prior to 2011, when the USA began working to foment civil war in the context of the Arab Spring, Syria had begun constructing an oil pipeline, connecting Iran to Mediterranean.

Prior to its destruction by NATO bombs in 2011, Libya was the most prosperous country on the African continent. It had the highest life expectancy, and had constructed a huge irrigation system in order to spread water across this dry, desert country. The forces backed by the United States to topple the Islamic Socialist government in Libya were Wahabbis. Now ISIS and Al-Queda have set up shop in the country, and citizens are fleeing on rafts trying to reach Europe.

Different Definitions of Imperialism

In his 1917 book *Imperialism: The Highest Stage of Capitalism*, Russian revolutionary leader Vladimir Lenin argued that capitalism had entered a globalist phase. He talked about the rise of "monopoly capitalists" in Britain, France, Germany, and the United States. He spoke of how bankers had triumphed over industrial capitalists, and described how wealthy financial elites in the west teamed up with governments to battle against each other, carving out "spheres of influence" in Africa, Asia, Latin America, and elsewhere. He described how third world countries were utilized as "captive markets" in which western countries could sell commodities without competition.

Imperialism, as Lenin understood it, was about keeping the world poor, so that western bankers could stay rich.

364

Furthermore, imperialism meant dividing the working class within the western countries. A "labor aristocracy" of well paid workers was created. These were working class people who could be cultivated to identify with the western capitalists against the colonized people. With their rising standard of living, they would see their interests as identical to the interests of the monopolists that controlled their governments.

This understanding of imperialism was developed by Lenin, and adopted by figures like Mao Zedong, Che Guevara, Ho Chi Minh, Huey Newton. Even non-Marxists like Michel Aflaq, Juan Peron, and Moammar Gaddafi studied and came to understand imperialism this way. For various anti-imperialist figures of the 20th century, third world revolutions against imperialism were about raising their countries up from poverty, modernizing, and developing.

However, a large section of the modern political left has abandoned this understanding. The understanding of "imperialism" taught in Universities across the USA and western Europe is quite different.

Starting in the 1950s, the New Left, specifically beloved "cultural critics" in the Frankfurt School and elsewhere, began speaking about "cultural imperialism." Suddenly, among western academics and leftist activists, imperialism wasn't about holding back development and keeping people poor. Rather, it was about eroding "beautiful" "traditions" and "ways of life" and "imposing" supposedly "western" values.

So-called "Mcworld" & Wahabbi Extremists Work Together

When describing the supposed leftist critique of imperialism in his book *On Paradise Drive* New York Times-Columnist David Brooks said that "anti-American" and anti-imperialist forces oppose "McDonalds, Barnes and Noble, and boob jobs." Those who object to Wall Street running the world are depicted as Native American mystics, Islamic fanatics, or others who object to the industrialization, commercialization, and sexual freedom of western life.

This misrepresentation is widespread. The false dichotomy is often stated as "Mcworld vs. Jihad," and was widely promoted in the USA, prior to, but especially after 9/11. In this "Clash of Civilizations" narrative, the forces said to represent "Jihad" were the Saudi Monarchy and Osama Bin Laden, while the forces said to represent "Mcworld" were the IMF, the World Bank, and Wall Street.

In reality, Mcworld globalizationists and the forces represented as "Jihad" are on the same team. They have never been enemies. Washington has been on friendly terms with Saudi Arabia since 1945. The CIA worked with Wahabbi extremists in Afghanistan to topple an independent, modernizing government called the People's Democratic Party. The USA and Saudi Arabia worked with Wahabbis in Chechnya to fight against the Soviet Union and afterwards the Russian Federation. The USA currently funds and arms Wahhabis in Syria, and cooperated with these forces in Libya to topple the Islamic Socialist government.

The conservative forces in the Middle East that oppose modernization and development, and embrace the Wahabbi

ideology of the 1700s are not enemies of Wall Street or the
London Stock Exchange. Unlike the Shia revolutionaries, or
the Baath Socialists, which represent legitimate resistance,
the Wahabbi forces do not wish to modernize or industrialize
the region. They want to keep it a mess of impoverished oil
plantations ruled over by autocratic vassals. Wall Street has
no objection to this setup, and it can largely be traced back to
the Sykes-Pickot agreement, crafted by western colonizers.

However, in the west, especially in circles considered to be
"progressive" there is a strange mystical and cosmopolitan
admiration for the forces of primitivism. For example,
those who defend the Syrian government, and point out the
terrorist nature of the anti-government forces are labelled
"Islamophobic." Liberal crowds in the United States swoon
over the pro-Saudi demagogue named Linda Sarsour as
she wears a headscarf, uses exotic sounding Arabic words,
accuses those who oppose her of racism, and holds rallies
calling for the USA to topple the Syrian government.

This degeneration of leftist politics has been a long time
in the making. In the 1960s, the Hare Krishna movement, an
extremely right-wing Hindu sect in India, suddenly became
a beloved staple of Peace Marches. Gurus from India, figures
who promoted drug use for "spiritual" purposes, all suddenly
became the fixture of the left. Previously these kinds of
bohemian elements had been embraced by the far-right and
fascists.

In the 1950s, it was Republicans and the "China Lobby"
that rallied support for the Dalai Lama and his insurgency
in the Tibet Autonomous Region. Republicans accused
the democrats of "losing China." However, in the present
context it is liberals who sport "Free Tibet" bumper stickers,

while the right-wing is less interested in foreign meddling and applauds to the words "America First." No matter what region is being discussed, in the present context, it is the liberals, not the conservatives, whose hearts bleed the loudest for US proxy fighters around the world.

While in the 1980s, it was conservatives like Ronald Reagan and Oliver North who championed the fight against the Sandinistas in Nicaragua, it is now liberals who moan for the "indigenous cultures" that are supposedly being "oppressed" by the Marxist government, which dares challenge the hegemony of the Panama Canal.

The US Central Intelligence Agency is probably the most involved with supporting forces of primitivism around the world, as they work to battle independent modernizing governments that threaten the monopoly of western capitalism. It should be no surprise, that since the 1950s, the CIA has also been heavily involved in supporting the anti-communist political left, which seems now fully dedicated to their latest crusade.

The CIA began its infamous "Congress for Cultural Freedom" in the 1950s, hoping to direct anti-capitalist activists and artists away from the pro-Soviet Communist Parties in the USA and Europe. The CIA funded the art of Jackson Pollack, experimental music, and all kinds of cultural strata intended to clash with Marxist-Leninist dialectical materialism and socialist realism. The CIA also launched a program called MKULTRA which involved distributing drugs on college campuses.

368

The Monument Fights in the USA

The media in western countries, as it champions various primitivist forces, has essentially embraced Julius Evola's critique of the "demonic nature of the economy." Like Mother Teresa who infamously said "There is something beautiful in seeing the poor accept their lot, to suffer it like Christ's Passion. The world gains much from their suffering," the non-Marxist, "liberal" element now sees social, economic, and technological progress as its enemy, and looks on poverty, ignorance, and primitivism in a condescending admiration.

While once it was the right-wing that pushed malthusian ideas about "overpopulation" it is now billionaire liberals like Bill Gates that work to decrease the global population. Often in the name of ecology, liberals will boast about how they refrain from shopping, and live frugal lives.

Now in the USA, a political clash that is very dangerous is unfolding. The fight involves monuments to various historical figures who did reprehensible things, such as owning slaves or fighting for the Confederacy in the hopes of preserving the slave system.

While it easy for anyone who hates racism and the racist mythology of films like *Gone With The Wind* and *The Birth of a Nation* to celebrate the destruction of Confederate Monuments, and they are absolutely right to do so, the context of their destruction, and who is destroying them, presents a new danger.

The forces that seek to defend the Confederate monuments are white supremacists, Ku Klux Klansmen, admirers of Hitler, traditionalists, and others. These are forces that want the USA to return to segregation, racial division, and other things overcome through decades of struggle. These forces are known to use violence, and they are widely hated and unpopular, though their prestige is slowly growing due to the absurd political context.

The problem is not that reactionary symbols are being destroyed. This is a positive thing. The problem is rather that the forces who line up against them do not seek to replace their hateful ideology with something new. In Charlottesville and elsewhere, the battle is taking place in which bigots who think Robert E. Lee was a hero are facing and off and violently clashing with those who believe society should have no heroes at all.

Racism Battles Post-Modernism

While the racist, hateful messaging and views of White Nationalists fill the airwaves, and become the subject of debate, what does Anti-Fa believe in? The media refers to crowds opposing the "Alt Right" as "anti-racist activists." The White Nationalists are quick to call them "Communists." But what ideas does "The Resistance" believe in? What alternative vision do they hold up to combat the right-wing?

The crowds of post-modern, non-ideological leftists largely do not seek to replace statues they destroy with statues of progressive figures like Frederick Douglas, Huey Newton, or William Z. Foster. Rather, they rally around the concept that "no one should be worshipped" and "there is no truth." Images of Abraham Lincoln, the man who defeated Robert E. Lee and led the fight against slavery are now being destroyed, alongside the Confederates.

While "Anarchists" and liberals who destroy monuments are quick to point out and emphasize these leaders real crimes, the slogan they rally in opposition with is "No Gods and No Masters." They fall back on concepts like "think for yourself" "question everything" and more subtly: "don't believe in anything" "there is no truth."

As media eulogized Heather Heyer, who was murdered by a white nationalist in Charlottesville, very few reports mentioned that she was a member of the Industrial Workers of the World. The IWW, an anarcho-syndicalist labor union formed in 1905, also known as "the wobblies," indeed has an ideology and belief system of its own. The IWW believes in creating a society in which the major industries and workplaces are controlled by those who work in them. Throughout its history, it was known for working in favor something, it syndicalist vision, not simply for the destruction the old. Not surprisingly, US media, which largely cheers for the opposition to the Alt-Right, obscures this important aspect of the woman who recently died opposing them.

As the media champions the fight against the Alt-Right, they work to obscure any solid ideology that would oppose them. The primary voices opposing the Alt-Right are post-modernists from middle class backgrounds, trained at elite Universities. They tear down the statues of confederate monuments as they cheer for the "Syrian revolution" that reduces Syria to chaos, or the various "oppressed" primitivist groups that fight against China or the government of Nicaragua.

Bill Maher, a left-wing TV commentator interviewed Leah Remini about her painful history in the Church of Scientology. In the interview, Maher outrageously compared

371

scientology to Communism. The outrageous comparison was in reference to the low income of scientology practitioners.

As the polarization continues, the dangerous reality is that this is not the 1930s. Those who are fighting "fascists" are not armed with Marxism-Leninism and guided by the Soviet Union, fighting for the ideal of Communism. Unlike the anti-fascist of the 1930s, anti-fa and the liberals who support them are not fighting to impose their own ideology onto society. Rather, they are fighting in the hopes of destroying ideology itself.

This is a hopeless mission. Every society since the dawn of agriculture has involved ideas, religions, and some concept morality, however incorrect or distorted they may have been. These things are the foundation of human civilization. Even pre-historic tribes of hunter gathers had some rules or beliefs to guide their actions. Post-modernism and relativism cannot lay the foundations of a healthy society.

Western capitalism now rallies around the belief that "there is no truth." At home it promotes free market capitalism and austerity, an economic model in which selfishness rules, and many people are left in poverty and misery. Meanwhile, it emphasizes a social liberalism based on hedonism and shallow values. Internationally, the west aligns itself with forces that seek to stop economic and technological progress, and freeze their societies in poverty and ignorance, so that Wall Street can maintain its monopoly.

As Americans, like all human beings, long for something to believe in, and long for their lives to improve, not get worse, they are likely to rally around forces who offer them such things. If no alternative is presented, only the now marginal far right-wing will be available to offer such things.

While its easy to call Trump a fascist, something far more deadly, and far closer the reactionary regimes of Nazi Germany and Mussolini's Italy could gain support. A population told to chose between either anarchy, chaos, and nihilism, or the hateful "truths" of reaction, could be pushed toward a very dangerous trajectory.

Originally published in New Eastern Outlook

Native Americans and the New Confusion in US Politics

When it comes to the genocide of Native Americans, the people of the United States seem to face an existential crisis. The cultural clashes and recent diversification of rhetoric around this issue illustrates how deeply confused the people of the United States truly are about their identity and their history.

Ethnic Cleansing, Cultural Genocide and Mass Murder

Long before the creation of the United States, or the signing of the Declaration of Independence in 1776, massacres of Native people by settlers had already begun. Incident such as the Gnadenhutten massacre of 1782, or the Massacre at Wounded Knee in 1890, cannot be described "accidental" or as outliers.

The forced removal of Native Americans ordered by US President Andrew Jackson in 1838 and carried out against the wishes of the US Supreme Court resulted in at least 10,000 deaths. It is hard to honestly describe the "Trail of Tears" as anything but ethnic cleansing.

The Native American Schools operated by the Bureau of Indian Affairs conducted a cultural genocide. Children were forcibly removed from their parents and taken to government run facilities in which they were not permitted to speak their own language, and indoctrinated with Christianity. Native American religion was illegal in many parts of the United States until the passage of the Federal American Indian Religious Freedom Act in 1978.

374

In 2004, the British white supremacist leader John Tyndall told a group of sympathizers in Louisiana: "I've always been greatly interested in America. No one with the least knowledge of history, the history and development of your country could possibly believe in the current madness of racial equality. Here is a great continent of boundless wealth, but it was just a wilderness before the coming of the white man. It was the white man and white women who tamed it, build it and created a civilization here."

Defending Crimes Against Humanity

In 2004 John Tyndall, and former US Congressman David Duke, who sat in the audience as Tyndall spoke, were on the political fringe. These statements glorifying the crimes against Native Americans and justifying them had been marginalized to only the extreme right-wing. In 1980s, 90s, and the early years of the 21st Century, mainstream conservatives and Republicans spoke of the genocide of Native Americans as a horrific reality from America's past, and crime that should be atoned for.

However, this was not always the case. Until the mid-1970s, arguments attempting to justify the slaughter of indigenous people were commonplace among conservatives. Ayn Rand, the free market philosopher and novelist who is held up by Congressman Paul Ryan as his main inspiration was unafraid to make such statements.

The book "Ayn Rand Answers" which compiled materials from Rand's various interviews throughout her life quotes her saying the following about Native Americans:

"Now, I don't care to discuss the alleged complaints American Indians have against this country. I believe, with good reason, the most unsympathetic Hollywood portrayal of Indians and what they did to the white man. They had no right to a country merely because they were born here and then acted like savages. The white man did not conquer this country. And you're a racist if you object, because it means you believe that certain men are entitled to something because of their race. You believe that if someone is born in a magnificent country and doesn't know what to do with it, he still has a property right to it. He does not. Since the Indians did not have the concept of property or property rights–they didn't have a settled society, they had predominantly nomadic tribal "cultures"–they didn't have rights to the land, and there was no reason for anyone to grant them rights that they had not conceived of and were not using."

During the 1970s, the mass protests of the American Indian Movement, and the efforts of New Left activists to spread awareness about US history, changed the terms of national debate. It no longer became acceptable to defend what had taken place, and US media, educational institutions, and political leaders openly admitted that horrendous, indefensible crimes had been committed.

A New Wave of Denial

However, in the age of Trump, the terms of discourse have shifted once again.

Highly popular conservative commentator Dinesh Dsouza denies that such well documented incidents took place. On July 3rd, 2014, appearing on FOX news, Dsouza declared: "We shouldn't flagellate ourselves for things we didn't do...

The main reason for that was not because of warfare or systematic killing, it's because …diseases, …did not have any immunities, so they perished in large numbers."

According to Dsouza, mass killing, forced deportation, cultural genocide are all figments of a "radical leftist" imagination. The mass death of Native people was merely the result of unintentional spreading of disease.

Dsouza's words could be easily dissected by any scholar of American history. Unlike those who attempt to deny the Nazi holocaust, D'souza doesn't even bother to try and debunk the many documented massacres. D'souza simply bluffs and says something that a certain audience badly wants to hear.

More recently, *PragerU* the widely advertised and promoted youtube channel of conservative commentator Dennis Prager, posted an odd video on November 20th, 2018. An individual identified as Will Witt walked around California State University in an outfit intended to mock Native American clothing. Witt then portrayed himself as a victim when students shouted at him and criticized his behavior.

The video does not deny the genocide, but seems to hint that somehow Witt is being victimized. The fact that anyone might take offense at such a costume is portrayed as some scandalous example of left-wing extremism.

Organizations such as the Proud Boys, started by Gavin Mcguiness, speak of celebrating "western civilization" in a defensive manner, angrily decrying those who speak of "western civilization" in negative terms.

Post-Modernism vs. Marxism

The question must be raised, why would anyone listen to Dsouza's denial of historical facts? Why would anyone sympathize with a student in a mock Native American costume, and believe he is the victim when others object to his offensive outfit?

Now that decades have passed since the 1970s, a number of white Americans have begun to take criticism of the crimes against Native people as a personal attack. The widespread discussion of "white privilege" and "man-splaining" has created an atmosphere in which millions of Americans believe that acknowledging the actual history is somehow the equivalent of calling them bad people, and saying they to deserve to be less prosperous.

The narrative of the post-modern campus based, academic "oppression theory" leftists is that white Americans "have it to good" and should feel deep shame on behalf of their ethnic group. With such arguments abundant, those who feel the sting of such rebukes, hear Dsouza claim saying the deaths were unintentional and then sigh with relief. Dsouza gives them permission to say "see, I'm not a bad person after all."

But a classical leftist interpretation of the crimes against indigenous people, as opposed to the post-modern and identity politics narrative pushed on the campuses, draws a different conclusion, and does not blame the working class for the crimes of the capitalist system.

Marx's book *Capital* described the killing of Native Americans, along with the colonization of Africa, as "primitive accumulation." Marx put it into the same category as the land-seizures and clearing of the commons that killed millions of white European peasants during the same historical epoch.

The seizing of the Americas from the Native people was carried out as the emerging class of merchants and capitalists was setting itself up to rule, replacing the decaying order of feudalism. Serfs and peasants were forced to become wage laborers, and sell themselves to survive. During this time period, thousands of Britons were executed for "vagrancy" i.e. the crime of being homeless. Millions of Scottish people were forced off of their lands during the clearing of the highlands.

Like the transatlantic slave trade, the seizing of Mexican territory, and the many wars waged by western governments, these crimes were not carried out for the benefit of average Americans who happen to be white. Most certainly the horrendous realities surrounding the origins of the United States of America were far, far worse for those who came to the US as African slaves, or those who were driven from their lands and exterminated. However, the brutal drive for profits by a small wealthy elite did not spare the white working class from harm. The crimes of slavery and Native genocide were carried out and driven by the same wealthy monopolists who worked millions of white people to death in sweatshops or the building of the railroads for low pay in horrendous conditions.

The Global System of Imperialism

In fact, the very forces that have more recently de-industrialized the United States, driven wages down, and presided over the in-flow of opioids, built up their wealth through seizing US territory. The way US land was distributed was widely corrupt, with railroad "Robber Barons" and bankers bribing politicians and acquiring most of America's vast wealth and natural resources for themselves. Those who own the huge multinational corporations and banks have no loyalty to the United States or its population, and have presided over the creation of a global financial system which has impoverished millions of Americans. The 1950s "American Dream" of a prosperous middle class has been largely eroded, as international monopolists play workers all across the world against each other in a "race to the bottom" with lower wages, less secure employment, and austerity.

In his book *Outline Political History of the Americas* the Marxist William Z. Foster described the slaughter of the indigenous people, not as a crime to be blamed on all whites, but as a crime of capitalism. The small group of bankers based in Wall Street and London who now rule the world, seized it through the horrendous process of colonialism, and now maintain a system of global monopolism, labelled by Vladimir Lenin as "Imperialism: The Highest Stage of Capitalism." Exposing the founding crimes of this international economic order is not an attack on workers who happen to be white. On the contrary, it lays out how their anger and outrage is justified, and how they share a common foe with those around the world demanding self-determination and economic independence.

Opposing capitalism and fighting for the establishment of governments that represent the majority of working people, rather than merely the billionaire elite, is in the interest of all Americans, of all backgrounds.

It is the absence of this once common, class conscious understanding among the "American Left" that has laid the basis for so much confusion in recent politics.

Originally published in New Eastern Outlook

TALK OF SOCIALISM STIRS CONTROVERSY
IN THE USA

Alexandria Ocasio-Cortez is only 28 years old. She is a New Yorker of Puerto Rican heritage, and after an upset primary vote, she will be the Democratic Party's nominee for U.S. Congress in November. Ocasio-Cortez is almost guaranteed to be elected to Congress, as the district is overwhelmingly controlled by the Democratic Party. Her victory in the primary was over Joe Crowley, a longstanding figure in New York City politics.

Alexandria Ocasio-Cortez is at the center of a debate regarding socialism in the United States, as many Americans question the free market.

Ocasio-Cortez is a member of the Democratic Socialists of America and aligns herself with Bernie Sanders and other members of the Democratic Party who reject the pro-market, neoliberal economic policies long favored by the party's National Committee.

After her victory, all across U.S. media a debate about "socialism" has taken place. Among Republicans and conservatives, alarm-bells have sounded. Ocasio-Cortez is accused of wanting to "turn the USA into Venezuela." Because Ocasio-Cortez has criticized capitalism, her critics equate her to Marxist-Leninists, and invoke Cold War rhetoric against her.

Meanwhile, supporters of Ocasio-Cortez insist that "socialism" simply refers to government policies intended to deliver economic justice. TV host, Joy Behar, defended Ocasio-Cortez in a heated exchange on national TV, saying that socialism had been successful in Norway and Sweden.

The Neoliberal definition of socialism

Both sides of the new "socialism" debate seem to agree with the definition of socialism that emerged in the 1970s and 80s, as U.S. discourse became dominated by advocates of economic neoliberalism such as Milton Friedman and Ayn Rand. Both sides define socialism as government involvement in the economy.

For example, defenders of "socialism" say the U.S. already has a "socialist post office," "socialist fire department," and "socialist roads." Critics of "socialism" claim the U.S. government is too large, taxes are too high, and that the problems of U.S. society can be attributed to a lack of free market policies.

This discourse lacks the standard definition of socialism used for well over 200 years. The invention of the word "socialism" is attributed to the French utopian thinker, Henri de Saint-Simon. Simon began utilizing the term "socialisme" in aftermath of the French revolution, contrasting his vision of a highly organized and rationally planned society, with "liberalism," the philosophy of the emerging French capitalism, in which production was organized to serve the interests of individual business owners.

Long before the emergence of Marxism as a political force, "socialism" referred to the centers of economic power being controlled by the community. Marx and Engels later spoke of "workers controlling the means of production." Throughout the Cold War, "socialism" referred to societies in which the commanding heights of the economy were controlled by the state.

Even non-Marxist socialists, such as the Baathists of the Arab world, or figures like Kwame Nkrumah or Julius Nyerere in Africa, understood socialism in this way. Socialism did not refer to progressive taxation policies, or government merely providing services. It was viewed as an alternative to the rule of profits, in which the economy is planned by the state and made to function in the interest of the public overall.

Amid the height of McCarthyism in the United States, propaganda pushing the merits of the "free market" was routinely shown to U.S. school children. As a result, many Americans now believe that socialism and communism is "everyone getting the same wage, no matter how hard they work" among other confused definitions.

However, as the increase in the U.S. standard of living has slowed, millions of Americans have come to reject the neoliberal principles contending privatizations are always best and the population should be left to "pull itself up by its bootstraps." Despite being told that government activity is "socialism," a large number of Americans still want the government to be involved in providing services and regulating financial activities.

The organization that Ocasio-Cortez is affiliated with, Democratic Socialists of America, emerged during the early 1980s from the Democratic Socialist Organizing Committee of Michael Harrington. The group emerged as the "New Communist Movement" of young activists inspired by Mao Zedong in China, as the Soviet-aligned Communist Party USA, declined.

Harrington recruited many former organizers of the Civil Rights and Anti-Vietnam War movements to his organization, publishing "In These Times" magazine and encouraging young activists to distance themselves from Marxism-Leninism, and put forward a "democratic" vision of socialism that was contrary to it. Harrington also encouraged his followers to be involved in the Democratic Party's election campaigns rather than street protests.

Harrington's organization has certainly evolved since the 1980s, and it seems to be increasingly influential as the Democratic Party struggles to define itself. Other than opposing Donald Trump, the Democrats are greatly confused about what they stand for. Figures like Howard Shultz, former CEO of Starbucks, are greatly disturbed by the rise of "socialists" like Bernie Sanders and Ocasio-Cortez and seek to counter it within the Democratic Party. Meanwhile, many young Americans are deeply inspired by the new socialist trend, and have become politically active in order to support it.

The conversation about socialism continues in the United States, as many Americans, on both the right and left, reject the economic policies that have defined the country for the last few decades and look for a solid alternative that can restore growth and allow living standards to keep rising.

Originally published at China.org.cn

FEAR OF RUSSIA AND THE RISE OF THE LEFT BIRCHERS

In 1963, folk singer Bob Dylan, whose left-leaning lyrics seemed to define the liberal politics of the era, composed a song which was a mockery of the right-wing anti-Communist organization known as the John Birch Society. He wrote:

Well, I was feelin' sad and feelin' blue
I didn't know what in the world I was gonna do
Them Communists they was comin' around
They was in the air
They was on the ground
They wouldn't gimme no peace

The John Birch Society was easy to laugh at. This far-right organization was made up doctors, lawyers, and other middle class elements and operated in a clandestine manner. Its members were reportedly shown a "secret book" claiming to prove that Republican President Dwight Eisenhower was a Communist, receiving orders from the Russians.

Invoking Russia To Attack Dissidents

However, for those involved in peace marches and activism for civil rights, the Birchers were more than just a joke. As McCarthyism ebbed after the death of Stalin and talk of detente dominated mainstream politics, the far-right took up the task of mobilizing to attack and silence left-wing activists.

The John Birch Society, the Ku Klux Klan, the American Legion and other right-wing organizations claimed to be against the entire political establishment. They accused both major parties of being corrupt and tied to Communism. Their rhetoric often called for some kind of revolt in order to "restore the republic."

But at the end of the day, the main activity of far-rightists was simply to silence critics of US foreign policy while accusing them of being Soviet agents. In 1965, as the first large protests and teach-ins against the Vietnam War took place across the country, the far-right mobilized for the purpose of silencing them.

The well-known intellectual,Noam Chomsky described the scene in Boston: "We tried to have our first major public demonstration against the war on the Boston Common, the usual place for meetings. I was supposed to be one of the speakers, but nobody could hear a word. The meeting was totally broken up—by students marching over from universities, by others, and hundreds of state police, which kept people from being murdered."

The *Harvard Crimson* described the scene this way: "The speakers were continually interrupted by organized cheers of "Stay in Vietnam" and "We want victory" from the hecklers, who also sang the national anthem." In New York City, the anti-war protesters were splattered with a can red paint. In Berkeley, the Hells Angels Motorcycle Club attacked protesters, and broke the leg of a police officer who stepped in to try and protect them.

The same year, right-wing activists called in a bomb-threat in order prevent professors at the University of Michigan from holding an anti-war teach-in. As the activists continued to have their anti-war conference outside in the snow, far-rightists heckled them and displayed placards saying "Nuke Hanoi."

It was easy to tell what the far-right of the early 1960s was opposed to. They were against Communism and anyone who seemed even slightly sympathetic to it. But what exactly did the Birchers believe in? Their answers were vague: "Freedom" "Liberty" "Americanism" and not much more.

Despite whatever rhetoric, the main activity of the Cold War far right was to defend the political establishment. The right-wing groupings of the period existed simply to shut down and silence those who opposed the Vietnam War, advocated Civil Rights, or otherwise challenged the status quo. Their ideology and critique of overall society was secondary and marginal, as their primary activity was to shut down the forces that constituted an actual threat to the existing order.

Meet The "Left Birchers"

In contemporary America, styles from the John Birch playbook have re-emerged, but this time from sections of the so-called left. Leftism has long been a wide ideological tent including those who advocate a new political and economic order. The political left is made up those who believe in Social-Democracy, Communism, Anarchism or other egalitarian visions for a new world.

Leftists have been known to call the mainstream media "bourgeois propaganda." Leftist students in the past were known for arguing against the ideas their professors and teachers extolled and in some cases were expelled from their Universities for acts of protest. But increasingly the contemporary "left" is made up, not of dissidents and free thinkers, but of those who watch MSNBC and CNN religiously. Many leftists can perfectly recite an "anti-oppression pedagogy" taught to them by their professors chapter and verse. These most conforming and obedient university students are then dispatched to silence those who break the politically correct rules they have carefully studied.

Much like the Birchers couldn't really argue against left-wing ideas, but simply pinned the label of "commie" or "pinko" on those who disagreed with them, the new, campus based liberal "anti-fascist" thinks they have won a debate simply by declaring their opponent's arguments to be reminiscent of some form of oppression. If an opponent can somehow be declared "racist," "sexist," or otherwise oppressive, his arguments are null and void, no matter how much truth they contain.

Many of the leftists who attend "Stop Trump" rallies cannot tell you what they believe in or what policies they advocate. Instead they can simply tell you about the evils of systemic racism, white privilege, homophobia, transphobia, and other injustices that they oppose, and demand the establishment join their efforts against such atrocities. The cold war far-right advocated outlawing the Communist Party and leftist organizations because they were "too dangerous to American democracy." These Left Birchers will go on to argue that those who extoll "harmful" ideas must never be allowed to speak, because what they say is oppressing those who may hear them.

In the 1960s, anti-communist fanatics could not really explain the ideology of Marxism, simply seeing it as "dictatorship" "redistribution of wealth" or "taking my money away." Likewise, the new Birchers often cannot tell you what a "fascist" is, or offer a comprehensible definition. However, these folks are happy to draw complex charts and graphs, in attempts to convince you that someone is a fascist, utilizing classic "guilt by association." Furthermore, much like the Birchers of Cold War era, due to some strange leaps in logic, all the "transphobia" "slut shaming" "mansplaining" "white supremacy" and "fascism" they are opposed to is somehow being imported from Russia, directed as part of a Kremlin conspiracy to hurt the US status quo.

Purging Left-wing Circles

While the left birchers rarely hold rallies demanding specific reforms, and hardly ever convene conferences on socialist ideology, they are happy shout down speakers they disagree with, tear down statues or monuments, and call for TV programs and books to be outlawed.

Like the Birchers of the 60s, these leftists may claim they oppose "the system" but in reality, they spend their time mobilizing to defend and protect the liberal order against those who oppose it. Much like the Birchers accused critics of the Vietnam War of being "Commies" who needed to "Go Back To Russia," leftists now declare that those who criticize US and NATO policies are "racists" who "have ties to Moscow." No anti-Trump rally goes by without signs featuring a Hammer and Sickle or the face of Vladimir Putin. Wanting more hostility toward Russia is considered an essential aspect of "opposing oppression" and "fighting for justice." Russians are accused of "undermining faith in the U.S. democratic process" i.e. encouraging Americans to have ideologically incorrect thoughts.

Members of the far-left who don't jump on board with the new trend in left-wing politics are labelled as "Red Browns" and "Nazbols." Across the internet, certain liberal-minded "experts" insist that groups like the Workers Party of Belgium, websites like Black Agenda Report, and even former African-American Congresswoman Cynthia Mckinney are somehow actually "fascists." The logic is that if a leftist dares speak up against the social media censorship of Alex Jones, or questions the "Russiagate" narratives of the Intelligence Agencies, he must be a closet Nazi, no matter how outspoken he or she may be on vital political questions.

The Bernie Sanders wing of the Democratic Party, adherents of which often fall in line with new trend of Left Mccarthyism, increasingly face charges of disloyalty and accusations of Kremlin ties. During the 2016 election, the argument from these forces was that favoring Sanders made one a "sexist" "mansplaining" "Bernie Bro." Since then, liberal voices have endlessly spouted the idea that the Berniecrat movement, advocating policies that rank-and-file democrats actually want, is somehow a Russian plot to get Trump re-elected by making sure Democrats don't obediently march behind the National Committee.

Antifa from the Pentagon

During the Cold War, US foreign policy was justified in the name of opposing Communism. So, Communists and leftists in the United States, who challenged the notion that Marxism was evil, were seen as the primary ideological threat. Those who opposed war were deemed to be "soft on communism." Today, US foreign policy is justified in the name of "spreading freedom" "promoting human rights" and overthrowing "oppressive regimes."

The USA now presents itself to the world as a bastion of sexual freedom, racial equality, and liberation, and when it attacks a country, the regime is accused of being "racist" "sexist" or "homophobic." So, those within the United States who oppose gay marriage, or advocate social conservatism, are seen as extolling the ideology of the enemy. Furthermore, those who oppose attacks on countries like Syria, Russia, or China are deemed as being "soft on fascism."

At the end of the day, the existing white nationalists and fascists of the United States are indeed a big public relations problem for the government. Mainstream media would like the world to believe that Obama's presidency and the actions of Martin Luther King Jr. made the USA a benevolent, tolerant place, free from racial injustice. Klansmen and Neo-Nazis are an ugly reminder of the actual history of the United States, from the slaughter of Native Americans to Jim Crow segregation. Furthermore, racism towards people from Latin America, or bigotry against Muslims, makes it more difficult for the USA to sell itself as a trusted ally to people in certain regions.

Trump's words often present a big problem for those who work overtime to convince the world to trust the United States. The fact that the "post-racial" Presidency of Barack Obama occupied the White House in 2011 was pivotal in the fall out of the Arab Spring. Imagine how differently such upheavals would play out if Trump had been the president at the time. One could hypothetically imagine Gaddafi and Assad emerging stronger, with Wall Street's Saudi puppets taking big losses.

"Anti-Fascism" in an age when Wall Street and the Pentagon accuse all of their geo-political rivals, even the Communists and Bolivarians, of somehow being fascists, is totally different from the often glorified activism of the late

1930s. We are in a new era in which war, monopolism, and economic neoliberalism present themselves as humanitarian and enlightened. Shouting down Ben Shapiro is not the equivalent of fighting with the International Brigades in Spain. Demanding that Donald Trump be impeached for allegedly being friendly with Vladimir Putin cannot be compared to the Battle of Cable Street.

The biggest threat to the "Left-Birchers" who defend the political establishment from the "fascist" menace, is not Trump or his base of supporters. Rather, it is the emerging "democratic socialist" opposition within the Democratic Party. By speaking in favor of social-democratic policies, and not merely accusing people of being "racist" "sexist" and "fascist" the Berniecrat element is pointing leftists away from simply being defenders of the status quo.

The call for "unity" within the Democratic Party, in order to "focus on defeating Trump" should be exposed for what it is. The opposition to Bernie Sanders and Alexandria Ocasio-Cortez from the mouths of figures like Starbucks CEO Howard Shultz is not well intentioned Democratic Party strategism; It is a maneuver to trap leftists in a position of defending the very establishment that many of them strongly oppose.

Originally published in New Eastern Outlook

Anti-Totalitarianism & Confusion on the American Right

Jordan Peterson is not a political scientist or an ideologue and does not purport to be. The wildly popular clinical and academic psychologist packages his lectures as self-help. His best-selling book *12 Rules for Life* is not by any means a political tirade or manifesto. However, regardless of his wishes or intent, the Canadian Professor has become a key face of American conservatism.

But this points to the bigger question: what does it mean to be a conservative in the United States in 2018?

Donald Trump, the Republican President, is hardly a right-wing archetype. Trump is a wealthy real-estate tycoon known for his foul mouth and sexual promiscuity. Trump has been known to insult his opponents in ways that would cause conservatives of previous eras to vomit. Trump insulted John McCain for being captured during the Vietnam War. Trump boasted about his own lack of military service, and referred to his struggles with venereal disease during his youth as his own "personal Vietnam."

Trump's Vice President, Mike Pence, is a highly masculine evangelical Christian who grabbed national headlines as Governor of Indiana. Trump's policies have certainly involved de-regulation and privatization. But overall, anyone who is familiar with the Post-World War Two American right-wing from William F. Buckley to Ann Coulter must look at Trump and wonder "What has happened?"

The Decline of Cold War Liberalism

In order to understand the Neoconservative American right that seemed so powerful in the age of Reagan, it is first necessary to understand Cold War Liberalism. By the mid-1950s the civil defense drills and Congressional witch-hunts left the American public weary, and soon a new brand, loved by Hollywood and TV producers, stepped up to dominate American politics.

Rod Serling's television program *The Twilight Zone*, the novels of George Orwell, and the eventual rise of John F. Kennedy pointed toward a new interpretation of the geopolitical confrontation with the Soviet Union. The way to beat the Soviets was to be true to the "American ideals" of democracy and freedom.

The widely celebrated Science Fiction film *The Manchurian Candidate* portrayed a right-wing, extremist politician who was mind controlled by Chinese Communists. The intent of the Communists was to push these extreme right-wing politics in order to make the United States seem hypocritical and foolish. The message was that right wing authoritarianism, militarism, and repression helped America's enemies.

The Civil Rights Movement, which became part of the national conversation during the Montgomery Bus Boycott of 1955-1956, was the biggest expression of Cold War Liberal sentiments. The Soviet Union had long portrayed US human rights rhetoric as hypocritical by pointing to Jim Crow Segregation. The response of the Cold War liberals was to prove them wrong, correct an injustice, and steal their thunder.

Cold War liberalism plowed onward after the assassination of John F. Kennedy with the expansion of the welfare state. Lyndon Johnson expanded social programs arguing that poverty among urban African-Americans and Appalachian and southern whites was a stain on America's conscience.

However, Cold War liberalism met its climax in 1969. The Civil Rights Movement had left many Black people unsatisfied, and the Black Liberation Movement of Marxist-Leninists and Nationalists arose to fill its shoes. Young American liberals who opposed the Vietnam War also became increasingly radical as the war continued. Student protests became more violent and confrontational. Students for a Democratic Society, founded as a liberal social-democratic activist group, was eventually dominated by Marxist-Leninists.

Neoconservatism swept in to beat back the storm created by the unsatisfied promises of Cold War Liberalism. The message was "my country, right or wrong" and "if you don't like it here, move to some other country." Nixon famously referred to anti-war protesters saying "These are not romantic revolutionaries, but the same kind of common thugs who have always plagued the good people." The FBI cracked down on the Black Nationalists, the US withdrew from Vietnam, and ultimately the short-lived episode of social unrest was halted.

Neoconservatism, rooted in a kind "know nothing patriotism" and loyalty to a vague concept of America emerged to ride high and dominate American politics. The Reagan-era, Newt Gingrich's "Contract with America," and the George W. Bush administration all continued this tradition of the Nixon-era blend of militarism, patriotism, evangelical

Christianity, and neoliberal economic reforms.

The New Post-2008 Conservatism

For years conservatives tended to focus on cultural issues, and would dismiss talk of poverty and income inequality with claims that poor people were simply lacking motivation and intelligence. The response to liberal calls for economic reform would be "don't fix it if it ain't broke." The unemployed and low income Americans were told to "go get a job." Welfare was portrayed as nothing more than rewarding laziness.

Such arguments became rather ineffectual when Midwestern neighborhoods were dotted with foreclosed homes, household debt was rising, and unemployment was high during the aftermath of the 2008 financial crash. As Obama took office, suddenly conservative anti-intellectualism was scaled back and ideological free market theories took center stage. The Tea Party movement pushed *Atlas Shrugged*, and Paul Ryan, a conservative who cited Ayn Rand as his great influence, became the voice of Congressional Republicans. Glenn Beck's nightly FOX news program told of how Marxism and left-wing economic ideas were contrary to the very definition of Americanism, and every effort must be made to deregulate, lower taxes, and let the private sector flourish.

But the rise of Trump seems to indicate that among the base of the Republican Party free market economics was not satisfactory. Populist style rhetoric about "Make America Great Again" and fighting for the forgotten, silent majority against "globalist" elites seems to be filling the gap. Trump's big target was international trade deals. He promised to end foreign interventions and focus on "America First."

Almost immediately this rhetoric was jumped on by the far-left as proof of fascistic and totalitarian aspirations from Trump. The "Alt-Right" of conservatives who obsess with "western civilization" and "white identity" became a favorite talking point of Hillary Clinton and Trump's many detractors.

Protests against Trump often became hectic and violent with his campaign rallies being shut down. After his election, the protests intensified with airports being crowded in the aftermath of the travel ban. In Charlottesville, activist Heather Heyer was killed after a white supremacist charged his car into a crowd of left wing demonstrators.

Presenting Totalitarianism as Chaos

The right-wing psychologist Jordan Peterson was hailed by the *Wall Street Journal* as "conservatism's rebirth." His self-help lectures meander around in their anecdotes, diagnoses, and personal advice, but almost always Peterson finds his way to quote the Russian anti-Communist Aleksandr Solzhenitsyn. He also tends to frequently invoke the book *Ordinary Men* by Christopher Browning which describes Nazi atrocities.

Peterson seems to warn his audience about the evils of those who attempt to recreate or socially engineer human civilization. His anti-totalitarianism seems focused on urging people to simply live moral lives and let hierarchies and traditional structures continue to exist. He argues that inequalities between demographics and income differentials are natural, not the result of the "patriarchal tyranny," a phrase he utters with scorn. He portrays attempts to correct inequality and push diversity as having largely negative consequences.

Peterson's Anti-Totalitarianism is the mirror opposite of the Cold War Liberalism of Rod Serling. To Serling and the Cold War liberals, opposing totalitarianism meant being more egalitarian. In order to disprove the allegations of Communists and agitators who opposed the American system, it was necessary to loosen social constraints, correct historic injustices, and prove that the Marxist revolution was unnecessary.

However, in the post-cold war era, the Cold War liberals have evolved into the post-modern left. Instead of urging power to loosen its restraints, often those in seats of power justify their actions with post-modernist and left sounding rhetoric. Countries are invaded supposedly to liberate homosexuals and women from oppression. Big corporations speak of a "global community" as they expand across the planet. The Marxist ideology has faded into the background, most especially its economic basis, but the liberal calls for diversity, sensitivity, and social justice have become the rallying cry of the powers that be, that rule over a global, capitalist market.

As global capitalism makes the world less stable, the left seems to celebrate the instability and chaos as "freedom." Free markets, free speech, freedom of information in an increasingly unstable world, is called progress.

Peterson equates this crusade to bring chaos against alleged oppression with totalitarianism. Unlike the Cold War liberals who urged more chaos in order to make society better, Peterson urges respecting existing authority and hierarchies in the hope of preserving social peace and order. While Cold War anti-totalitarian liberalism warned of the danger of authority and repression as the equivalent of Fascism or Communism, Peterson's right wing anti-totalitarianism presents the enemy as chaos. Peterson presents what he fears as mob rule, unleashed when people are given permission to rebel amid attempts to correct injustice.

It has been speculated that perhaps Peterson's sudden popularity is not accidental, and that he has been selected as a voice to calm the brewing storm of young working class white males who are the main demographic of recruiting for the alt-right. Instead of telling them to engage in some kind of fascist insurrection, Peterson is urging them to obey the rules and be personally responsible while maintaining their contempt for feminism and other "anti-oppression" constructs pushed by the establishment. His message, while mocking and holding contempt for leftist narratives, seems to be focused on warning against any big effort to reconstruct society.

The fact that an obscure Canadian psychologist is now the main ideologue for American right-wingers is a sign of the time. Peterson's rise indicates that the US right-wing, much like the American left, is facing a strange identity crisis. The old messages are not working in a new era full of new political ideas and increasing instability.

Originally Published in New Eastern Outlook

ODINIST AMERICA?

Across the southern and midwestern United States, it is common at high school sporting events to see the players join hands in prayer. This tradition has even become the subject of court cases, as it violates the US Constitution for any public school or government institution to promote religion.

Regardless, in many football fields and basketball courts, you will see American high school athletes joining hands, and led by their Coach or instructor, bow their heads, and ask for the blessing of Jesus Christ before they go out and engage in competition.

Now, what purpose does this tradition serve? High School Athletes and Coaches will be very open and honest about this. The prayer is asking God's assistance in helping the players to fully concentrate, give their most full efforts, play to their best ability, and vanquish the opposing team.

Yes, many Coaches and Principals have joined hands with football players and basketball players and muttered the name of Jesus Christ, but to those who understand the Christian religion and its history, something seems to be oddly misplaced about this tradition. Jesus Christ, let us recall, said: "the last shall be first and the first shall be last." Christ's message and teachings, according to the Christian gospels, contained very little if anything advocating that one go out and struggle to the best of one's ability, put forth gigantic efforts, in order to defeat a group of rivals in order to win a competition.

But yet, many Americans seems to have placed this "work ethic" at the center of their worldview. Conservative

American Christians have many misattributed bits of wisdom aligning such sentiments with the Christian Gospels. For example, polls have numerous times revealed that a majority of American Christians mistakenly believe that the often quoted phrase "God helps those who help themselves," written by Benjamin Franklin in 1736, can be found in the scripture.

If one looks into not simply the widespread interpretation of Christianity in the United States, but into wider US culture itself, one can see the unmistakable stamp of another deity, whose worship predates Jesus and Christianity among the European ancestors of many Americans. Odin, or Wotan, the god of the Germanic tribes and the Norse men, has a deep influence on US Culture.

The God of Valor and Sacrifice

Thomas Carlyle, the Scottish intellectual whose text *On Heroes, Hero-Worship, and The Heroic in History* published in 1841, had a groundbreaking impact on European political thought, examined the influence of the pagan deity known as Odin. Carlyle described the ritual of dying Norse men slicing themselves open, in the hopes that Odin would believe they had died in battle, as only war-dead were allowed to spend the afterlife in his mystical hall of Valhalla.

As one read's Carlyle's description of Odin as a God of grit, self-sacrifice, and hard work, one is forced to think of American phrases like "pull yourself up by your bootstraps."

American culture is no doubt deeply influenced by Germany. The most stereotypical American foods, Hamburgers and Hot Dogs (Frankfurters) both have

Germanic origins. The most common American surname is Miller, often an Anglicization of "Mueller." The religious beliefs of most evangelical Christians can be traced back to the Anabaptists, who were central in the 1848 German revolution. The very concept of being "born again" is rooted in the arguments of the German radical protestants in opposition to baptizing infants, arguing that until adolescence, a child was incapable of truly accepting Christianity.

A great deal of American "motor mindedness" and entrepreneurial culture is rooted in a kind of Odinist worldview. Americans will say "mind over matter" and argue that anything is possible if enough effort is simply put forward. Americans will blame those who are economically destitute for their own situation, arguing that if only they had put forward substantial effort they would not be impoverished. Americans routinely attribute the geopolitical position of the United States in the world to the belief that the country is more "hard working" than other nations.

A great deal is written and discussed regarding the "protestant work ethic" and the influence of French theologian John Calvin on American history and thinking, but the influence of the Germanic pagan ethos is rarely explored.

However, the American consumerist celebration of Christmas, complete with decorated pine trees, long hours worked by retail workers, running up of credit card debt, and a mythical figure with a long white beard who appears once a year for Yuletide, reveals that Odin is quite well alive, though perhaps deeply buried, in the American psyche.

Neoliberalism & The Odinist Mindset

Neoliberal economics, promoted by globalist financial institutions, has latched on to this spiritual current among the American people very effectively. Milton Friedman was the child of Jewish immigrants from Hungary. Ayn Rand was born in Russia. Ludwig Von Mises and Fredrick Von Hayek were anything but American. Yet, the economic theories they pushed were very easily swallowed by the American people. The American culture of "hard work pays off" and "a man's house is his castle" became a very welcome host for free-market economic theories and parasitical international banking institutions and corporations. The Odinist values of Americans have been channeled to argue for policies of de-regulation and full integration of the country into the "open international system."

As a result of decades of privatizations, deregulations, and globalization treaties, the USA is in a state of overall economic decline. Across the USA roads are being unpaved because municipalities cannot afford to maintain them. Water is not being properly purified. The US Department of Agriculture reports that a number of households across the country are "food insecure" with access to basic nutrition at risk. The industrial middle class has been eroded by both technological advances eliminating labor, and a global race to the bottom, as corporations are free to scour the globe searching for the lowest paid workers.

The vast natural resources of the country produce huge amounts of wealth for Wall Street oil and fracking companies, while the people who inhabit the vast territories of the country, where the oil and gas is extracted, become poorer and poorer over the years.

While such circumstances in other nations might results in some kind of socialist or nationalist upsurge, blaming the corporations and banks that have swept away prosperity, Americans have largely internalized a kind of Odinist interpretation of their hardships. They watch TV programs talking of "rags to riches" and Horatio Alger-like stories in which other people have become rich through hard work and sacrifice. Americans suffer in silence, believing only they themselves can be blamed for their suffering, and if only they work harder and sacrifice more they can be better off.

Efforts to understand the economic situation in an overall or collective sense is largely absent among the population. Americans happily consume books about how to personally save money better, how to start their own businesses, and learn to think like a wealthy person, but books on the nature of the economy itself, and the economic condition of the country do not sell very well.

As their incomes decrease and their lives become less and less stable, Americans increasingly turn to opioids in the hopes of finding some level of solace. The "diseases of despair" such as narcotics, alcoholism, and suicide, are claiming the lives of increasing numbers of Americans.

Neoliberalism, which largely guts and undermines the US economy, has hijacked the "work hard to get ahead" and "go out and make something of yourself" sentiments that once were quite a boon to US society overall.

Can Socialism Fit Into American Odinism?

Among younger people in the United States, figures like Alexandria Ocasio-Cortez and Bernie Sanders are certainly popular. These figures have openly called for expanding the US welfare state, guaranteeing education and healthcare to the population, and imposing a heavier tax burden on the ultra-rich.

Millennial Americans who face a much harder economic situation than their parents are much more sympathetic to social democratic rhetoric. However, a right-wing current remains very widespread in critiquing this rising "Democratic Socialism" as un-American in its world outlook. Those who follow Sanders and Ocasio-Cortez are labeled as "lazy" "spoiled" "pathetic." They are portrayed as wanting "handouts" and "begging the government to give them stuff for free." The term "snowflake" referring to a kind of cultivated oversensitivity and a lack of harsh consequences in the educational system has been linked to the left economic turn among the younger generation by right-wing critics. Young people who are attracted to socialism are presented as simply weaklings and who do not understand the Odinist values of grit and sacrifice that once made America great.

Some of these criticisms are absolutely valid,. The majority currents of the contemporary left, largely controlled and crafted by academia, are very much guided by post-modernism, identity politics, and ultra-sensitivity. The campus-based activist groups tend to begin meetings with each attendee stating their preferred gender-pronoun, and the rhetoric creates a kind of "self-care" therapeutic atmosphere in which victimhood is aspired to as an ideal state of being. The right accurately critiques the prevailing left as unleashing sentiments largely rooted in jealousy and resentment, and a desire to tear down those who "have it too good" and have benefited from "white privilege" or "cys-gender hierarchy."

However, the overall history of leftism in the United States and the world tells a different story. The history of socialism in America is not limited to post-modern whining about "its unfair" and calls for an expanded welfare state and along with a ban on "mansplaining."

The socialist current in US society, going back to the 1800s includes figures like Daniel DeLeon, Eugene Debs, Elizabeth Gurley Flynn, William Z. Foster, Henry Winston, Claudia Jones, and Huey Newton, among others. These figures, despite being leftist and anti-capitalist, espoused almost the same kind of American and Odinist values of grit, self-sacrifice, and struggle. Their rhetoric includes burning anger as well as a call for selfless courage and relentless effort to change the world.

Furthermore, their vision of socialism is not an expanded welfare state, but rather a centrally planned economy in which the people of the United States are mobilized to reconstruct the country along egalitarian lines.

When one reads the work of American Marxists from the 1930s, and see how they marveled at Stalin's Five Year Plans, one can see a clear identification of an "Americanism" within it. Anna Louise Strong, the American journalist who became a leading pro-Soviet voice, argued in her memoir *I Change Worlds* that the Soviet construction efforts were the greatest example of the American mindset being applied.

During the Second World War, the US Marine Corps popularized the phrase *"Gung Ho,"* a Chinese slogan utilized by the Mao Zedong's Eighth Route Army that means "all together" and "joint effort." A Hollywood movie called Gung Ho was produced and circulated, to this day, American slang refers to having great enthusiasm as being "very gung ho." This again shows Americans seeing their Odinist values enacted by communist, rather than capitalist and individualist forces.

The Odinist spirit of the American culture has so far only been utilized by neoliberalism. The free market advocates have effectively presented themselves as defenders of "The American Way" of hard work and entrepreneurialism. However, as the socialist movement expands and anti-capitalist ideas become more and more popular, socialism will most likely need to adjust, and also find a way to adapt itself with the "motor mindedness" and "will to power" sentiments that are central in the minds of so many working people across US society.

Americans believe in hard work, sacrifice, grit, valor, and struggle. Such sentiments are present all throughout world history, and though Americans have more than a small streak, these values are hardly unique to our shores. However, the efforts glorified by such values are most effective when they are combined. When nations are no longer held back by the irrationality of greed and the anarchy of production, whole peoples and communities are capable of being mobilized to "pull themselves up by their bootstraps" and achieve results that are highly impressive. Collectivism is not inherently a rewarding of weakness, and grit and struggle are not limited to liberal individualism.

When groups of human beings learn to pull together, their ability to achieve tremendous results is much greater. If the Americanist sentiments could be combined with socialist economics, the results could indeed be astronomical.

Originally published at United World International

COMPUTERS, CAPITALISM & THE CRISIS OF CIVILIZATION

The fight between the Chinese government and Apple is about far more than copyright laws and regulations within international business. The current tension between one of the most powerful governments in the world and one of the world's most powerful corporations points to key lessons about what both drives and restrains the advances of human society.

iPhones & "The Fall of Man"

Once, in a conversation I had while traveling overseas, someone told me an interesting theory about the origins of the logo of the Apple computer corporation. The person believed it was biblical symbolism. To him, the silhouette of an apple with a bite taken out of it represented fruit from the tree of knowledge, plucked and eaten by Adam in the Garden of Eden.

I have no way of knowing what the Apple corporation had in mind when it designed its logo many years ago. However, the theory is interesting because the Apple corporation in many ways incarnates the essence of the "fall of man" described throughout centuries of Christian theology.

According to the biblical story, in the Garden of Eden, the first two humans, Adam and Eve were forbidden from eating from the tree of knowledge. God did not want human beings to become enlightened, because he knew of their moral weakness. If humans became capable of thinking and reasoning, there was no guarantee that they would use this ability in a moral way.

If one holds an iPhone or an iPad in their hands, one can certainly see the vast achievements of human civilization. Over the course of the last six thousand years, human reason has empowered us as a species. We are now capable of transforming rocks, dirt and other natural resources into a compact device, which can project pictures and video across the planet.

Each and every Apple product is the result of collective efforts. Tens of thousands of people, hardware and software engineers, miners and smelters, factory workers, and retail employees all come together and coordinate their actions in such a way that this amazing piece of communication technology can be in the palm of your hand, allowing you to update your Facebook status, check your e-mail, text, and call up your friends.

Human beings are capable of all the complex cooperation and discipline necessary to produce millions of iPhones and iPads, and send them across the planet. Yet, with all of this brilliance, innovation, creativity, and ability to work together, we still allow 30,000 of our species to die every single day due to malnutrition-related illnesses. We still slaughter each other in wars. We live in a world where every day women are sexually assaulted, and people are driven from their homes to become unwanted refugees.

Despite all of our great advances in terms of civilization, the worst problems we face are not being solved. In the 21st century of the Common Era, these problems are intensifying. For many people, life is becoming less secure and less safe than ever before.

The contradiction articulated at the Garden of Eden is very

well apparent when one looks at an iPad, iPhone, or laptop computer. These items tell the story of human beings who have bitten into the fruit of knowledge, and gained the ability to reason and think, while lacking the morality and collective self-control needed in order to fully utilize it. This logo is very appropriate in a society that has accomplished amazing feats in terms production, scientific research, discovery, and technological achievement, yet focuses these efforts almost exclusively toward making corporate profits.

Innovation in the Battle for Democracy

In addition to speculation that Apple's logo is inspired by the Book of Genesis, other theories exist. Among those familiar with the history of computers, many uphold the theory that the Apple logo is some kind of ironic joke or statement, related to the death of a scientist named Alan Turing. For those who know the history of computers, it is common knowledge that the work of this British mathematician and cryptologist is largely responsible for the development of modern computers.

The way the history of computers is popularly told, we get the impression that computers are the product of brilliant men like Bill Gates and Steve Jobs, who tinkered in their garages, invented something new, lived as billionaires, and were rewarded for their creativity. Such narratives about the lives of software millionaires are often held up as a defense of capitalism. It is argued that their individual initiative, motivated by greed and unhindered by the government, is the cause of the computer revolution which has forever changed humanity.

The drawn-out series of technological advances that

culminated in what is now called the "computer revolution" is a great example of the pure stupidity of free-market concepts like "intellectual property." No one can own an idea. Ideas don't exist in isolated vacuums. Human intelligence has always been collective in nature.

However, the innovations of Alan Turing, without which modern computing would not be possible, were not achieved in the private sector. Alan Turing never became a billionaire, and was clearly motivated by something other than greed. Turing's work was carried out during the Second World War, a unique moment in the history of the United States and Britain.

In the lead-up to the war during the late 1930s, there were many wealthy people who wanted the United States and Britain to align with the Nazis. Sir Oswald Mosley, Henry Ford, Walt Disney, the American Liberty League, the German-American Bund, and the America First Committee, all admired the Nazis and preferred that the United States be on friendly terms with the Axis Powers. King Edward VIII abdicated the throne in 1936 because he was so well known to be a Nazi sympathizer. At one point, many powerful people in Britain were proven to have been conspiring with Hitler, hoping to put the pro-Nazi monarch back on the throne.

During the Second World War, the United States was led by Franklin Delano Roosevelt, a president who aligned himself with labor unions and unemployment councils, while being hated in corporate boardrooms. In 1934, it was revealed that some of the richest and most powerful people in the United States had been conspiring to depose Roosevelt and establish a fascist military dictatorship. The infamous "Business Plot" was revealed by Marine Corps General Smedley Butler in a testimony before the US Congress.

It is because of popular power and the mobilization of millions of working families into a "People's Front" that the United States and Britain did not fall under the rule of fascism. At the Battle of Cable Street, the Flint Sit-Down Strike, and in many other instances, popular power pushed back the forces of greed and dictatorship. Henry Ford, the British Royal Family, the Morgans, and Charles Lindbergh would have preferred that things to have turned out differently, but the people's coalition of labor unions, unemployment councils, and community organizations ultimately prevailed.

Just as the Russians stood with Lincoln during the American Civil War, and the Russians embraced the American colonists in their fight for independence, the United States and the Soviet Union were friends and allies during the fight against Hitler. Britain was also an essential part of the global anti-fascist coalition. As the fighting raged across Europe and Asia, neither the United States nor Britain functioned as free market economies. Industry and corporations were tightly controlled by the government in order to coordinate production and ensure victory.

In the free-market society of post-Victorian Britain, Alan Turing had been an outcast. Turing was a socially awkward academic who lived in near poverty. It was only in the midst of nationally coordinated efforts to defeat the Nazis that leading figures in British society began scouring the universities, looking for someone capable of helping to de-code Nazi transmissions. Once Turing was discovered, he was immediately put to work. His unique ability and talents were seen as an asset.

It wasn't just Alan Turing. Almost everyone throughout Britain and the United States was assigned a task in the struggle against fascism. Even today, elderly Britons tend to positively reminisce about the war years, despite the tremendous hardships. They recall how it seemed like every man, woman, and child had a role to play in the struggle against the fascist menace that dropped bombs from the sky. While Alan Turing decoded Nazi transmissions, the Royal Air Force flew missions, soldiers carried guns, and civilians collected scrap metal and dug out bomb shelters. It was a national effort with no human potential left unspent.

Working around the clock, Alan Turing made gigantic leaps in the field of mathematics and engineering, developing his groundbreaking decoding machine. Once it was completed, Turing's machine effectively cracked the German Naval Enigma, allowing a secret transmission to be translated and for millions of lives to be saved.

Computers Are Collective Human Brilliance

After the war, when Britain returned to its normal cold, punitive, imperialist way of functioning, Turing's life returned to its previous state of misery. His technological achievements and his role in the allied victory were classified state secrets, and barely anyone knew about them. Alan Turing died in 1954, when the battle for democracy was over and western society was descending into the Cold War. Turing took his own life in the same year that Julius and Ethel Rosenberg were sent to the electric chair, while left-wing political activists and Communist party members across the United States were locked in prison.

In Post-War Britain, while living once again as an

impoverished, lonely academic, Turing was eventually arrested under British sodomy laws. The courts forced him to ingest hormones in hope of curing his homosexuality. After experiencing the ongoing misery that normally results from the process of chemically induced castration, Turing killed himself by eating an apple he had dipped in cyanide.

While society at large was mostly unaware of Alan Turing's work, there's no question that the creators and owners of the Apple corporation knew of it. Those who think that Apple's logo is a reference to Alan Turing's method of suicide, suspect that this is some kind of twisted joke. The computers they invented and made astronomical amounts of wealth from selling could never have been built without Turing's amazing leaps in scientific reasoning. Yet Alan Turing never received any royalties from Steve Jobs or Bill Gates. The only compensation Alan Turing ever received from British society was ostracization, isolation, and punishment, ultimately driving him to take his own life.

Turing's groundbreaking contributions during the war point to the fact that computers are not proof *of the greatness of capitalism*. This is shown as computers further developed from the 1960s through the 1980s. During the Cold War years, the Soviet Union pioneered computer technology at roughly the same rate as the western world. Soviet scientists were forced to make their breakthroughs without utilizing the achievements of the western world, due to international treaties that prevented sharing technological breakthroughs with the Eastern Bloc.

Some have called the Soviet Union's record with computers a "story of missed opportunities." Many times, because of a lack of resources while facing constant attack, the Soviet government was forced to cut funding for very groundbreaking projects, which were full of potential. Despite the technological blockade and lack of resources, scientists in the Warsaw Pact countries developed home computer systems along with many other advancements in computer technology.

There's no question that even in the hostile circumstances the Soviet Union faced, an economy based on five-year plans and directed by a centralized party is very capable of making technological breakthroughs. Those who claim "Communism doesn't work" because it makes innovation impossible, always seem to forget that the Soviet Union was the first country to reach outer space.

Even though western leaders have invested millions and millions of dollars in a military industrial complex (the US economy is in many ways centered around militarism), it was the planned economy of the USSR that brought us the most efficient firearm ever invented. No one disputes that the invention of the AK-47 Automatic Rifle took place within a socialist planned economy.

Human intelligence has always been collective in nature. The history of civilization involves millions of minds building on each other and collaborating, with all of society eventually reaping the benefits.

So, who invented the computer? To answer this question with one name would be a dramatic and obvious falsehood. If the names of each individual who was essential in the technological leaps that brought us modern computer technology were to be listed, tens of thousands of people, if not millions, would have to be included. No single person "invented" the computer, just like no one in present civilization, except perhaps an obscure craftsman, can point to anything and say "I made that." Nearly every commodity in the world at this time is the result of the collective effort of thousands of people, working together in the complex process of production.

Squandering Human Potential

A rational society should be constantly looking for people with skills in order to unleash them. However, the British educational system deemed Turing to be quite useless, and he received very poor marks throughout his years of schooling. Turing's childhood teachers actually referred to his "stupidity" in notes to his parents. It was only Turing's personal passion for mathematics and physics that drove him to pursue these studies.

Why did it take the Second World War, a disaster that killed tens of millions, for the talent of Alan Turing to be discovered by British society? Because during the Second World War, *out of desperate necessity, the societies of Britain and the United States stopped functioning according to their normal economic laws. Capitalism was temporarily put on hold for the purpose of national defense.*

What is capitalism? One of the best definitions of capitalism can be found in the writings of Frederick Engels. Engels says, "In capitalistic society, the means of production can only function when they have undergone a preliminary transformation into capital, into the means of exploiting human labor-power."

To put Engels' words into more common language: nothing gets done in a capitalist economy, unless profits can be made from it. Under capitalism, houses are not constructed because human beings need shelter. Rather, houses are constructed so that landlords and bankers can make profits. People don't get paid wages to do work because it is useful for society, but rather, because a capitalist can somehow make a profit from their labor.

The present situation in the United States, which is facing a deep societal and economic crisis, is a prime example of capitalism's inefficiency. Neighborhoods throughout the United States are dotted with empty, foreclosed homes. At the same time, there are six empty housing units for every homeless person. There is nothing rational about such a state of affairs.

The much decried and criticized "millennial" generation of Americans is the best educated in the country's history. The numbers of young Americans who are either currently in college, or have graduated, is the highest ever. However, the highly educated millennials, many of whom have racked up thousands of dollars in student debt in order to receive their education, are more unemployed and under-employed than ever. Among the millennials lucky enough to be working, a great number of these highly educated young people work in service sector jobs, which do not require even a high school diploma.

At this moment across the United States thousands, if not millions, of young people, full of potential, with degrees in physics, mathematics, history, or computer science, are sweeping floors at Wal-Mart or McDonald's. Instead of solving the crisis of global climate change, or working to eradicate starvation and cure diseases, they are struggling to pay back their student debts. Many more are unemployed, making no money, and spending their early adulthoods living as miserable dependents, locked out of the dignity that comes with economic independence.

There is no shortage of tasks they could be performing. If anything, the present turmoil of the United States cries out for a mobilization of young people to tackle society's problems. Drug addiction is rising across the United States, and each day 78 people die from overdosing on heroin. Suicide rates are the highest they have been in decades.

The prison population is the highest in the world, in terms of both numbers and percentage. Water isn't being properly purified. Bridges are not secure.

Young Americans, who could be mobilized to solve these problems, have instead been cast aside, because Wall Street bankers can't make money from hiring them. The irrationality of an economy organized to make profits, is causing a huge reservoir of human potential to be squandered.

Why is China different?

While the United States is in a state of societal decay, China is rising. In 1949 China was an agrarian third world country, where the overwhelming majority of people were illiterate. Today, China is the world's second largest economy.

The Chinese mainland has been transformed into a high-tech fortress of production. China is home to the famous "Three Gorges Dam," which is the largest hydro-electrical facility in the world. More than half of the steel in the world is now produced in China. More than half of the cooper in the world is also produced in China. As China's productive capacity rises, so does the people's standard of living. The wages of Chinese industrial workers increased by 71% between 2008 and 2012. contamination.

Because of China, the world tourism industry is having a boom. Chinese people whose parents and grandparents were born as peasants, living as the property of feudal landlords, are now going on vacation to Paris and London. CNN confirms that almost every week another Chinese person becomes a millionaire.

On June 20th, 2016 at the International Supercomputer Conference in Frankfurt, Germany, it was declared that China had constructed the world's fastest supercomputer system. Like Alan Turing's decoder machine, this innovation was not developed by the private sector. It was developed by National Research Center of Parallel Computer Engineering & Technology. The machine was installed at the National Supercomputing Center in the Chinese City of Wuxi.

China's ability to pull together and advance as a country is often attributed to some crude racial stereotypes about Asians or a "lack of freedom." Analysts in the United States will often characterize the differences between the United States and China as cultural, saying that Asian societies are inherently collectivist and authoritarian. The racist trope of "Asiatic Despotism," often used in the past to demonize Asian societies, and justify wars against them, is very much alive today.

Western analysts tell us that China is advancing because Asians are heartless, natural-born totalitarians. However, there is plenty of authoritarianism and repression in the Asian countries of Bangladesh, Cambodia, Indonesia, Malaysia, and Thailand, but they have not experienced anything close to China's economic achievements. The various central Asian countries like Afghanistan, Kazakhstan, and Georgia serve as a similar case study.

The secret to China's successes cannot be found in the outdated, debunked pseudo-science of Eugenics. The "Great Revival" of Chinese civilization did not begin with some genetic mutation, but with kicking out western capitalism and the triumph of the Communist Party in 1949.

Sometimes, when analyzing China's economic rise, western analysts will point to the influx of western investment which began in 1978. Those who think western investment is the secret to eliminating global poverty should look at the China that existed prior to 1949. Corporations from Britain and the United States did plenty of "investing" at that time.

The British empire used heroin to dumb down and enslave the Chinese people. In the two famous "Opium Wars" Britain actually declared war in order to prevent China from erecting protective tariffs and stopping the flow of narcotics.

A few decades after the Opium Wars, when Chinese Nationalists called "Boxers" confiscated opium pipes, lynched drug dealers, and boycotted foreign products, the United States deployed the Marines. The US military was sent to the Chinese mainland in order to maintain the ability of British and American corporations to "invest" and prevent the Chinese people from developing an independent economy.

Imperialism is About Destruction

Prior to 1949, China had experienced over a century of "free trade" with western corporations. As a result it was the "sick man of Asia" who was burdened by starvation, drug addiction, forced prostitution, and almost no industrial production. China was kept impoverished with a primarily agrarian, primitive economy because of imperialism. So, what is imperialism?

Across the United States, progressive activists are making huge efforts to tear down monuments to Confederates and slaveholders, but there has been very little outcry about the fact that Warner Brothers recently released a new film based on *The Jungle Book* written in 1894 by Rudyard Kipling.

There is no individual whose name is more closely associated with racism and the demented psychology of the British Empire than Rudyard Kipling. In addition to The Jungle Book, Kipling wrote a poem defending racism and colonialism, referring to the plundering of the world as *The White Man's Burden*. His writings, most of which are intended for children, profess that it is the duty of white people to colonize the world, and to "civilize" the peoples of Africa, Asia, and Latin America.

Beyond Kipling's propaganda, the actual logic of imperialism can be discovered in the words of Cecil Rhodes, the racist settler for whom Rhodesia (now Zimbabwe) was named. Cecil Rhodes is quoted as saying: "I was in the East End of London (a working-class quarter) yesterday and attended a meeting of the unemployed. I listened to the wild speeches, which were just a cry for 'bread! bread!' and on my way home I pondered over the scene and I became more

than ever convinced of the importance of imperialism....
My cherished idea is a solution for the social problem, i.e.,
in order to save the 40,000,000 inhabitants of the United
Kingdom from a bloody civil war, we colonial statesmen
must acquire new lands to settle the surplus population, to
provide new markets for the goods produced in the factories
and mines. The Empire, as I have always said, is a bread
and butter question. If you want to avoid civil war, you must
become imperialists." prejudices.

In the mid-1800s, British people were being worked to
death in mills and factories. The increasing mechanization
of production created high levels of unemployment. The
hardships of the industrial revolution unleashed a wave of
strikes, protest, and uprisings. Revolts of British workers
demanding better conditions threatened the very foundations
of society. It was then discovered that this looming threat
of a working-class uprising could be reduced by sending
white European workers across the world to act as settlers
and overseers. The starving and unemployed who languished
in the urban industrial centers could be used to staff armies
enforcing the global dominance of British corporations.

As British capitalists seized global markets, a strata of
working-class people called the "Aristocracy of Labor" came
into existence. Though they worked and received wages from
an employer, the "Labor Aristocrats" were better paid, and
came to identify with their white-skinned bosses, with whom
they stood against the world's dark-skinned peoples.

Imperial Britain depended on cotton picked by African
slaves in the southern United States in order to develop its
textile industry. In order to maintain their monopoly, the
British forcibly destroyed the textile industry of India. The

occupied people of India then had no choice but to purchase imported cloth from Britain. Because their textile monopoly relied on cheap, slave-picked cotton, British bankers supported the Confederacy during the American Civil War.

This method of controlling the world market with military force, while dividing the working class at home was pioneered by the British, with the United States, Germany, France, and other western powers catching up shortly afterward. This setup is called imperialism. Imperialism is a system where western bankers are at the center of the world economy, raking in super profits by dominating markets across the planet, and enforcing their rule with violence.

Kipling's portrayals of India and Africa give the impression that these places were just jungles and deserts until the white Europeans showed up and started "civilizing" things. In reality, Africa had vibrant civilizations at Timbuktu and elsewhere. India has a long history of civilization that predates Rome and Greece. Who built the pyramids? Who first developed mathematics and geometry? The idea that western Europeans have always been "the most advanced" is a harmful myth.

While Europeans were living in the Dark Ages, people inspired by the Prophet Mohammed, living in Arabian Peninsula, Palestine, Syria, Iran, and Iraq were centuries ahead, making amazing contributions to human development. The terrorism of Al-Qaeda and ISIS, mass refugee crises and instability; these are not the natural products of Middle Eastern peoples, nor of the Islamic faith.

Look at the situation in Iraq, Afghanistan, Libya, and Syria. Is western military intervention and the toppling of independent, nationalistic governments bringing civilization to these countries? Is it bringing even basic stability or peace? The whole world can see that this is not the case. Even when the interventions are justified in the name of a 'War on Terror,' the forces of terror and chaos only get stronger wherever western bankers and soldiers are deployed.

Contrary to what Kipling and years of propaganda have constantly repeated, neither the East India Company, the Slave Ships, the settler armies back in the 1800s, nor the IMF, the World Bank or the Pentagon are actually developing the world today. These are forces of destruction, holding back humanity in order to maintain a monopoly for the bankers who own them. Imperialism is not about developing, or helping impoverished countries. It's about keeping them poor and dependent, at the barrel of a gun.

Murder and the Imperialist Mindset

There is indeed something inherently sick, destructive and immoral about western colonizers. British settlers were known to laugh as they slaughtered entire African villages with early machine guns. The British army committed a slew of atrocities in Asia, the Caribbean, and in many other regions where they were deployed.

These extreme acts of cruelty are not actions human beings naturally engage in. A specific kind of molding is required to make humans capable of such cruelty and indifference to the suffering of others. In the works of Rudyard Kipling, among others, we can see how generations of westerners were mis-educated and trained with a mindset that allowed them carry the rifles of colonial armies, and the whips to beat colonial slaves.

425

In Kipling's *The Elephant's Child or, How the Elephant Got His Trunk*, a tale intended for children, we read about a baby elephant whose relatives continuously subject him to corporal punishment for his "insatiable curiosity." After many spankings the youthful pachyderm gives up on trying to get an answer about what the alligator "eats for dinner." The young elephant goes to the river to see for himself, only to have his nose elongated as he struggles to wrench it from the alligator's jaws. Now equipped with a long trunk, the elephant returns to his kin. In his new state of being he is no longer subject to being spanked because he can effectively return the favor, using his lengthy sniffer against his relatives.

Kipling's demented fairy tale seems to be almost an allegory for the aspirations of white settlers: endure horrific mistreatment and be exploited in your homeland before being unleashed on to the world. Go out into the world with the hope of returning somehow stronger and crueler than before. The only hope for a happy ending in this constructed mindset is that, once unleashed on the world, you will gain the ability to dish out an even fiercer version of the cruelty you previously endured.

At the height of its power on the global stage during the 1880s, Imperial Britain had spawned some dangerously insane people. The press in London endlessly publicized and fawned over the sexualized murders of "Jack the Ripper." British newspapers received tens of thousands of letters from people, falsely claiming to be Jack the Ripper. The letters came from individuals throughout a British public, brought up to worship and admire cruelty from parents and educators. It's clear that in 1888, many people within the homeland of the British empire were in awe of the anonymous Jack who would be the first of many serial killers in the western world

The dominance of Britain is merely history. British bankers have been usurped as the top exploiters and monopolists on the global stage. The billionaires of the United States now hold this title. The society they lead has one-upped Britain's "serial killers" by unleashing the new phenomena of "mass shooters" who slaughter large numbers of often random people in a wave of bullets.

Xi Jinping:
"Prosperity for the People is the Primary Goal"

The Chinese government doesn't exactly have a cozy relationship with Wall Street corporations. When OSI, a Chicago-based meat supplier was caught serving rotten meat to the public in Chinese McDonald's, KFC, and Pizza Hut restaurants, the corporate executives were dragged away in handcuffs. China is the only country in the world that has executed billionaires. In fact, executions of extravagantly wealthy people on the Chinese mainland have taken place multiple times.

The Chinese government is currently battling the Apple corporation, insisting that as the recognized government, the People's Republic has to right to dictate the manner in which Apple's "intellectual property" is utilized, and by whom. Apple is furious because the Chinese government is allowing domestic companies to utilize technological advances which they insist they "own."

As the owners of Apple go head to head with the Chinese government, they are witnessing the rise of a very strong competitor. The Chinese multi-national Huawei, which is the largest telecommunications manufacturer in the world, is challenging Apple's dominance in computer and smartphone technology around the world. Huawei has announced that it intends to take smartphone technology to a whole new level, releasing "Superphones" by 2020. *China Daily* quotes Huawei's Richard Yu who says, "The superphone will be a living organism, like our families and friends, recording our behaviors and habits, and understanding our likes and preferences."

Huawei is technically not a corporation, but a "collective" under Chinese law. A large number of the shares of Huawei are owned by the Communist Party aligned trade union, which represents the Huawei's 170,000+ employees. Many of Huawei's top executives have been leading figures within the Chinese military or the government itself. Though Huawei often insists that it is not "government controlled," it clearly does not operate like an American corporation, following the flow of the market, seeking to maximize its own profits. This Chinese multinational's activities are closely coordinated with the Chinese government as part of a strategy for advancing the economy, fitting in neatly with the Five Year Plans.

When speaking at the ceremonies commemorating the 95th anniversary of the Chinese Communist Party, Xi Jinping said "Prosperity for the people is the primary goal of the Communist Party of China, and it is this goal that distinguishes Marxist parties from other political forces." For a party that began with less than 30 people in the basement of women's college dormitory in 1921, the organization that now holds 87 million people among its ranks definitely has a record worth boasting about.

China's vast market sector is tightly controlled by the government and the party. This has allowed China to avoid the chaotic boom-bust cycle of capitalism, and to steadily advance from the "sick man of Asia" to the powerful global center it is today.

In July of 2015, when the Chinese stock market dropped by 30% in a single day, almost nothing happened. Less than 2% of the Chinese public is invested in the Chinese stock market. A similar drop in the United States, where 55% of the population is invested in the stock market either directly or through retirement pensions, would have resulted in riots in the streets.

When the stock market in China "crashed" in June of 2015, the government immediately instituted a ban on short-selling with the threat of arrest. Communist Party leaders made a few phone calls, and the economy had bounced back within a month. Despite such a dramatic drop on the Shanghai Stock Market, Chinese society just kept going, insulated from market turbulence. In China the "Preliminary Transformation," by which Frederick Engels defined capitalism, is not in control. To paraphrase the terminology employed by China's founder, Mao Zedong, "Profits are not in command." China has a planned economy.

When it was revealed that some of Apple's products were being manufactured in a sweatshop facility in Chungqing owned by the Taiwan-based corporation called Foxconn, the world was horrified by the conditions that existed at this facility on the Chinese mainland. People across China and around the world denounced Apple for the way they mistreated industrial workers.

Most people in the United States are unaware of what happened next. In 2014, workers at laid down their tools and went out on strike to demand better conditions. The Chinese

Communist Party supported and protected the striking workers, who eventually won some dramatic improvements in their working conditions.

Currently, the Chinese government is waging a massive crackdown on corruption. President Xi Jinping has articulated that many practices that go against the principles of "Socialism with Chinese Characteristics" have become entrenched and widespread since the late 1970s. In 1978, Deng Xiaoping's reforms and openness moved China away from the extremist "poverty communism" of the Gang of Four, and from international isolation. Today, Xi Jinping's "Mass Line Campaign" is reigning in and controlling sectors of Chinese society where market forces seem to be out of control.

There is nothing inherently Chinese or Asian about these successes. In China, greed and profit is not allowed to run rampant, with the state having the final say on economic decision making. When it comes to setting government policy, the Communist party and its 87 million members are in charge, not corporate executives.

Guided by the power of human reason, and not by the anarchy of production, China's one billion people are pulling together and marching forward. What the United States and Britain were briefly forced to do in order to defeat fascism during the Second World War, China has been doing since 1949. The result has been one of the most dramatic advances of any society in history.

How Should We Direct Human Intelligence?

If one opens the newspapers of the United States, you will

read about mass shootings, the rise of heroin addiction, and children being poisoned with lead in their drinking water. Our government allows this kind of news to be published, not out of a love for "freedom of the press," but because most Americans don't bother to read about it. The United States is a country where the state is not officially pushing any ideology, and the public is widely depoliticized.

Foreigners often laugh about the fact that Americans boast that they are "free" and arrogantly proclaim that people in countries like Iran, Russia, Venezuela or Cuba the people are "brainwashed." While Americans think they are "free," a large percentage of them cannot even find their country on a world map.

In the United States, "think for yourself" has become a euphemism for not thinking at all. The leaders of the western capitalist world do not mobilize their populations. Americans and western Europeans are not part of any continuing revolution, national project, or collective vision. Americans feel little, if any, obligation toward the country, or even each other. Westerners are "free" to live their lives chasing after material comfort as their own society crumbles around them.

As things get worse, with rising poverty and societal instability, many Americans are becoming interested in what is commonly called "conspiracy theories," hoping to explain why everything in the country seems to be going wrong.

The breakdown of US society is happening on a number of different levels. The educational system is very poorly rated. Intelligent people in US society are generally put to work figuring out derivatives on Wall Street, or designing the latest high tech weapons for the Pentagon. A number of corporations have discovered that a rise in poverty and crime isn't so bad, because locking people in prisons can be a way of making money. The existence of a "prison industrial complex" is widely decried.

There isn't much of a "labor aristocracy" anymore. International bankers have wrecked the midwestern and southern United States, in a similar manner to the way they have wrecked much of the planet. The once prosperous industrial heartland of the United States has become known as the "rust belt." While shipping jobs overseas, presiding over an inefficient healthcare system, and watching the country growing poorer and less stable than ever, a small group of people in the United States have continued to make lots of money.

From within this societal collapse some kind of new American collectivism needs to emerge. Some kind of swift, dramatic central planning and mobilization of the population must be enacted in order to liquidate the crisis. American society must get beyond the notion that the answer to our problems will involve corporations making lots of money, and with the government keeping its "hands off."

The history of human civilization has been the story of our struggle to restrain our animalistic impulses and our drives toward selfishness and aggression. As we advance we have, more and more, allowed our rational minds to take the helm. Tremendous progress has been made. Human beings have gone from being a species of hunter gatherers and cave dwellers to being space travelers and computer manufacturers.

In the fight between Apple and the Chinese government, we see a looming question about how human intelligence should be directed. Should it be used to fill up the bank accounts of corporate executives—a puny segment of humanity? Or should the brilliance that enabled humanity to create the iPhone be unleashed to save civilization? The human race will soon have no choice but to resolve this burning question.

Originally published in Greanville Post

Lightning Source UK Ltd.
Milton Keynes UK
UKHW040022150620
364910UK00005BA/848